INTERFACE

Library Automation with Special Reference to Computing Activity

Edited by
C. K. Balmforth
and
N. S. M. Cox

THE M.I.T. PRESS

Cambridge, Massachusetts

First M.I.T. Press Edition, 1971

ISBN 0 262 02084 X (hardcover)

Library of Congress Catalog Card Number 70-158649

Printed in Great Britain

CONTENTS

The papers asterisked were presented at the *Newcastle Seminar on the management of computing activity in academic libraries*, 10–13 January 1969, and were circulated as preprints. Some alterations have been made to the original texts.

iii

Foreword

by Dr J. Swift

The first Professor I saw was in a very large Room, with Forty Pupils about him. After Salutation, observing me to look earnestly upon a Frame, which took up the greatest Part of both the Length and Breadth of the Room; he said, perhaps I might wonder to see him employed in a Project for improving speculative Knowledge by practical and mechanical Operations. But the World would soon be sensible of its Usefulness; and he flattered himself, that a more noble exalted Thought never sprang in any other Man's Head. Every one knew how laborious the usual Method is of attaining to Arts and Sciences; whereas by his Contrivance, the most ignorant Person at a reasonable Charge, and with a little bodily Labour, may write Books in Philosophy, Poetry, Politicks, Law, Mathematicks and Theology, without the least Assistance from Genius or Study. He then led me to the Frame, about the Sides whereof all his Pupils stood in Ranks. It was Twenty Foot square, placed in the Middle of the Room. The Superficies was composed of several Bits of Wood, about the Bigness of a Dye, but some larger than others. They were all linked together by slender Wires. These Bits of Wood were covered on every Square with Papers pasted on them; and on these Papers were written all the Words of their Language in their several Moods, Tenses, and Declensions, but without any Order. The Professor then desired me to observe, for he was going to set his Engine at work. The Pupils at his Command took each of them hold of an Iron Handle, whereof there were Forty fixed round the Edges of the Frame; and giving them a sudden Turn, the whole Disposition of the Words was entirely changed. He then commanded Six and Thirty of the Lads to read the several Lines softly as they appeared upon the Frame; and where they found three or four Words together that might make Part of a Sentence, they dictated to the four remaining Boys who were Scribes. This Work was repeated three or four Times, and at every Turn the Engine was so contrived, that the Words shifted into new Places, as the square Bits of Wood moved upside down.

Six Hours a-Day the young Students were employed in this Labour; and the Professor shewed me several Volumes in large Folio already collected, of broken Sentences, which he intended to piece together; and out of those rich Materials to give the World a compleat Body of all Arts and Sciences; *which however might be still*

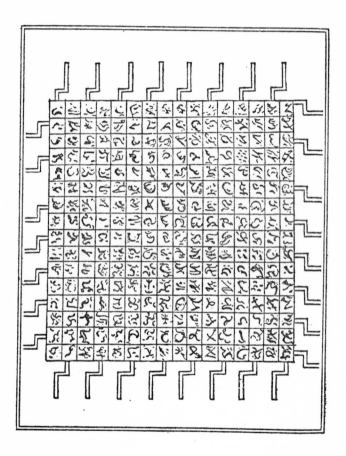

improved and much expedited, if the Publick would raise a Fund for making and employing five Hundred such Frames in Lagado, *and oblige the Managers to contribute in common their several Collections.*

He assured me, that this Invention had employed all his Thoughts from his Youth; that he had emptyed the whole Vocabulary into his Frame, and made the strictest Computation of the general Proportion there is in Books between the Numbers of Particles, Nouns, and Verbs, and other Parts of Speech.

I made my humblest Acknowledgments to this illustrious Person for his great Communicativeness; and promised if ever I had the good Fortune to return to my native Country, that I would do him Justice, as the sole Inventor of this wonderful Machine; the Form and Contrivance of which I desired Leave to delineate upon Paper as in the Figure here annexed. I told him, although it were the Custom of our Learned in Europe to steal Inventions from each other, who had thereby at least this Advantage, that it became a Controversy which was the right Owner; yet I would take such Caution, that he should have the Honour entire without a Rival.

Gulliver's Travels: Part 3
(italics by the Editors)

Editors' Introduction

About half of the papers in this collection were presented at the Seminar on the Management of Computing Activity in Academic Libraries, held in Newcastle in January 1969. These have been abridged, extended and up-dated by the editors, who offer their apologies to any author who feels that he has been misinterpreted. Other papers presented at the Seminar and circulated with the pre-prints have not, for various reasons, been reprinted here.

The remaining papers were solicited and we are particularly grateful to those authors who responded to the call for topical material at short notice.

The editors feel that this is an appropriate time to be offering a volume containing a high proportion of papers on management techniques, and especially those relating to cost and benefits. Some views expressed may be controversial but we hope that the book will stimulate further consideration and practical application of the methods discussed.

Our thanks are particularly due to the members of the Symplegades Research Group and the staff of the Computing Laboratory who helped to organize and run the original Seminar, and to Professor E. S. Page, Director of the Computing Laboratory, and the Librarian, Dr. W. S. Mitchell, who jointly sponsored it.

C.K.B.
N.S.M.C.

SECTION I

The Current Situation in Library Automation

The Computer/Library Interface: the Last Five Years
by C. K. Balmforth, M. W. Grose and A. E. Jeffreys

The State of the Art in Academic Libraries
contributions from
J. M. Bagnall, Newcastle upon Tyne University Library
P. Brown, Bodleian Library, Oxford
*R. M. Duchesne, Birmingham Libraries Co-operative
    Mechanization Project*
G. Ford, South-West Library Systems Co-operative Project
J. W. Jolliffe, British Museum, London
A. Tucker, Trinity College, Dublin

Computers in British Public Libraries
by C. D. Batty

Work in progress in the Book Trade
D. Whitaker and J. Blackwell

The Computer/Library Interface: the Last Five Years*

C. K. BALMFORTH, M. W. GROSE and
A. E. JEFFREYS

THE LAST FIVE YEARS

> University printing presses exist, and are subsidised by the Government for the purpose of producing books which no one can read; and they are true to their high calling. Books are the sources of material for lectures. They should be kept from the young; for to read books and remember what you read, well enough to reproduce it, is called 'cramming', and this is destructive of all true education. The best way to protect the young from books, is, first, to make sure that they shall be so dry as to offer no temptation; and, second, to store them in such a way that no one can find them without several years' training. A lecturer is a sound scholar, who is chosen to teach on the ground that he was once able to learn. Eloquence is not permissible in a lecture; it is a privilege reserved by statute for the Public Orator.
>
> F. M. CORNFORD, Microcosmographia Academica

Universities are not what they were five years ago; they are certainly not what they were fifty years ago. We have only to compare Cornford's caricature of Cambridge opinion at the turn of the century with the report of the Hale Committee (1964) to see how far attitudes have changed. The attempt is now being made to shift the emphasis from the formal lecture to learning how to educate oneself by private study with guidance from seminars and tutorials. Second, there has been a rapid growth in both the number of universities and in their size; university education is no longer a privilege for a favoured few, and as a result we now have a far higher proportion of first-generation students whose home may not have encouraged the habit of study.

---

* This article was intended to provide background for the 1969 Newcastle Seminar, and was not an exhaustive review. Since the preprint was circulated, some statistics and statements of fact have been up-dated; but few additional examples have been given, since many of the most recent projects are described fully elsewhere in this volume.

Third, the subjects taught at university have changed. While it is still too soon to be predicting the demise of Classics, the Social Sciences have certainly arrived, and cross-disciplinary courses have found a new popularity.

We will leave you to judge for yourselves whether University Presses have changed since Cornford's day, or even whether they should; however you cannot but be aware how the other changes have brought changing pressures on university libraries—and not only on university libraries. In all university towns there is an under-world of students at less favoured institutions of further education, whose libraries are even less able to cope with the pressure, and often it is the public library which suffers. Libraries are having to move from an attitude of guardianship to one of service; instead of sitting dragon-like upon their wordhoard, they are called to become dis-pensers of 'information'. ('Information' is enjoying a vogue at the moment; combine it with 'scientist', 'officer', 'transfer' and it be-comes an even more potent talisman.)

There are economic pressures also: we have had a period of rapid expansion, in which library staff, never underworked at the best of times, have had their traditional procedures tested by the flood of work—often to destruction. Now it has become clear that the Govern-ment cannot afford to allow the expansion to continue at the same rate. Not so the price of library materials; in 1968/69 the average price of all books listed in *BNB* rose by 7·1% over the previous year, to £2 6s. 10½d. giving an index figure of 158·9 measured against the 1964/65 figures (Average Book Prices 1968, 1969).* Periodical prices too have shown a steady rise, from a base of 100 in 1965 to 141·3 in 1968 and 155·0 in 1969 (Veasey, 1968, 1969). It is clear therefore that libraries are facing an even bleaker financial climate than usual.

Many large institutions find their size a source of inertia, more politely called 'tradition': libraries are rather worse off than most because their long history (the Bodleian, for example, was opened on 8 November 1602) has given them a vast bookstock, which is expen-sive to re-arrange and even more expensive to re-catalogue. But now many libraries are finding that the pressures caused by the changes in their functions, and the approaching or actual breakdown of their traditional methods, are becoming stronger than the weight of inertia. Much of the credit for this must be given to the computer,

---

* It was learnt just before this book went to press that the corresponding figure for 1969–70 was 193·3: representing a *percentage* increase of 21·4 over 1968–69.

which, by seeming to offer a solution to some traditional problems, has acted as a catalyst. The manufacturer's publicity is certainly enticing, and its effects are reinforced by the popular conception of computers as giant brains. Reports of experience from early users have almost universally been enthusiastic but it is hard to discover the truth without recourse to the grapevine unless someone with knowledge of the institution blows the gaff, (Shaw, 1965, quoted below; Bryan, 1966). Certainly we all ought to take to heart Barbara Markuson's warning in her chapter in the 1967 *Annual Review of Information Science and Technology*:

> The most distressing feature of the literature is the failure of the writers to disclose what is actually operational and what is proposed or conjectural in the automation projects they describe.

On the other hand it is not hard to explain such optimism; the writers are working in a new and rapidly developing field, and, with the optimism of pioneers, feel justified in writing of their plans as if they were already accomplished, because they expect them to be by the time the account can appear in print. What they overlook is the quite considerable chance that the successful completion of the project may need far more work than was taken to produce the promising interim results which prompted them to write them up. Mechanical translation provides a striking example of this, though perhaps not entirely fair as the problem is considerably more difficult than most library work. There the later stages were found to need so much more effort than was expected from the results of a decade ago that now almost all work has been abandoned.

This sort of experience in other fields lends a good deal of support to those librarians who have decided to wait until library automation has proved itself before applying it to their libraries. Quite rightly they do not want the expense and upheaval of altering their present systems only to find that the automated one has its own new deficiencies. They have after all libraries to run. But if we do not gain experience by having a go, library automation will never get the chance to prove itself. Fortunately however there are some libraries which have begun to experiment either because they are new and have no built-in inertia, or because their manual systems are so overloaded that they are facing disaster in any case. It is perhaps significant that libraries in this second class where problems are drawing attention to themselves seem to have been more successful than those new libraries which one would have expected to have had more success just because they were starting from scratch.

In the review which follows we consider some of the more interesting happenings in the field of library automation over the last few years. This is not a complete review of even the most significant events We have excluded all consideration of information retrieval and have concentrated rather on the housekeeping operations, for example, ordering, accessioning, cataloguing and circulation systems. University libraries have for a long time been deeply involved in the manual operation of these activities; they are not yet committed in the same way to information retrieval. This does not imply that we do not consider information retrieval relevant or important to the activities of a modern university library. Information retrieval is included in the reviews of e.g. Stein (1964), Coblans (1966), Lynch (1966) and Kimber (1967).

TRANSATLANTIC CONTRASTS

'We should be thankful that librarians are often equated with God, Mother and Country, because if they were not, the faculty and administrators would begin to ask why other programs must be curtailed because of continually increasing budgets for the libraries.'

(R. E. Chapin, 'Administrative and economic considerations for library automation'. University of Illinois Graduate School of Library Science. *Proceedings of the 1967 Clinic on library applications of data processing.* Edited by D. E. Carroll. Champaign, Illinois, Illini Union Bookstore, 1967, p. 58)

'The simple fact is with libraries and computers that we are not going to be able to make a case for computers purely on the cash savings aspect. Cash savings, in the main, come from staff savings, and most libraries do not employ enough staff; you can't save them because they're not there.'

(H. A. J. Marshall *in* N. S. M. Cox and M. W. Grose, *Organization and handling of bibliographic records by computer.* Newcastle upon Tyne, Oriel Press 1967, p. 181.)

CONFERENCES

The conference on libraries and automation held at the Airlie Foundation, Virginia, in 1963 was an important meeting between librarians and technologists. Its published proceedings (Markuson, 1964) are a valuable review of the state of the art and go some way towards providing librarians with at least a broad acquaintance with the technology relating to library mechanization.

The Brasenose conference on the automation of libraries, which took place at Oxford in the middle of 1966 (Harrison and Laslett,

1967), brought together a group of American and British librarians involved with the application of automation to libraries, with the Americans having more to report by way of practical experience and achievement. The balance was partly redressed at Newcastle in July 1967, when a conference on the organization and handling of bibliographic records by computer was more concerned with work in progress and projects in hand in Britain, particularly those centring on the Newcastle File Handling System designed by Cox and Dews (Cox and Grose, 1967).

TOTAL SYSTEMS
Library of Congress
One of the more significant events in the last few years in the field of automation and libraries was the publication of the King report on automation in the Library of Congress (King et al., 1963). The main conclusion of this report was that 'the automation of major operations within the Library of Congress is shown to be both desirable and feasible'. A useful summary of the report is given by Markuson (1965), who lists its major findings as:

1. Automation can, within the next decade, augment and accelerate the services rendered by large research libraries and can have a profound effect upon their responsiveness to the needs of library users;
2. Automation of bibliographic processing, catalogue searching and document retrieval is technically and economically feasible in large research libraries;
3. The retrieval of the intellectual content of books by automatic methods is not now feasible for large collections, but progress in that direction will be advanced by effective automation of cataloguing and indexing functions;
4. Automation will enhance the adaptability of libraries to changes in the national research environment and will facilitate the development of a national library system;
and 5. Automation will reduce the cost-to-performance ratio; however, the library should aim at the expansion of services rather than the reduction of total operating costs.

An important part of the automation programme at the Library of Congress was its project to test the feasibility of distributing bibliographic data in machine-readable form. This was immediately christened *MARC* (Machine-Readable Cataloguing) and began in November 1966 with the weekly distribution of cataloguing data on magnetic tapes to sixteen participating libraries. These libraries were mainly occupied with experimental attempts at producing catalogue

B

cards from it. During this pilot project, cataloguing data were supplied for current English language monographs only. *MARC I* has now been superseded by *MARC II* and this is closely linked with an experimental project being carried out in this country under the aegis of the British National Bibliography Limited. The *BNB MARC* Record and its applications are described elsewhere in this volume by Richard Coward. A short description of *MARC I* is given by Reimers (1967), and a report has been published (Avram, 1968).

Florida Atlantic

Three or four years ago we were hearing quite a lot about the first computer-based university library system to go into operation in the United States, Florida Atlantic (e.g. Perreault, 1964; Becker, 1965). Here were computer-based cataloguing, circulation, serials and acquisitions systems.

There were to be supplements to the catalogue every three months for 1965 and monthly thereafter. Daily circulation lists were produced by call numbers and by borrowers' numbers, together with lists of books overdue. There was talk of putting the entire contents of the catalogue into random access store, made available as required to users via remote consoles.

But after the initial outburst of enthusiasm there was silence and some of the staff who were involved have now turned up elsewhere.

Chicago University

The University of Chicago is one of a small number of American university libraries (others include Washington State and Stanford) which have the long range goal of a totally automated system, or as Chicago somewhat awkwardly call it 'an integrated, computer-based bibliographical data system for a large university library'. (Payne, 1967). The costs of this developmental project are being supported, in part, by a grant from the National Science Foundation. The overall aim is the incorporation of all the data relating to a single item into one machine record. All production will be output from this master record, including such things as orders and claims, catalogue cards, bindery records, spine labels, and so on. Chicago had a lot of trouble with their computer because of inefficient programs supplied by the manufacturer. A Data Processing Unit has been established within the library which is responsible not only for the implementation of the automated system but also for a prior study of the existing operations, planning any necessary changes and explaining the new system to the library staff. It is intended to make cost/benefit studies of the situations existing before and after the establishment of automated systems. Discussions are being held with other university libraries (e.g. Stanford and Columbia) on the possible problems and benefits of collaboration in joint library systems development.

In concluding his account of developments at Chicago, Payne (1967) makes five points, predictions rather than conclusions:

1. Library systems development will become open-ended: the library systems analyst will not reach the end of his (or her) job since there is almost unlimited opportunity for change and improvement;
2. Library systems development staff, computer staff and programming staff will thus become permanent parts of the library;
3. The future lies with large time-sharing computers rather than with a smaller computer for use of the library alone. This is because of the combination of large core-storage requirements together with low computer utilization;
4. Remote on-line terminals are expensive and it is unlikely they will be scattered around; it is improbable, for example, that there will be one at every cataloguer's desk;
and 5. The library needs staff trained both in library operations and in computer science so that it can successfully communicate with computer men.

No university library in Britain has the financial resources to undertake a project on the same scale as at Chicago. Until recently there has been little in the way of co-operative or co-ordinated effort in this country: this is perhaps because of the jealous autonomy of British universities as institutions and the dearth of hard facts about what their libraries are really trying to do and the best ways of doing it. But a number of libraries are now appointing systems analysts to their staff and several projects are under way, the latter guided by the beneficent hand of the Office of Scientific and Technical Information. Projects in the first and later generations are described elsewhere in the present volume.

Bochum

The University Library at Bochum began its life in 1963 with the intention of achieving a fully integrated computerized system within five years. They have made further advances towards this than any other German library but after five years are achieving only a gradual integration of cataloguing, acquisition, binding and circulation. They now consider that fifteen to twenty years is a more realistic timetable (Pflug, 1968). Pflug gives three main reasons for this reappraisal:

1. Prior theories have to be modified and developed in the light of practical experience;
2. Automated systems must of necessity evolve from traditional manual systems because there is as yet no generally established body of practice for an automated library. The changeover from the manual to the automated system may involve difficult organizational changes, but a breakdown in library processes cannot be tolerated;

and 3. Bochum has no separate planning team. Those responsible for planning the automated systems have numerous other tasks to carry out as well.

But Bochum's achievement of some 260,000 entries (as of April 1968), in its computerized author catalogue is nevertheless impressive, although one may consider that its form and appearance fall below what is traditionally acceptable.

The Deutsche Wissenschaftsrat gives its opinion that the cataloguing of a book costs about DM 3·90 on the average (Pflug, 1968). According to the calculations carried out by the University of Bochum Library the price is DM 3·15 per title. But these figures presumably refer to author cataloguing only and in any case one would want to know a lot more about the criteria used in arriving at and assessing such figures before reading anything at all into them. And this is quite apart from the difficult problems of whether the cost of constructing any particular catalogue is justified by the user needs it fulfils.

CATALOGUING

Harvard

Compared with university libraries in Britain, Harvard is very big and very rich. It has approximately 8 million volumes and an annual budget of over $8 million. It adds some 200,000 volumes each year and has a staff of more than 600.

The Widener Library is the central unit of the Harvard library system and has some three million volumes. Widener is of some age and developed its own cataloguing system, subject headings and classification schemes around the turn of the last century.

Harvard sees the introduction of automated systems into the

library as progressing in stages, with each stage building on its predecessors (De Gennaro, 1968). In this way the staff gain experience in dealing with automation and thus become capable of developing and adopting more sophisticated systems as they become practicable. The library suffers no traumatic changes and is able to maintain its services without interruption. The immediate aim is to raise the level of housekeeping operations, such as circulation, shelflist maintenance, book ordering and accounting, and so on, from the manual stage to a relatively simple and economical machine system.

The library's introduction to data processing equipment and techniques came with the design and installation of a punched card circulation system in July 1963. The old manual system could no longer cope with the steadily increasing load that had been placed upon it. The success of the new circulation system proved to the library that data-processing techniques would be of value.

About a year later the IBM Corporation embarked on a study with the assistance of the library staff to determine how computer technology might be used to assist in certain housekeeping operations. This resulted in a recommendation that the library embark on a major automation program, a recommendation which was set aside by a joint decision of the library administration and the university's computing centre because it was 'overly ambitious and prohibitively expensive'. Instead it was decided to work on something simpler which would have direct value for the library's readers.

Attention was thus focussed on the Widener Library shelflists. A shelflist is a record of a library's books arranged in the order in which they appear on the shelves and has traditionally served two main purposes: as an inventory of the books in the library and as an aid in placing new material. The Widener Library still used the old sheaf form handwritten shelflist in loose-leaf volumes which was started in the nineteenth century. As might be expected, this was showing signs of wear. The idea was developed that this shelflist, with the aid of computer technology, could be upgraded and transformed into a kind of classified catalogue with alphabetical and chronological indexes which would be useful to readers and library staff alike. These indexes were obtained by a programmed computer sort of the original entries. The chronological listing has been particularly useful to the Harvard libraries themselves: the Houghton library goes through this list before each volume is published to see if any unsuspected treasures have turned up.

The conversion of the shelflist into computer printout is proceeding class by class, beginning with a small section of some 1200 entries of historical works on the Crusades. Several volumes have now been issued and a full-scale publication programme for the Widener shelflist is under way. The library considers the cost of converting the shelflist worth while for its own record purposes while the publication part of the programme is conceived to be self-supporting. Sales and subscriptions for the series have reached a level that provides a secure financial base for the venture.

The first volumes of the new shelflist were in standard, upper-case only, computer printout, but later volumes are in upper and lower case. The published volumes are reduced by about 50%. Examples of the old and new Widener shelflists are given in the article by De Gennaro (1968), and one may judge for oneself what degree of success there has been in the upgrading process. Palmer gives a technical description of the project in its earlier stages in the *Brasenose conference on the automation of libraries* (Harrison and Laslett, 1967).

As the shelflist conversion proceeds the library is building up a data bank in machine-readable form and other developments become possible, for example the creation of new finding lists based on combinations of language, date and place of publication. Particularly interesting is the attempt by the Institute of Latin American Studies at the University of London to use the Latin American shelflist tapes as the basis for building a union list in machine-readable form of Latin American holdings in British libraries.

The Widener shelflist project has enabled the library to establish its own Data Processing Department so that it can take on new projects in a routine manner. These included the preparation in multiple copies for internal use of revised versions of the classification schedules and the subject-heading list, which had previously existed only in two typewritten copies some thirty years old.

Baltimore County

The Baltimore County Public Library in Maryland, U.S.A. issued a computer-produced book catalogue in July 1965, and just over a year afterwards produced a refreshingly frank report giving an account of their new catalogue and detailing the problems it brought. This report compares in some detail the cost of the computer catalogue with the cost of maintaining a card catalogue (Childers, et al., 1967) A catalogue in book form was decided on for two reasons:

1. The need for a union catalogue of the complete holdings of the system at each branch in place of the earlier card catalogues covering only holdings of the individual branch;

and 2. Several new branch libraries were to be opened and a union catalogue did away with the need to establish separate card catalogues for each one.

This was a small catalogue consisting of a basic set of three volumes of some 55,000 titles between them, one volume each for authors, titles and subjects. The original plan was for monthly cumulative supplements for 1965 and a second basic list after two years.

The catalogue was produced under contract by a commercial firm which had no previous experience in producing book catalogues. The library personnel had no previous experience with computers or with programming. It seems that both sides underestimated the amount of work to be done.

Filing problems were particularly apparent among the difficulties on the library's side: the computer did not disregard such designations as 'ed.', 'comp.', 'illus.', etc. in filing and they were consequently omitted; abbreviations and numerals were arranged as written and not as if spelt out. 'Mc' was thus filed as written and not as 'Mac'; for acronyms it was necessary to have periods either always or never, and they chose never.

As you can see from the examples*, both upper and lower case was used (printout was from an *IBM* 120-character chain). Baltimore County Public Library had always used simplified cataloguing and this was maintained, cut down even more, in the computer catalogue: each catalogue entry consists of from two to four lines, in double columns. Added entries were given sparingly (e.g. none for joint authors and only occasionally for editors). The library was firmly of the opinion that its catalogue was to be a finding list, not a bibliographical tool.

Input was by punched cards. Errors were from three sources:

1. Mistakes in cataloguing (mainly misspellings);
2. Key-punching errors;

and 3. Errors in programming.

The last two mainly affected corporate authors, especially those with subheadings.

It was difficult to say how much staff time was saved by the computer catalogue, if any. The only time saved for the cataloguers was

* Figures 3 and 4.

by being able to consult the catalogues at their desks. The two main conclusions were:

1. The adoption of a computer-produced book catalogue proved an added expense: it cost £9.57 per title in the book catalogue in the first year of its operation against £8.19 per title in the last year of the card catalogue. But the costs of the continuations of the catalogue were expected to remain stable or to decrease. We are reminded that the figures on costs can be taken as applying only to the Baltimore County Library system;

and 2. The provision of multiple copies of a portable union catalogue in book form resulted in an increase in the services provided by the library. There was a marked increase in inter-library loans within the system, and this could not be attributed to any other factor. And it was possible to distribute copies of the catalogue to over a hundred schools in the county. The increase in the inter-library loans meant of course that this service cost more overall.

C. W. Robinson, the Baltimore County Librarian, concluded his report (1965) with 'a few general observations':

'In common with many librarians, we were aghast at the difficulties. . . . We were convinced that we would never understand the difference between *ADP* and *EDP*, the intricacies of programming, the principles of systems analysis and so on. We still don't know many of the details or even the principles, but neither do we understand the electrical and mechanical theory which is involved in the design and construction of the heating and air-conditioning equipment in our libraries. Our main job was not the comprehension of data processing as such, but the setting up of specifications. . . . We would recommend that others entering such a project should consider carefully every item that should or should not go in the catalog. . . . Then confer long and soul-searchingly with the programmer to make sure that there is a genuine meeting of minds and that everyone concerned is agreed on every single item involved and the way in which it is to appear in the book catalog. Insist on your own terminology; do not be overawed by documentationese.'

The New London Boroughs*

In 1965 there was a re-organization of local government authorities in London. New boroughs were formed by the amalgamation into one authority of a number of the former boroughs. One of the most immediate and complex problems which faced the libraries of these new boroughs was the provision and maintenance of public catalogues of the bookstock. The new boroughs inherited a variety of different catalogues, of different physical forms and constructed on

* See also the paper by Batty (pp. 55–61).

different systems. Some of them decided that computer technology offered a means of constructing a union catalogue of the holdings of all their libraries which would be available in several copies, so that each branch would be able to have one. Catalogues in book form occupy much less space than card cabinets and thus even mobile libraries were able to have a union catalogue. The computer catalogue could be produced either by using the local authority's own computer (if there was one available) or by contract to an outside firm. Only current accessions would be included, at least to begin with; the older stock could be taken into the computer catalogue later.

The original intention at Barnet (Meakin, 1965) was to produce three sequences which would be updated and cumulated every few months: a classified catalogue, an alphabetical author catalogue, and a subject index. These three sequences are still used but are now cumulated at six monthly intervals. They are supplemented by fortnightly lists in author order.

The catalogue is produced under contract by *ICT* (now *ICL*) and is restricted to adult non-fiction only. 24 copies of the catalogue are produced by Rank-Xerox *Copyflo* with computer printout of 11″ × 15″ reduced to 8″ × 12″ (i.e. to about 75%). Since February 1968 Rank-Xerox have been using their new 2400 printer and this is said to result in a more readable image.

The estimates given by *ICT* were based on an intake of 400 titles a fortnight, leading to a maximum stock of about 100,000 titles by the tenth year. *ICT* quoted the cost for the first year as £840 for one copy and £1540 for 24 copies. By the ninth year, the cumulations would bring the cost to £1840 for a single copy and £6170 for 24 copies. In addition to this there was an initial charge of £630 for programming plus £150 for magnetic tapes. £75 was set aside for an initial supply of binders. This order of finance was not considered by the library authority to be excessive when viewed (in 1965) against a total annual expenditure for the library of some £360,000.

In order to keep costs down Barnet accepted a very short entry, one or, at most, two lines per item, giving Dewey number, author, short title, edition, date and holding library or libraries. (Perhaps this is all that is needed in a finding list type of catalogue.) They also accepted some oddities in filing.

There were worried by the delays in production time: fortnightly batches of 400 titles were sent to *ICT*, who in two or three days sent a print out to Rank-Xerox. Rank-Xerox in their turn sent reduced copies to the central library in three or four days and these were then distributed to the branches via a regular twice daily delivery service. This time scale of about seven days does not seem excessive by university library standards.

After three years practical experience with a computer-produced catalogue, Barnet are now concerning themselves with the next stage of development. This will include an automated order system.

Barnet's original programming costs were reduced when the London Borough of Camden adopted the same system from *ICT*. Camden (Maidment, 1968) now have separate catalogues of children's books and adult fiction as well as non-fiction. They are introducing developments to the system, including the elimination of the strait jacket brought about by the use of fields of fixed length. (This, for example, restricted the classification number to ten spaces, the author's name to 40 spaces and the title, edition, publisher and date to 76.) Camden plan to build up an entry starting from the original ordering of the book. Selective printing from the master record will then be used for different purposes (e.g. author+brief title for the order to the bookseller); the catalogue entry will be fuller but will exclude the accession number and the bookseller.

Greenwich Public Libraries use the computer available in their own local authority, (Howard, 1967) but like Barnet and Camden believe the advantages of having a union catalogue available at each service point outweigh the disadvantages of sometimes strange filing and of truncated entries in nasty upper case printout. Their former union catalogue on cards is being edited for conversion to machine-readable form and as these entries are prepared they are included in the next annual printout. An original estimate of two years to complete this conversion was later revised to five years, when it is estimated that the catalogue will be in 20 volumes, ten for authors and ten for subjects, with some 15,000 entries to each volume.

Tower Hamlets is one of the new London boroughs which decided not to use a computer for the job of integrating the catalogues of three formerly separate systems, Stepney, Poplar and Bethnal Green. Instead, they have been building up a new union classified catalogue on cards since 1965. This work is being absorbed by their existing staff and they estimate it will take six years to complete. Some 50,000 titles have been dealt with in $2\frac{1}{4}$ years. They give four reasons for not using a computer (Bennett, 1968):

1. There was a vast amount of bibliographic work to be done before data were ready; a whole library system had to be reclassified from one scheme to another and a mixed bunch of catalogues, classified, author and dictionary, needed to be united into one central catalogue;
2. The local authority's computer was already fully occupied by other departments;
3. A single-line print out was unacceptable as a catalogue entry;

and 4. They were worried about the probable costs.

Ontario New University Libraries Project

The uncouth brevity of the catalogue entry used by the London boroughs may be contrasted with the more sophisticated product from the Ontario New University Libraries Project (*ONULP*). This project was established in 1963 to develop and maintain five new 35,000-volume academic libraries (Bregzis, 1965). Their computer-produced catalogues are in upper and lower case, with a range of diacritical marks, and the main entry in the author catalogue is in full and traditional detail. The filing is designed to give a traditional alphabetical sequence, including, for example, the disregarding of initial articles. For this a comprehensive list of articles in 27 languages is used. Such modifications of the normal computer alphabetical sorting are unfortunately impressively costly in terms of programming and operational factors. Improved appearance and legibility has had to be paid for, as a later report on the *ONULP* cataloguing system indicates:

> 'Experience has determined that this system of producing catalogues is prohibitively expensive. Two cost factors contribute to this circumstance first the cost of machine time, with existing programs and equipment, is considerably more than was anticipated; and the actual costs of printing the catalogues from the machine-produced printout have also proved to be unexpectedly high. The conclusion of those working on the project is that book catalogues not only do not satisfactorily meet the needs of a growing collection, but also cost substantially more to produce than card catalogues.' (Stuart-Stubbs, 1966.)

German Libraries

Although we do not intend to say very much more about the use of computers in libraries on the continent of Europe, a brief mention must be made of the situation in Germany. Fuller information about automation in German libraries is given in the recent report by Lingenberg (1968). Two years ago only Bochum and the Technical University of Berlin were involved with computers; now there are some dozen libraries with automated systems in being or planned.

The Germans seem to have taken the author catalogue as one of the first candidates for automation. This may be because of their experience in the computerization of the *Deutsche Bibliographie*. (It is interesting to note that the *Deutsche Bibliographie* is studying the use of computer-controlled Digiset photocomposition.) Lingenberg comments, 'in Germany a degree of success has already been achieved with computer-produced book catalogues and bibliographies. . . . We have chosen to go straight ahead without too much thought for theory. Time alone will show whether the resulting pattern of bibliographical data collection and recording, based partly on documentation models, will prove a valid one'. There is as yet no agreement among the German libraries on a standard format for a catalogue entry. The decision of the University libraries of Bremen and Ulm to develop a joint computerized cataloguing programme may be a first step in this direction and the influence of the *MARC II* format another.

FILING PROBLEMS

Filing problems become apparent when libraries use computers. If a fairly small file is involved, such as in an order or accessions system, then these problems can perhaps be ignored. It is after all only the library staff, not the public, who notice them. Such is the present filing situation in the computerized order and accessions system at Newcastle. But a library's catalogue is a much larger file and is one used by the public.

The trouble comes not so much because of the seemingly endless variations possible among different libraries on the theme of alphabetical filing, of which 'letter by letter' or 'word by word' is but one among many (although a greater degree of standardization in this might be helpful to all concerned), but rather because existing filing rules are not sufficiently explicit for successful computer manipulation.

A typical computer alphabetization follows the rule 'space before A–Z, then 0, 1–9'. This appears to be delightfully simple until it is realized that it results in odd (i.e. unaccustomed) spaces appearing here and there and orders like:

Charles County, Md.
Charles d'Orleans
Charles family
Charles, John.

This is a strict alphabetical sequence*; unfortunately a computer will not recognize that the different categories of persons, places and titles affect their filing order, that is unless something is done about it.

A human filer can easily file 'Mc' as if it were 'Mac' and 'St.' as if it were 'Saint'. But to the moronic machine they are different and file in different places.

Then there is the problem that certain kinds of words have to be ignored; non-significant filing words, like initial articles, are of this kind. Terms added to the end of a heading, like 'ed.' and 'joint author' are other examples.

The degree of precision necessary when using a computer to order a sequence is well illustrated in the example of 'The Chinese; their history and culture' (Richmond, 1966)†, where variations in spacing and punctuation and the two forms of 'and', spelt out and as ampersand, present forty different titles to the machine, in place of one title for the human filer.

Some libraries have accepted many of the disadvantages of computer alphabetization, and so may have headings like Newton, Isaac, Sir instead of Newton, Sir Isaac. Others have attempted to program their computers to give an order more acceptable to traditional library practice, but have found that this is costly.

An attempt at a code suitable for both computer and manual filing was issued by Hines and Harris (1966). This met with some criticism of inadequacy. Both the American Library Association and the Cataloguing and Indexing Group of the Library Association have been studying problems of filing, the latter having set up a working party for this purpose in 1966, including representatives of computer firms as well as librarians and documentalists. A particularly interesting attempt to achieve a sophisticated filing standard, in a parallel field, is reported by Cox and Davies (1970 d).

The moral to be drawn from the problem area of filing again seems to be that diversity is costly and that librarians must rethink their own problems before someone else does it for them.

INDEXES

A good example of a small computerization project which is a means of familiarizing both librarians with the basic techniques of

---

* Though note the intrusive comma.

† Reproduced in the paper by Barraclough, Dews and Smethurst (figure 3).

mechanization and computer men with the mysteries of librarianship is the production of a subject index and associated authority file
to the classification scheme. Such a project has the advantage of
being of immediate practical value. Subject indexes and authority
files of this kind have been produced, for example, at Dorset County
Library, Loughborough University and The City University.

These libraries were already maintaining on cards their own
subject indexes to the classification scheme used. This was fed into
the computer. Authority files to the classification scheme were then
obtained by sorting on the classification numbers and both this and
the original alphabetical subject index were produced in book form
in multiple copies. These can be made available to the public at all
strategic service points and each classifier can have his own copies of
the index and the authority file.

The computerized subject index in The City University Library is
particularly interesting in that no modification of conventional
indexing procedure has been necessary (Cowburn, *et al.*, 1968). The
alphabetical subject index uses a conventional variety of punctuation
symbols to present a fairly sophisticated but traditional acceptable
alphabetization (this is also achieved in the computerized alphabetization of British Technology Index). The City University Library
uses the Universal Decimal Classification and the authority file print
out maintains an accurate *UDC* order with all arbitrary symbols and
auxiliary numbers in correct sequence.

CIRCULATION SYSTEMS

An enthusiastic article about the University of Hawaii's new computerized circulation system appeared in the May 1965 issue of
College and Research Libraries (Cammack, 1965). This system was
designed to operate at approximately the same cost as the unsatisfactory manual system which preceded it. 'Machine costs turned out
to be considerably lower than expected. . . . The new system literally
paid for its own implementation and operation. Significant savings
are expected to accrue over an extended period of time as workload
increases are absorbed by machines rather than by additional staff.
These "savings", however, are far less important to the library, its
staff and its users than are the time saving advantages of a really
efficient, reliable, circulation system.'

Unfortunately this glowing account was completely rebutted in
the September 1965 issue (Shaw, 1965): 'Computer costs were double

the preliminary estimate. . . . The net cost of computer charging was found to be substantially more than double that of the old manual charging system, which was no model of efficiency. . . . In the old system it sometimes took from 15 to 30 minutes to locate a book. Under the computer charging system . . . it was always a day before the charge got into the files since the computer was run once a day only. . . . The mean time for getting a charge into the computer file was 3·3 days, and on several occasions the delay ran two weeks or more before the location of a book could be determined.' Shaw concludes that his is not a generalization about computer charging, but a factual report on the system as actually applied at the University of Hawaii. 'It may very well be that some system still to come and some machine configuration still to come may give us better control of loans for less money, but that remains for the future.'

Elsewhere experience with computerized loan and circulation systems have been less unhappy. Chapin (1967) reports on the system at Michigan State University. Here the former manual system was breaking down (in spite of Sunday shifts). The automated system which replaced it cost 20% more to run, but the improved efficiency made it acceptable. Chapin gives six criteria for judging the new system:

1. Cost;
2. Capacity for increased work-load;
3. Better use of library resources (one result of the Michigan State system was that books got back onto the shelves more quickly after being returned from loan);
4. Capacity to give operational reports;
5. Acceptance by the library's users and staff;
and 6. Its accuracy and currency.

In this country, Southampton University introduced an automated circulation system in the latter part of 1966. It has been documented in *Program* (Woods, 1966 *a* & *b*, 1968, 1969).

A university library needs to know as soon as possible when a book has been taken out on loan from the library, ideally say within minutes. The manual systems typically operated in university libraries have been able to achieve this, theoretically at any rate. Public libraries do not demand the same precision from their charging systems and so have been quite happy with a computerized book issue system where the record is updated weekly. West Sussex County Library have such a system (Bearman, 1968) and point to two advantages over a manual system: the mechanized system takes up less space and machines can be handled by non-professional staff. A further development was introduced in May this year when the library had an on-line terminal to the computer, through not operational for the whole of the working day, enabling reservations to be checked against the master file. An enquiry in coded form, quoting the book number, is typed on the keyboard. Within three seconds, the reply is automatically received, in type, giving the reader's name, address and number, date the book was borrowed and the number of overdue notices (if any) already sent.

ORDERS
Newcastle University Library

The Newcastle order system has been described twice before (Line, 1966, and Cox and Grose, 1967: p. 158), so that only a brief summary here is necessary.

The system could not have been set up without the Newcastle File Handling System, on which work was begun in 1964 by N. S. M. Cox and J. D. Dews (Cox and Grose 1967, p. 1). Planning of the order system itself was started in mid-1965, and the system has been in operation (for the first three months in parallel with the old system) since April 1966. Roughly speaking, the first year was employed in removing some of the more noticeable errors and inconveniences in the design, while the system was dealing with the routine of ordering and accessions. Since then the system has been progressively refined and developed, to reduce punching time for input and to produce the printouts and statistics that were required.

By Easter 1968 the Library had more or less accepted full responsibility for input punching, with a *Friden Flexowriter* and *Creed* punch in the Library and Library typists employed on the work. Experiment is being carried on to find the optimum frequency of reminders to booksellers (which has to be commensurate with the bookseller's capacity to cope) and of departmental accessions lists and other printouts; and refinements of the kind needed to deal effectively with, for instance, situations like 'Vol. 2 supplied herewith, Vol. 1 O/P, Vol. 3 NYP', are added as the need becomes known. Stationery design has also been modified several times, especially to help clerical staff working on input data.

It is impossible to be dogmatic about the cost effectiveness of the new system, if only because no cost-study of the old manual system could be done. What is indisputable is that the old system was breaking down and that things can now be done easily which could not be done at all before: reminders to booksellers are a standard printout, and so are the departmental accessions lists, which have been well received as a new service.

Running costs are reasonable, and are almost certainly less than staff salaries for providing the same service. Development costs, as far as they can be identified, would be enormous if reckoned at full commercial rates: they would include a great deal of one programmer's time for three years, salary for Library and Computing Laboratory staff heavily involved at different times, and of course machine time on the computer.

The result, however, is an effective, flexible system which has now reached the stage where routine handling is done by junior and clerical staff; and the experience built up during these years should help to reduce very considerably the development period needed on new systems of the same kind. When the system is transferred from *KDF9* to the *IBM 360/67*, in one or two years' time, the opportunity will be taken of not only re-programming but also redesigning in the light of experience.

Book trade

Developments in the book trade affect all librarians, directly or indirectly; and it may be expected that as automated techniques become better understood and more widely introduced some links will be created between libraries and suppliers via the computer. The exchange of machine-readable records, automatic invoicing and stock-control, and other peripheral advantages will be greatly facilitated by the *ISBN* as a unique identifier and the *MARC* record as a communications format.

A report on the present situation in the book trade was made recently by Julian Blackwell (Blackwell (1970)) who with David Whitaker has also contributed a chapter to the Work in Progress section in the present volume.

CODA

Few libraries are blessed with 'extra' funds or staff. The computer, to the extent that it is a labour-saving device, should, in the long run, help with this problem. In the short run (say under five years) it won't—it will make it worse. Explicit recognition of this fact will prevent a number of problems arising in the planning operation.   (Cox, *et al.*, 1966)

Even this brief survey of the variety of approaches makes it quite clear that local conditions and individual interpretations of the purpose and needs of libraries have played a considerable part in determining the extent and direction of automation. In some cases both librarians and their institutions have been forced through circumstances to find some way of improving existing methods. A good example of this is the shot-gun marriage of London boroughs, when barely compatible records have had to be merged at fairly high speed; another is the Newcastle University order system, which was no longer able to cope with demand in its old form. In the latter case resource, both hardware and software, was available; and it has often happened that local authorities have had spare capacity on machines installed for payroll and other similar work. In at least one case this spare capacity has become one of the main reasons for a public library's becoming involved in automation.

University libraries have been fairly fortunate in that a computer and some programming and systems design are often available either free or at less than commercial rates; and in this connection universities have also benefited by help from the Computer Board which has relieved pressure on internal resources and made development possible where it could not otherwise have taken place. Few libraries have so far started an automation project in this country with their own programmers and systems analysts, though some have gradually acquired trained staff as projects developed. An obvious limiting factor has therefore been the extent to which the computing side of the institution is able and willing to co-operate in the development of library programs.

The computing people themselves, assuming considerable time and enthusiasm on their part, have been and will be limited in turn by the librarians' comprehension of the problems involved in automating library processes; and both sides are limited by their resources in hardware and software, and by the difficulty of obtaining information about successes and failures in relevant experiments elsewhere.

One of the important recent developments in this country has been the gradual appearances of groups and working parties with special interests, which are attempting to co-ordinate research into common problems. Librarians and computing staff have been involved in such groups, along in some cases with manufacturers so that research is following various lines: not only the discussion of problems and the exchange of programs and other documents, with some attempt to share out research on different aspects of Library work, but also the production of 'package deal' programs by the manufacturers themselves, specially designed for library applications. Notable among these groups have been the *SUN* Working Party, based on the *ICL 1900* range of computers, and the Newcastle Symplegades Research Group which has published work and arranged courses and seminars.

The formation of *OSTI* in 1965 was an important point in the development of computer applications in libraries, both in the provision of funds and in the circulation of information. *OSTI* has financed many of the plans referred to in this paper, and its staff has played a considerable part in linking people of like interests and approach and avoiding the duplication of research in the subject.

It seems clear that in present economic circumstances in this country and at the particular stage that computerization in libraries has reached, the immediate future is likely to be a period of consolidation, exchange of information and education. When those libraries that have pioneered applications in various fields are able to report in detail on their experience, to an extent that permits others to apply the findings to their own circumstances, it is likely that those who have waited will be encouraged to advance, and that those who have developed one aspect will be able to proceed to others. We can hope that the period of wholesale and disastrous commitment is over, to be succeeded by a more cautious and more certain advance.

FURTHER READING

This is in no way a full list but merely a guideline to suggestions for keeping up-to-date. It is restricted to material in English.

Short general reviews are by Stein (1964), Lynch (1966) and Adkinson and Stearns (1967). Cox, Dews and Dolby (1966) originated from a series of lectures given in Newcastle in early 1966.

Critical bibliographical reviews were published by Coblans (1966) and Kimber (1967).

A good bibliography was compiled by McCune and Salmon (1967). This is usefully arranged according to particular subject areas (e.g. acquisitions, cataloguing) and is restricted to material relating to the automation or mechanization of traditional library functions.

Apart from the more general library periodicals there are at least three serials devoted to library automation. *Program* is edited by Richard Kimber, at the School of Library Studies at the Queen's University of Belfast, and is published by Aslib. The *Annual review of information science and technology* is issued by the American Documentation Institute, and the recently formed Information Science and Automation Division of the American Library Association publishes the *Journal of library automation*. There is also an annual *Clinic on library applications of data processing*, organized by the Graduate School of Library Science at the University of Illinois the *Proceedings* of which are issued as annual volumes. The quarterly *OSTI Newsletter* includes notes on projects supported by other bodies.

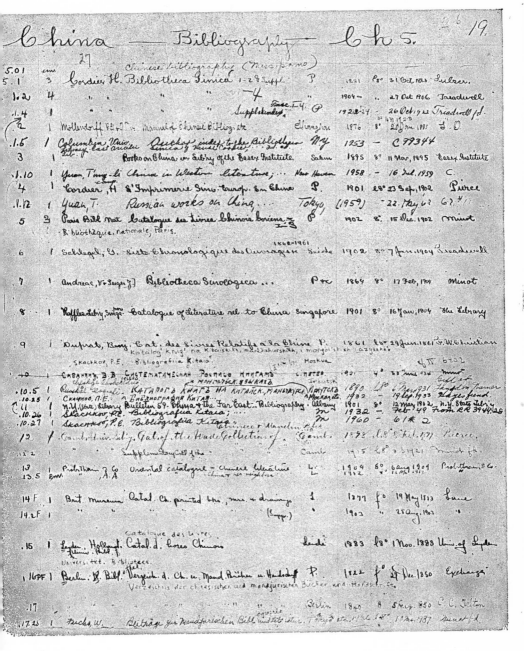

Figure 1. Sample page from the original Widener Shelflist started in the 19th Century in De Gennaro, R., 'Automation in the Harvard College Library', *Harvard Library Bulletin*, vol. 16, No. 3, (July, 1968).

- 16 -

Ch   2   Chinese history - Periodicals (.1-.26, A-Z) - Continued

Ch 2.18.12.5   Royal Asiatic Society of Great Britain and Ireland. North China Branch. Index to
                     Journal, v.1-54. Shanghai. 1924

Ch 2.18.13   Royal Asiatic Society of Great Britain and Ireland. Hongkong Branch. Journal.
                     Hongkong. 1,1960+

Ch 2.18.14   Royal Asiatic Society of Great Britain and Ireland. North China Branch. Rules of
                     the North China of the Royal Asiatic Society. Shanghai, 1911?

Ch 2.18.15F   Royal Institute of International Affairs. Summaries of leading articles.
                     London. 2-5,1933-1937

Ch 2.18.25   3v   Revue de l'Extreme Orient. Paris. 1-3,1882-1887

Ch 2.19   3v   Shanghai almanac. Shanghai. 1852-1857

Ch 2.19.2F   Shanghai International Red Cross. News bulletin. Shanghai. 1938-1939

Ch 2.19.3   The Straits Chinese magazine. Singapore. 1-5,1897-1901

Ch 2.19.7   Supreme court and consular gazette. Shanghai. 5,1869

Ch 2.19.13   Sinica. Frankfurt.

Ch 2.19.15   Sinica. 1,1938?

Ch 2.19.18   13v Sinica Leidensia. Leyden. 1,1931+

Ch 2.19.20   Sino-Japanese issue series. Nanking. 1-8,1937-1938

Ch 2.19.22   Sputnik po Dal'nemu Vostoku. Kharbin'. 1910

Ch 2.19.24   Social research publications. Monograph series. Peiping.

Ch 2.19.30   Studies in Chinese Communist terminology. Berkeley.

Ch 2.20   38v T'oung Pao. Archives. Archives pour servir a l'etude de l'histoire, des langues, de
                     la geographie et de l'ethnographie de l'Asie orientale. Leide. 1,1900+

Ch 2.20.5F   28v Trans-Pacific. Tokyo. 1-39,1919-1950

Ch 2.21.10   8v   United States. Central Intelligence Agency. Documents Division. Weekly report on
                     Communist China. 1960+

Ch 2.22   19v Vladivostock. Vostochnyi Institut. Izvestiia. Vladivostock. 1-30,1899-1909

Ch 2.22.5   Vladivostock. Vostochnyi Institut. Spravochnais knizhka. Vladivostock. 1909

Ch 2.22.10   Voice of China. Shanghai. 1,1936

Ch 2.22.15   Voice of new China. Shanghai.

Ch 2.23   2v   World's Chinese student's journal. Shanghai. 2-3,1907-1909

Ch 2.23.5   9v   Week in China. Peking. 1926-1932

Ch 2.23.8   3v   West China Border Research Society. Journal. Chengtu. 1-9,1922-1937

Ch 2.25   Yenching journal of Chinese studies. Peiping.

Ch 2.25.5   11v Harvard-Yenching Institute studies. Cambridge. 1,1950+

Ch 2.26   Zheltyi lik. Shankhai. 1,1921

Ch 2.30   United States. Consulate. Hongkong. Summary of New China news agency.

Ch 2.31F   38v United States. Consulate. Hongkong. Current background. 1950-1965

Ch 2.31   2v   United States. Consulate. Hongkong. Current background. 1966+

Ch 2.32F   369v United States. Consulate. Hongkong. Survey of China mainland press. 1950-1965

Ch 2.32   15v United States. Consulate. Hongkong. Survey of China mainland press. 1966+

Ch 2.33F   16v United States. Consulate. Hongkong. Index to survey of China mainland press, extracts
                     from China mainland magazine, and current background. 1956+

Ch 2.33   United States. Consulate. Hongkong. Index to survey of China mainland press, extracts
                     from China mainland magazine, and current background. 1966+

Ch   3   Chinese history - Societies [Discontinued]

Ch 3.1   2v   China Association, London. Annual report. London. 1911-1912

Ch 3.9.5   China. International Institute. Pamphlet. Shanghai. 4

Ch 3.12   5v   Verband fur den Fernen Osten. Schriften. Berlin. 1-5,1915-1920

Ch   4   Chinese history - Registers, directories, yearbooks
Deposit

Ch 4.2   24v Chronicle and directory for China, Japan. Hongkong. 1889-1941

Ch 4.3   Hongkong almanack and directory. Hongkong. 1846

Ch 4.5   Hongkong directory with list of foreign residents. Hongkong, 1859.

Ch 4.7   Rosenstock's directory of China and Manila. Manila. 15,1909

Ch 4.9F   Mayers, S.F. List of the higher metropolitan and provincial authorities of China.
                     Shanghai, 1907.

Ch 4.53   4v   Manchuria year book. Tokyo. 1931-1942

Ch 4.53.9   Manchuria year book. 3rd ed. Tokyo. 1931

Ch   5   Chinese history - Bibliographies

Ch 5.01   Pamphlet box. Chinese bibliography.

Ch 5.1   3v   Cordier, H. Bibliotheca Sinica. Supplement. Paris, 1881.

Ch 5.1.2   4v   Cordier, H. Bibliotheca Sinica. Paris, 1904.

Ch 5.1.4   Cordier, H. Bibliotheca Sinica. Supplement et tables. Paris, 1922-24.

Ch 5.1.5   Columbia University. Library. East Asiatic Library. Author index to the Bibliotheca
                     sinica of Henri Cordier. 2nd ed. N.Y., 1953.

Ch 5.1.10   Yuan, T'ung-li. China in Western literature. New Haven, 1958.

Ch 5.1.12   Yuan, T'ung-li. Russian works on China. Tokyo, 1959.

Ch 5.2   Mollendorff, P.G. Manual of Chinese bibliography. Shanghai, 1876.

Ch 5.3   Books on China in library of the Essex Institute. Salem, 1895.

Ch 5.4   Cordier, H. L'imprimerie Sino-Europeenne en China. Paris, 1901.

Figure 2. Sample page from computer printed Widener Shelflist in De Gennaro, R., 'Automation in the Harvard College Library', *Harvard Library Bulletin*, vol. 16, No. 3, (July 1968).

```
940.545
M      Morison, Samuel Eliot
            Battle of the Atlantic: September 1939-
       May 1943.    Little, c1947.
            (History of United States naval operations
       in World War II. v.1)



6      1. World War, 1939-1945--Atlantic Ocean
       2. World War, 1939-1945--Naval operations
       3. T  4. Series
```

```
940.545   WORLD WAR, 1939-1945--ATLANTIC OCEAN
M      Morison, Samuel Eliot
            Battle of the Atlantic: September 1939-
       May 1943.    Little, c1947
            (History of United States naval operations
       in World War II. v.1)



6      1. World War, 1939-1945--Atlantic Ocean
       2. World War, 1939-1945--Naval operations
       3. T  4. Series
```

See overleaf

Figure 3. Samples of multilith catalogue cards, superseded by a computer produced book catalogue; compare figure 4. Childers, T., *et al.* 'Book Catalog and card catalog: a cost and service study', Baltimore County Public Library (1967).

940.545   WORLD WAR, 1939-1945--NAVAL OPERATIONS
M   Morison, Samuel Eliot
            Battle of the Atlantic: September 1939-
      May 1943.   Little, c1947.
            (History of United States naval operations
      in World War II. v.1)

6   1. World War, 1939-1945--Atlantic Ocean
      2. World War, 1939-1945--Naval operations
      3. T 4. Series

            History of United States naval operations
940.545   in World War II. v.1
M   Morison, Samuel Eliot
            Battle of the Atlantic: September 1939-
      May 1943.   Little, c1947.
            (History of United States naval operations
      in World War II. v.1)

6   1. World War, 1939-1945--Atlantic Ocean
      2. World War, 1939-1945--Naval operations
      3. T 4. Series

            Battle of the Atlantic: September 1939-
940.545   May 1943.
M   Morison, Samuel Eliot
            Battle of the Atlantic: September 1939-
      May 1943.   Little, c1947.
            (History of United States naval operations
      in World War II. v.1)

6   1. World War, 1939-1945--Atlantic Ocean
      2. World War, 1939-1945--Naval operations
      3. T 4. Series

Figure 3 continued

, WILLIAM JAMES

, WILLIAM JAMES
tains to the northward. 1959
5015658   973.3 M
 S and I. 1957.
5018157   940.5486 M
N, WINONA LOUISE
ly meets the depression. 1939
4046336   392.3 M
NSTERN, CHRISTIAN
genlieder. 1963
4046337   837 M
NSTERN, GEORGE EDWARD
rl Harbor. 1947
4046338   940.54 M
NSTERN, OSKAR
the accuracy of economic observations. 2nd
 rev. 1963
4046339   330.18 M
ation of national defense. 1959
4046340   355 M
NSTERN, SOMA
my father's pastures. 1947
4046341
of the lost son. 1946
4046342
NTHAU, HANS JOACHIM
ssroad papers. 1965
5017251   308 M
emmas of politics. 1958
4046343   341 M
itics among nations. 3rd ed. 1960
4046344   341 M
itics in the twentieth century. 1962 3v.
4046345   320.1 M
pose of American politics. 1960
4046346   973.91 M
tnam and the United States. 1965.
5012708   327.597 M

LT, EVELYN
rcebook for the biological sciences. 1958
4046347   371.3 M
 OSAMU
ical Japanese gardens. 1962.
6017103   712 M
RTY, PHILIP
ingboard diving. 1959
4046348   797.2 M
R, JAMES JUSTINIAN
entures of Hajji Baba of Ispahan. 1937
4046349
, RELMAN
t wind rising. 1960
4046350   950 M
ON, DAVID L.
 S R and Africa. 1964
5021189   327.47 M
ON, ELTING ELMORE
rican style. 1958
4046351   917.3 M
, machines, and modern times. 1966
6019686   601 M
moil and tradition (H L Stimson). 1960
4046352   B S
ON, LUELLA JOSEPHINE
ppingstones to professional nursing. 3rd ed.
0
4046353   610.7 M
ON, NATHANIEL HOLMES
body Library. 1954
4046354   Ref 021 M
ON, SAMUEL ELIOT
niral of the ocean sea. a life of
istopher Columbus. 1942
4046355   B C
eutians, Gilberts and Marshalls; June 1942-
il 1944. 1951 (History of United States
val operations in World War II, v.7)
54046356   940.545 M
antic Battle won, May 1943-May 1945. 1956
story of United States naval operations in
ld War II, v.10)
54046357   940.545 M
ttle of the Atlantic: September 1939-May 1943.
7 (History of United States naval

operations in World War II. v.1)
    64046358   940.545 M
Breaking the Bismarks Barrier: 22 July 1942-1
May 1944. 1950 (History of United States
naval operations in World War II, v.6)
    64046359   940.545 M
Builders of the Bay Colony. Rev. and enl.
c1930
    65013249   974.4 M
By land and by sea. 1963
    64046360   973.04 M
Caribbean as Columbus saw it. c1964
    6501J250   972.902 M
Christopher Columbus, mariner. 1955
    64046361   B C

Figure 4(a).

Figure 4. Sample columns from a computer produced book catalogue showing the same entry in (a) author catalogue, (b), (c) title catalogue, and (d), (e) subject catalogue, printed two columns per page in Childers, T., *et al*, 'Book Catalog and card catalog: a cost and service study', Baltimore County Public Library (1967).

32

64022328   943.6 C
BATTLE OF MATAPAN
Pack, Stanley Walter Croucher 1961
64048874   940.545 P
BATTLE OF NEW ORLEANS
Chidsey, Donald Barr 1961
64020215   973.5 C
BATTLE OF NORTH CAPE
Ogden, Michael 1962
64048312   940.545 O
BATTLE OF PLASSEY AND THE CONQUEST OF BENGAL
Edwardes, Michael c1963
65011964   954.14 E
BATTLE OF POINT PLEASANT
Simpson-Poffenbarger, Livia Nye 1909
64056159   973.3 S
BATTLE OF THE ALMA
Gibbs, Peter Bawtree 1963
64030071   947.07 G
BATTLE OF THE ATLANTIC
Macintyre, Donald George Frederick Wyville 1961
64042956   940.545 M

BATTLE OF THE ATLANTIC: SEPTEMBER 1939-MAY 1943
Morison, Samuel Eliot 1947
64046358   940.545 M

BATTLE OF THE BOOKS
Swift, Jonathan Gulliver's travels, A tale of
a tub, The battle of the books 1950
64058746
Swift, Jonathan Tale of a tub, to which is
added, The battle of the books and the
Mechanical operation of the spirit 1958
64058752   827 S
BATTLE OF THE HUERTGEN FOREST
MacDonald, Charles Brown 1963
64042679   940.54 M
BATTLE OF THE LITTLE BIGHORN
Sandoz, Mari 1966.
66016893   973.82 S
BATTLE OF THE MARNE
Isselin, Henri 1965.
66014709   940.421 I
BATTLE OF THE NILE
Warner, Oliver 1960
64062523   942.07 W
BATTLE OF THE RIVER PLATE
Pope, Dudley 1956
64050519   940.545 P
Strabolgi, Joseph Montague Kenworthy, baron
1944
64058220   940.545 S
BATTLE OF THE V-WEAPONS, 1944-45
Collier, Basil 1964
65018199   940.54 C
BATTLE OF THE VILLA FIORITA
Godden, Rumer 1963
64030499
BATTLE OF THE WILD TURKEY
Johnson, Alvin Saunders 1961
64037084   S
BATTLE OF THE WILDERNESS
Schaff, Morris c1910
65013776   973.7 S
BATTLE OF TRAFALGAR
Taylor, A. H. 1950
66023166   940.27 T
BATTLE REPORT: ATLANTIC WAR
Karig, Walter 1944-1948
64037818   940.545 K
BATTLE REPORT: PACIFIC WAR: MIDDLE PHASE
Karig, Walter 1947
64037819   940.545 K
BATTLE REPORT: PEARL HARBOR TO CORAL SEA
Karig, Walter 1944
64037820   940.545 K
BATTLE REPORT: SELECTED POEMS
Shapiro, Harvey 1966
66020581   811 S
BATTLE ROYAL
Beamish, Tufton Victor Hamilton 1965
66023475   942.03 B
BATTLE STATIONS
Scoggin, Margaret Clara 1953
64054717   940.548 S
BATTLE: THE STORY OF THE BULGE

Hough, Richard Alexander 1966
66020052   629.227 H
HISTORY OF THE WORLD'S SPORTS CARS
Hough, Richard Alexander 1961
64035329   629.2 H
HISTORY OF THE WORTHIES OF ENGLAND
Fuller, Thomas 1840 3v.
64029155   920 F
HISTORY OF THE 175TH INFANTRY (FIFTH MARYLAND)
Brewer, James H. Fitzgerald 1955
65011277   Md. 356 B
HISTORY OF THE 94TH INFANTRY DIVISION IN WORLD
WAR II
Byrnes, Laurence G. 1948
64018528   940.54 B
HISTORY OF THOROUGHBRED RACING IN AMERICA
Robertson, William Harris P. c1964
65013621   798.4 R
HISTORY OF TOM JONES
Fielding, Henry 1885
64027516
HISTORY OF TOM JONES, A FOUNDLING
Fielding, Henry 1952.
66012374
HISTORY OF TORTURE THROUGHOUT THE AGES
Scott, George Ryley 1940
64054743   179.2 S
HISTORY OF TOYS
Fraser, Antonia 1966
66020509   688.7 F
HISTORY OF TRADE UNIONISM IN THE UNITED STATES
Perlman, Selig 1922
64049780   331.88 P
HISTORY OF TRANSPORTATION IN THE UNITED STATES
BEFORE 1860
Meyer, Balthasar Henry 1948
64045251   385 M
HISTORY OF TRAVEL IN AMERICA
Dunbar, Seymour 1915 4v.
64025291   Ref 385 D 1915
Dunbar, Seymour 1937
64025290   385 D 1937
HISTORY OF TRUNCHEONS
Dicken, Eden Ronald Huddleston 1952
65011878   352.2 D
HISTORY OF TUNNELLING
Sandstrom, Gosta E. c1963
65013754   624.19 S
HISTORY OF TURKEY
Price, Morgan Philips 1956
64050876   949.6 P
HISTORY OF TWELVE CAESARS
Suetonius Tranquillus, Caius 1930
64058457   878 S 1930
HISTORY OF UNDERCLOTHES
Cunnington, Cecil Willett 1951
65011773   Ref. 391 C
HISTORY OF UNITED STATES FOREIGN POLICY
Pratt, Julius William 2d ed. 1965.
65018933   327.73 P 1965

HISTORY OF UNITED STATES NAVAL OPERATIONS IN
WORLD WAR II. V.1
Morison, Samuel Eliot Battle of the Atlantic:
September 1939-May 1943 1947
64046358   940.545 M

HISTORY OF UNITED STATES NAVAL OPERATIONS IN
WORLD WAR II. V.2
Morison, Samuel Eliot Operations in North
African waters,October 1942-June 1943 1950
64046372   940.545 M
HISTORY OF UNITED STATES NAVAL OPERATIONS IN WORLD
WAR II, V.3
Morison, Samuel Eliot Rising sun in the
Pacific: 1931-April 1942 1948
64046373   940.545 M
HISTORY OF UNITED STATES NAVAL OPERATIONS IN
WORLD WAR II. V.4
Morison, Samuel Eliot Coral sea, Midway and
submarine actions: May 1942-August 1942 1949
64046362   940.545 M
HISTORY OF UNITED STATES NAVAL OPERATIONS IN WORLD
WAR II, V.5
Morison, Samuel Eliot Struggle for
Guadalcanal: August 1942-February 1943 1949
64046378   940.545 M

Figure 4(b).

Figure 4(c).

hofield, Brian Betham Russian convoys 1964
65019006   940.545 S
D WAR, 1939-1945--ART AND THE WAR
rtt, Frederick Florentine art under fire
49
64033151   940.531 H
xan, David Rape of art 1964
65017470   940.531 R
D WAR, 1939-1945--ASIA
puy, Trevor Nevitt Asiatic land battles: the
pansion of Japan in Asia 1963
64025395   940.54 D
puy, Trevor Nevitt Asiatic land battles:
panese ambitions in the Pacific 1963
64025394   940.54 D
D WAR, 1939-1945--ATLANTIC OCEAN
puy, Trevor Nevitt Naval war in the west:
e raiders 1963
64025403   940.54 D
puy, Trevor Nevitt Naval war in the west:
e wolf packs 1963
64025404   940.54 D
cintyre, Donald George Frederick Wyville
ttle of the Atlantic 1961
64042956   940.545 M
rison, Samuel Eliot Atlantic Battle won, May
43-May 1945 1956
64046357   940.545 M
rison, Samuel Eliot Battle of the Atlantic:
ptember 1939-May 1943 1947
64046358   940.545 M
th, Ronald Fiercest battle 1961
64055117   940.545 S
D WAR, 1939-1945--ATROCITIES
stle, John, pseud. Password is courage c1954
65011539   940.54 C
oper, George Tyndale Ordeal in the sun 1963
64021848   940.548 C
n, Nerin E. Day of the Americans 1966.
66014618   940.5472 G
ewish Black book committee Black book 1946
64037021   940.54 J
aplan, Chaim Aron Scroll of agony 1965.
66010781   943.84 K
yiszli, Miklos Auschwitz 1960
64048123   940.54 N
eynolds, Quentin James Minister of death 1960
64052050   940.54 R
ells, Leon Weliczker Janowska road 1963
64063187   940.54 W
D WAR, 1939-1945--BAVARIA
nott, Rodney G. Fortress that never was 1964
64045722   940.54 M
D WAR, 1939-1945--BLOCKADES
omax, John Garnett Diplomatic smuggler 1965
66022374   940.5481 L
D WAR, 1939-1945--BORNEO
eith, Agnes Newton Three came home 1947
64038025   940.547 K
D WAR, 1939-1945--BURMA
upuy, Trevor Nevitt Asiatic land battles:
lied victories in China and Burma 1963
64025393   940.54 D
osely, Leonard Oswald Gideon goes to war (O C
ingate) 1955
65021196   B W
eagrave, Gordon Stifler Burma surgeon returns
946
64054861   B S
eagrave, Gordon Stifler Burma surgeon 1943.
66015158   B S
LD WAR, 1939-1945--CAMPAIGNS
lexander, Harold Rupert Leofric George
lexander, 1st earl Alexander memoirs, 1940-
945 1962
64010665   940.542 A
ltieri, James Spearheaders 1960
64010936   940.54 A
twell, Lester Private 1958
64012553   940.54 A
aldwin, Hanson Weightman Battles lost and won
966
66019354   940.542 B
anoist-Mechin, Jacques Gabriel Paul Michel,
aron Sixty days that shook the West 1963

Karig, Walter Battle report: Atlantic war
1944-1948
64037818   940.545 K
Karig, Walter Battle report: Pearl Harbor to
Coral Sea 1944
64037820   940.545 K
Karig, Walter Battle report: Pacific war:
middle phase 1947
64037819   940.545 K
Keating, Bern Mosquito fleet 1963
64037974   940.545 K
Kemp, Peter Kemp Key to victory 1957
64038149   940.545 K
Krancke, Theodor Pocket Battleship 1958
64039225   359.3 K
Langmaid, Kenneth Sea raiders 1963
64039842   940.54 L
Macintyre, Donald George Frederick Wyville
Battle of the Atlantic 1961
64042956   940.545 M
Macintyre, Donald George Frederick Wyville
Fighting ships and seamen 1963
65018703   940.545 M
Masters, David Epics of salvage 1953
64044444   623 M
Morison, Samuel Eliot Aleutians, Gilberts and
Marshalls 1951
64046356   940.545 M
Morison, Samuel Eliot Atlantic Battle won, May
1943-May 1945 1956
64046357   940.545 M
Morison, Samuel Eliot Battle of the Atlantic:
September 1939-May 1943 1947
64046358   940.545 M
Morison, Samuel Eliot Breaking the Bismarks
Barrier: 22 July 1942-1 May 1944 1950
64046359   940.545 M
Morison, Samuel Eliot Coral sea, Midway and
submarine actions: May 1942-August 1942 1949
64046362   940.545 M
Morison, Samuel Eliot Invasion of France and
Germany, 1944-1945 1957
64046366   940.545 M
Morison, Samuel Eliot Liberation of the
Philippines 1959
64046369   940.545 M
Morison, Samuel Eliot New Guinea and the
Marianas, March 1944-August 1944 1953
64046371   940.545 M
Morison, Samuel Eliot Operations in North
African waters, October 1942-June 1943 1950
64046372   940.545 M
Morison, Samuel Eliot Rising sun in the
Pacific: 1931-April 1942 1948
64046373   940.545 M
Morison, Samuel Eliot Sicily--Salerno--Anzio:
January 1943-June 1944 1954
64046374   940.545 M
Morison, Samuel Eliot Struggle for
Guadalcanal: August 1942-February 1943 1949
64046378   940.545 M
Morison, Samuel Eliot Supplement and general
Index 1962
64046379   940.545 M
Morison, Samuel Eliot Victory in the Pacific,
1945 1960
64046381   940.545 M
Newcomb, Richard Fairchild Abandon ship 1958
64047603   940.54 N
Norman, Albert Operation overlord 1952
64047949   940.542 N
Ogden, Michael Battle of North Cape 1962
64048312   940.545 O
Parkin, Ray Out of the smoke 1960
64049153   940.545 P
Pawle, Gerald Secret war, 1939-1945 1957
64049396   940.54 P
Payne, Donald Gordon Red duster, white ensign
1960
64049405   940.545 P
Potter, Elmer Belmont Great sea war 1960
64050656   940.54 P
Robertson, Terence Channel dash 1958
64052586   940.54 R
Roscoe, Theodore United States destroyer

ure 4(d).

Figure 4(e).

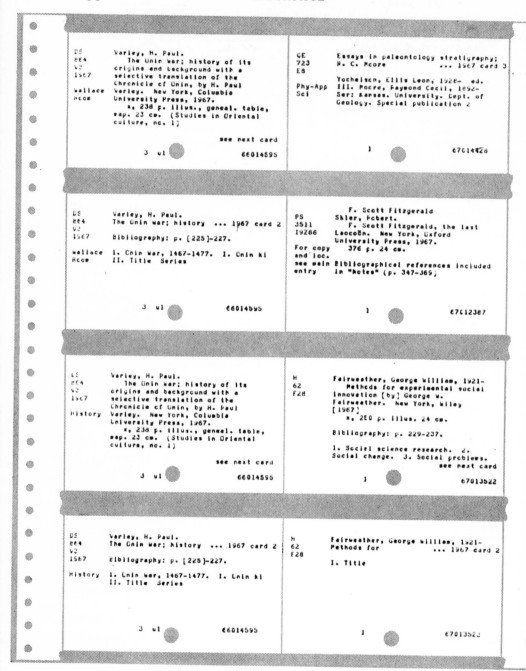

Figure 5. Computer produced catalogue cards from the University of Toronto. The cards are already cut along the top and bottom edges and perforated at the sides.

The State of the Art in Academic Libraries

INTRODUCTION

The six papers presented here describe six of the major projects currently in progress in academic libraries, and cover most aspects of library automation. Some current projects have been omitted because they have been, or are about to be, written up elsewhere. The sponsorship of *OSTI* has tended to ensure very little overlap, though the basic library operations have been approached from different directions.

Financial restraints in this country have imposed on university libraries a pattern of vicarious experiment; so that it is very important to establish the extent to which solutions can be generalized for the use of libraries where the environment may differ very considerably from that of the library carrying out the basic research. To this end, a period of analysis and evaluation will before long be needed, so that results can be published fully and discussed.

It seems likely that the report of the Working Party on the applications of *ADP* to the national libraries, which is due before the end of 1971, will have a very considerable influence on future development within the universities; though much will depend on the extent to which the Government is willing to provide finance to implement any plans which may be proposed. Certainly, the quinquennial estimates about to be prepared could be crucial for library automation, since the quinquennium 1972/77 ought to see increasing commitment to automated housekeeping routines and to research in information handling.

Progress in Library Automation at Newcastle University Library

J. M. BAGNALL

Newcastle University Library has had an active interest in automation for several years. The Library has had a rather chequered history, with the result that its basic systems, on which it depends totally for its operation, have been strained by frequent change and by problems in planning. With this background of difficulty with manual systems, automated procedures have seemed to offer the best solution, as the process of systems analysis and design would help to clarify our present problems, and would tend to enforce a systematic and consistent approach in the future.

The intellectual climate in Newcastle has been exceptionally favourable for work on automation in libraries. Largely responsible for this has been the good relationship between the Computing Laboratory and the Library, which has borne fruit in the Symplegades Research Group. The interests of several members of the Laboratory staff lie in areas of great relevance to library operations, and the corporate investigation of problems and expression of views by the Symplegades group have shaped in many respects the Library's attitude to future developments.

Perhaps the most influential concept in our thinking on library automation has been that of a general system for handling any type of record, bibliographical or otherwise, where the record structure is capable of showing logical relationships between the various data items contained in the record. The Newcastle File Handling System (*NFHS*) in its first version, on the *KDF*9 ,and its second version on the *IBM* 360/67 has provided such a system. *NFHS* is simple in concept and extremely flexible as a system for manipulating bibliographic records (Cox and Grose, 1967: pp. 1–21). When such a system is available, the librarian concerned with the problems of automation is able to concentrate much more on the content of records and the problems of manipulating them, and less on the mechanics of creating and maintaining records and files. The languages used in programming for library work are *IBM* 360 Assembly Language and *PL*/1 for the *IBM* machine, and Usercode for the *KDF*9.

There is only one major automated working system in the Library at the present time, namely the ordering and accessioning system. This has been working for about four years, and has been undergoing constant development during that time. It is based on the first version of the Newcastle File Handling System. It produces, from its input of orders and receipts, orders to booksellers and, where necessary, reminders, a list of books on order and recently received, and a register of books in accession number order, as well as other less frequently used listings. The turn-round period in this system is one week. On average, about one hour of computer time on the KDF9 per week is used by this system (Cox and Grose, 1967: pp. 158–167).

As well as providing a good standard of efficiency and reliability, the system has given Library staff four years' experience with an automated system, which we expect will be extremely useful in future development.

In September 1967 the Catalogue Computerization Project, an OSTI-supported research project, began work on converting the main author or name catalogue of the Library to machine-readable form. The purpose of the project was to investigate the problems involved in computer processing of library catalogue data, and to do use studies on various forms of computer-produced catalogue. One of the main objects was to eliminate errors, whether introduced during punching or already existing in the catalogue data, by various computer techniques. The investigations of error rates and of comparative costings for correction methods is another important object. At the moment, the entire original catalogue has been punched, and work is proceeding on correction techniques and on punching additions and amendments (University of Newcastle upon Tyne, 1968 and 1970).

The Catalogue Computerization Project is concerned with the conversion into machine-readable form of an existing card catalogue. Another project in the cataloguing field which is in progress is investigating the problems of producing catalogues of rare books, where the cataloguing is done with computer-produced catalogues specifically in mind. This is the 'Apple Pie' project, which is concerned with producing catalogues of the Bainbrigg Library of Appleby Grammar School and of the Pybus Collection of historical medical books and engravings, both housed in the University Library (Cox and Grose, 1967: pp. 137–149).

The catalogue entries are produced on specially designed forms, to facilitate punching onto paper tape. At the present time, cataloguing, punching and proof-reading are proceeding concurrently. It is hoped that the final printed catalogues may be produced by computer type-setting.

Another project of more immediate utility to the majority of users of the Library is aimed at producing a union list of periodicals within the University, for distribution throughout the many departmental libraries. The data has been punched, but a considerable amount of work remains to be done before the list becomes a reality.

Both the University Library and the Symplegades Research Group are working on *BNB MARC* tapes, and some degree of success has been achieved in various experimental projects to convert them to our local working format, as a prelude to closer investigation of the utility of the *MARC* record in library and information retrieval contexts.

Thus, we are committed to a number of automation projects, some of which could have a decisive influence on the Library's future. If they are brought to fruition, they will be the precursors of much wider and more comprehensive projects, embracing all of the Library's functions. The Library's present attitude to automation is that we should consolidate our position and work through the projects to which we have committed ourselves, but at the same time plan constantly for the future.

So far one could say that our approach has been fragmented, in applying automation techniques to specific problems. This was probably the right approach in a period of uncertainty about the future of automation in libraries, before much experience had been gained. Now it seems that we need to approach the library as a total system. Our future projects must be inter-related to a far greater degree than before. They must also be related to the development of other libraries, both at local and national levels. Once automated techniques have been mastered and some experience gained in their use, the systems analysis approach becomes vital, if we are to create unified and smoothly-running library systems, and give more and better services to our readers.

Computer Activities at the Bodleian Library

P. BROWN

The computer activities at the Bodleian Library arose from the recommendations of the Shackleton Committee on University Libraries in Oxford (University of Oxford, 1966). These recommendations were concerned in the first instance with the production of catalogues by computer.

CATALOGUE CONVERSION

The first and largest problem was that of the Bodleian Pre-1920 Catalogue. Revision of this catalogue had been under way since the early 1930s but the handwritten revised entries had never been typed or printed. The revision work has so far produced about one million entries; completion of the revision over the next five years will produce a further 250,000 entries. These catalogue entries would have to be set up by means of a keyboard for any form of printing. There were evident benefits in using the keyboard work to lead to computer records: more than one arrangement of the catalogue entries could be derived from computer records; further revision or modification could subsequently be carried out on the whole file more easily, both for the regular updating of printed catalogues and indexes of pre-1920 books, and for any major modification of the whole file such as the introduction into it of the Anglo-American cataloguing rules. Moreover, within the general concept of computer based catalogues and indexes to books the Bodleian has regarded the conversion of past catalogue records to machine-readable form as being intrinsically complementary to any handling of machine-readable records for new publications.

The Method

There are two aspects to the conversion of the Pre-1920 catalogue records. The first is the conversion of the characters of the handwritten records to machine codes. The cheapest and most satisfactory method of character conversion proved to be typing with optical character recognition (*OCR*) typewriters and subsequent *OCR* scanning of the typed sheets, the codes being written to magnetic tape. It was found that it was best to use a service bureau (Farrington Data Processing) for both the typing and the optical scanning. The

D

typists use conversion tables to represent characters not on their key-board; these tables cover modified roman alphabet characters, non-roman alphabets and special characters. The codes written by Farrington to magnetic tape are all interpreted by the Oxford *KDF9* and each original character is written as a 12-bit character showing alphabet, line printer character and case. The second and more difficult process is the identification of data fields within a record. The work done at the British Museum by John Jolliffe to do this identification by computer program was modified by him to deal with Bodleian catalogue entries. The structure and punctuation of each catalogue entry is interpreted to identify the data fields within it. Analysis had shown that there are five possible basic structural patterns to the Bodleian catalogue entries, each having its own range of sub-patterns. Over fifty possible data elements have been allowed for throughout the total range of sub-patterns. The computer record for each catalogue entry consists of a control word, a number of field labels (each with the address and length of the corresponding text data in the record) and the text data (in 12-bit character codes).

The results

After one year of testing and fault eradication, the *OCR* conversion began properly in June 1969 at the rate of 5000 records a week. As a result about 250,000 entries (covering letters A, B and C of the alphabet) have now been converted and the data fields in each entry identified. The results are printed out as proof (using two line representation with a line printer) so that the text and field identification can be checked by proof-readers throughout the Bodleian staff. Errors are marked by these proof-readers on the proof so that error correction messages may be punched, using the Bodleian Dura tape typewriters. The operation of the punching of error messages is well established but has always lagged far behind the rate of proof reading as a result of staffing difficulties. The printing of pages of catalogue entries (using the Oxford line printer) is the next stage. The display is sophisticated but the available character set imposes severe limitations. The initial preparations are already in hand for photosetting both for proof and catalogue page printing.

The standard of typing and the level of accurate field recognition are now both very high, with one error per thousand characters in the typing and 98% of fields correctly identified. The *OCR* process produces no errors. The fields that are identified do not match exactly the fields and sub-fields of a *MARC* record. This is due partly to the difference in cataloguing codes, partly to the lack of some recorded information in Bodleian catalogue entries, and partly to the impossibility of separating some fields by computer program. The only listing that can usefully be printed out during the next four years is an author catalogue. Only when conversion is complete can the records be sorted into other arrangements for additional listings. Selection of records for the creation of sub-files by date and place of publication has been carried out but this again requires the complete converted file before it can produce useful sub-files.

The implications

The Bodleian Pre-1920 Catalogue conversion is the first large-scale conversion of retrospective library records. Inexpensive solutions have been found to the two major problems of character conversion and field identification and these are likely to be of significance to retrospective conversion elsewhere. What is now necessary is national planning of retrospective conversion so that a national file of records is available for use by libraries generally.

EXPERIMENTS IN THE USE OF *MARC* RECORDS

The second computer activity at the Bodleian was more experimental in that it was to test the use of *BNB MARC* records in the context of producing and maintaining union catalogues of books acquired in a large number of Oxford libraries from the late 1960s onwards.

The Method

In order that *MARC* records should be subjected to a demanding test of flexibility, a sophisticated pattern of information was designed for inclusion in the catalogue entries to be produced from the *MARC* records. It was immediately evident that the *MARC* record structure was insufficient to meet these sophisticated demands efficiently so that it proved necessary to break down each *MARC* record into separately addressable sub-fields before catalogue entry production began. The basis of the Bodleian approach was that *MARC* records should be handled entirely automatically once they had been selected for use. This required that sufficient control information should exist within each *MARC* record to enable the computer program to set up and interfile all the necessary catalogue entries to be derived from it.

The results

Regular weekly *MARC* tapes were received at the Bodleian from December 1969. It was immediately apparent that there was insufficient control information in the *MARC* record to meet the demands of the Bodleian program. Reports on these inadequacies were made to *BNB*.

The experience at the Bodleian of *MARC* records during December 1969 and January 1970 led to the decision that the level of currency, coverage and accuracy of the *MARC* records being distributed by *BNB* was too low to permit the introduction of a working catalogue production system by the Bodleian. A new set of programs has now been written to monitor the performance of *BNB* in the production of *MARC* records so that improvement in currency, coverage and accuracy may be measured and reported.*

The implications

The concept of the distribution of bibliographical records in machine-readable form for widespread use in libraries may seem to offer no fundamental difficulties. In practice it is likely to be some time yet before libraries can without difficulty use *MARC* records to replace their present methods of keeping library records. This does not in any way invalidate the concept of the development of a *MARC* service by *BNB* but it is clear that such a service is not yet available.

Birmingham Libraries Co-operative Mechanization Project

R. M. DUCHESNE

INTRODUCTION
This article outlines the objectives of the *OSTI*-sponsored project and its major achievements up to June 1970 from the beginning of preparatory work which commenced in 1968; in addition, some implications of work are discussed.

Reference should be made to articles in *Program* (Cayless and Kimber, 1969; Duchesne, 1969; Driver, *et al.* 1970) for details of the history and administrative organization of the project.

* See paper by Cox (pp. 146–175).

OBJECTIVES

The immediate objective of the project is to investigate the co-operative use of *MARC* with locally produced machine-readable bibliographic records in a group of libraries. Libraries participating are those of:

> University of Aston in Birmingham
> University of Birmingham
> Birmingham Public Libraries.

Birmingham Public Libraries, it may be noted, comprises one of the largest public reference libraries and one of the largest city lending library systems in the United Kingdom.

A longer term objective is to investigate the feasibility of, firstly, a regional data bank of machine-readable bibliographic records and, secondly, of a library automation team to serve libraries in the region.

WORK TO DATE

Work to date is most conveniently summarized under a series of headings:

Fundamental Studies

The libraries have reached agreement to adopt the Cataloguing Rules used in the *MARC* service (Anglo-American Cataloguing Rules 1967), with only a very small number of minor exceptions which can in any case be effected by machine.

Surveys have been carried out, establishing *MARC*'s coverage of the libraries' intakes and prospects for using *MARC* records to speed their technical processing.

A set of computer filing rules has been constructed and will shortly be agreed, with any necessary modifications, with *BNB* and the Library Association Filing Working Party.

Book Selection

The libraries' requirements for a service using current *MARC* records have been specified in detail. A common machine system has been designed and completed, and is now ready for pilot operation.

Cataloguing of Serials

The requirements of the libraries have been specified in detail, and a common machine system using *MARC* format records has been designed in outline. 'Serial' is used according to the definition given in Anglo American Cataloguing Rules 1967; it includes periodicals, annuals, and newspapers.

Catalogue of Non-Serials (mainly monographs)

A co-ordinated schedule of catalogue outputs required by the libraries has been prepared, with detailed specification of name catalogue outputs. An outline schematic flowchart for a mechanized cataloguing system for non-serials has been prepared.

Computer Operations

A suite of programs to produce Book Selection Lists from *MARC* records has been prepared. *MTLT* (*MARC* Tape to Local Tape), the *ICL* 1900 decode/extract/copy program, has been made to work, made to process *LC* records and has had a print and merge routine incorporated.

Programs to process the *BLCMP* Intake Analysis Survey results have been obtained from the *OSTI* Documentation Processing Centre. These programs have been taken over and used to process the results. An additional program was written to correct certain fields on Intake Analysis data tapes.

OBSERVATIONS BASED ON WORK TO DATE
MARC

It is too early to draw final conclusions concerning the co-operative use of *MARC* with locally produced machine-readable bibliographic records. The final test of any projected system is its satisfactory performance on an operational basis, and it will be some months before any *BLCMP* machine-aided system achieves this. Nevertheless, work to date has shown in which areas cost-effective applications of *MARC* are most likely to be found for the *BLCMP* libraries: the book selection and cataloguing areas.

Regular lists of new books, especially of books published outside the United Kingdom, will be of considerable use as aids to book selection. At present the libraries do not have access to lists of new foreign books, and *MARC* will be very useful in providing regular, relatively comprehensive and up to date, lists of English language material published outside the United Kingdom. Copies of these lists, arranged by subject, will shortly be distributed to the libraries on a trial basis.

This system is likely to have particular advantages for Birmingham University Library; some 65% of the non-serial acquisitions of this library are published abroad. A further factor affecting the latter library is that nearly half of its non-serials acquisitions stem from suggestions made by users of the library: mostly, these are suggestions from staff of university departments. In these circumstances one could envisage a system whereby regular lists of new books, selected by subject area, are distributed to appropriate persons in departments of the university accompanied by financial information concerning available funds. These persons could mark suggested purchases on the lists and return them to the library who would order the books. Ultimately, such a system might be further extended by mechanizing the ordering operation, preparing the way for an integrated computer-aided system serving selection, ordering, accessioning, cataloguing functions.

Cataloguing is the other most promising area for potential use of *MARC* in the libraries. This is particularly true for the Reference Library, since a three year *UK/US MARC* backfile will cover some 85% of its intake, and there is every likelihood that a mechanized *MARC*-aided cataloguing system could substantially reduce the average time which this library takes to place an entry in its catalogue following the receipt of a book.

MARC's coverage of the libraries' intakes is of general interest:

	% Intake Covered by a three-year file of *UK/US MARC* Records*
Birmingham Public Libraries:	
Reference Library	85
Lending Library	76
University of Aston Library	66
University of Birmingham Library	32

While the immediate prospects for the use of *MARC* for cataloguing look best for the Reference Library, the University of Birmingham has very much to gain in the long run in this area. When *MARC*

* Source: *BLCMP Statistics Group Report, June 1970* (unpublished). Figures are based on a 1 in 4 sample drawn from the libraries' intakes received in the 24 weeks commencing 14 April 1969. The exception is the figure for the Lending Libraries which is based on a similar sample drawn from this library's intake received between 10 November and 3 December 1969. The short survey period makes the Lending Library figure less reliable: the true proportion is probably very much the same as for the Reference Library.

covers Slavic, Romance and German material*, its coverage of the latter library's intake will be similar in magnitude to its coverage of the other libraries' intakes. Possibly before, and certainly following, this expansion of coverage a *MARC*-aided cataloguing system will offer considerable advantages to the University of Birmingham Library with its relatively large intake, full cataloguing, and need to circulate lists of accessions; the greatest single advantage may be in speeding the appearance of catalogue entries for a book following its receipt in the library.

Further Developments

Experience to date indicates that co-operation in mechanization has very substantial advantages. Systems analysis may be carried out with a team a fraction of the combined size of many individual library teams. The use of a common machine system can make possible a several-fold reduction in the costs of designing, programming, and operating a system.

A common machine system has another advantage: the greater size of the system and its greater throughput may bring a whole range of special equipment and techniques into the area of economic feasibility. These might include:

> upper- and lower-case printing
> data links, data terminals
> computer generated microfilm
> computer typesetting
> OCR equipment
> on-line computing
> use of a computer solely for library purposes.

It is concluded that the development of library computing facilities on a co-operative or centralized (perhaps regional) basis, with a central team to undertake systems analysis and programming, looks feasible, desirable, and—in the long run—inevitable. The main impediment to these developments may be the difficulty and cost of obtaining sufficient access to suitable hardware: ultimately a medium sized computer with a number of data storage peripheral devices would be required, with access to a range of graphic output facilities.

---

* Proposals are set out in: *Conversion of Retrospective Catalog Records to Machine-readable Form*, Washington, Library of Congress, 1969. The commencement of work to implement these proposals is reported in: *Council on Library Resources. Recent developments, No. 287*, Washington, 13 February 1970. Progress is reported in *Journal of Library Automation* Vol. 3, part 2, June 1970, pp. 102–114.

South-West Universities Library Systems Co-operation Project

G. FORD

This project was set up in 1969 with a grant from *OSTI* as a co-operative venture of the Universities of Bath, Bristol and Exeter, University College, Cardiff, and the University of Wales Institute of Science and Technology. The Project Head is Norman Higham, Librarian of Bristol University; the project team consists of two systems analysts, one with library training (Geoffrey Ford) and one with computer training (Richard Hudson).

The aim of the project is to examine the feasibility of regional co-operation in the automation of library procedures. The possibility of sharing the high development costs of library automation is brought nearer by the proposed establishment of a computer network to be shared by the five university institutions mentioned above, all of which use *ICL System 4* machines. The existence of such a network argues a degree of compatibility between the computer systems, and gives the university librarians an added incentive to consider the extent of possible co-operation.

The main objective of the investigation is to discover how far regional sharing of automation is possible. The current activities of the institutions are being studied with two ends in view: the extent of compatibility between the various systems' requirements and the practical effects of standardization. Towards the end of the project it should be possible to determine whether computer programs developed in other libraries are applicable, and to what extent programs can be written to meet the requirements of all the co-operating libraries. One of the fruits of the project could be an indication of the practical extent to which special local requirements can be accommodated within a common systems design; another could be an estimate of whether it is worth while translating or transliterating other libraries' programs rather than writing from scratch.

The approach has been to start by making a detailed analysis of the library systems as they are operating now. Conventional techniques of interviewing, flow charting and diary compilation are used for data collection. Each Librarian was asked to prepare a statement of the objectives of his library; the research team are preparing a list of questions relating to the detailed system requirements.

For the initial analysis, each library has been treated as a separate entity. The library's activities have been grouped conventionally, acquisitions, cataloguing, and so on, and each of these is being studied in turn, in so far as this is possible within the limits imposed by the organization of the individual libraries. Thus, in Bristol, where the library administrative H.Q. is organized in functional departments, the acquisitions sub-system could be studied more or less in isolation, while in Exeter, where subject specialists are employed, data collection had to extend to cataloguing when acquisitions was the prime interest of the study. Considerable effort is required to obtain precise information on present systems performance: information which is not necessarily essential for the efficient operation of the system, but is important in the design of new systems.

As well as looking at the current library operations, the research team are gathering information on a variety of other relevant topics. Various library automation projects in the U.K. are in close touch for the mutual exchange of expertise and programs. Although programs written in high-level languages are theoretically transferable between different computers this transfer may still involve a great deal of work: for example, the differences between *KDF9 ALGOL* and *System 4J ALGOL* are considerable. The team are currently investigating the factors involved in getting programs written in *1900 COBOL* to run on a *System 4* computer. This kind of exercise is necessary to facilitate estimation of development costs. In addition, the team are developing their own programs to handle bibliographic data, to gain experience both of this kind of job and of the *System 4* capabilities.

At this (half-way) stage it is difficult to point to concrete 'results', as the nature of the project inevitably means that there are several strands of work which will be woven together only at the end. Analysis is proceeding, and some design work has been started.

A project of this nature depends not only on the goodwill of the top management, but also on the co-operation and hard work of the line management and workers. The systems analysts need good advance publicity—particularly when they are based on one library and visit the others mainly to collect data. Without good public relations, the motives of the analysts are almost certain to be misunderstood.

A development which becomes increasingly desirable is the meeting of equivalent personnel from the co-operating institutions. At some stages this is essential: in practical terms, it is only the cata-loguers who can say where and how their libraries deviate from a standard code of rules and how they can adjust in future.

The inevitable expansion of universities and the accompanying growth of demand for library services, coupled with an increasing desire to eliminate repetitive tasks ensure that automation will be-come increasingly desirable. The opportunities for economy afforded by co-operation suggest that the results of this and similar projects will be of considerable interest.

Project *LOC*

J. W. JOLLIFFE

Project *LOC* is directed at certain problems of union catalogue con-struction. The British Museum, the Bodleian Library and the Cam-bridge University Library, acting jointly with funds provided by the Old Dominion Foundation, have been attempting to discover practical approaches to the question of a union catalogue of early books in these three libraries and in the college and departmental libraries of Oxford and Cambridge.

It is known, from catalogues such as the two *Short Title Catalogues* of English books and from Adams' *Catalogue of books printed on the Continent of Europe, 1501–1600, in Cambridge libraries*, that the smaller libraries contain many early books not to be found in the great collections at the British Museum, the Bodleian and the Cambridge University Library. A union catalogue would thus be of considerable value to scholars; if it were indexed by date, place, language, title and so on, its value would be inestimable.

The contents of the smaller libraries are imperfectly suggested by the few available catalogues. In some cases, the library itself has no list of the works in an important collection. One of the first tasks of the union catalogue would thus be to provide homogeneous cata-loguing information for all the books.

Providing the cataloguing information will take manpower, as will the matching of entries. A constraint is the shortage of skilled cata-loguers and bibliographers. A further constraint is the necessity that any catalogue must be capable of completion in a reasonably short period of time.

The computer appeared to offer certain aids to the compilation of such a catalogue. It could be used to identify and report apparent duplicates; to provide flexible and rapid editing and correction facilities; to provide important statistical evidence of the distribution of the books both across the libraries and throughout the period of the history of printing; and to simplify the indexing of a completed catalogue.

The test 'sample' was made up of all the pre-1801 books in the libraries of Peterhouse and Hertford College, and of all books of the same date with 'O' headings in all the other libraries. Existing catalogue entries were used for the three large libraries; records were created from the books for the rest.

Owing to the constraint on staff, the level of skill required was deliberately kept low: intelligent but bibliographically untrained staff were used, graduates or undergraduates with some knowledge of Latin (the only skill explicitly insisted on). Selection of data was restricted, as far as possible, to what was available on the title-page and what could be recognized without too great effort. There was not a great deal of room for manoeuvre here: the traditional cataloguing exercise of 'establishing the heading' had to be eschewed or rendered unimportant and the effect of the diversity of individual judgments on what or how to include had to be minimized without the construction of an elaborate set of cataloguing rules. Preprinted forms were used, with boxes into which information was copied. The only 'regularization' was the recording of Latin names in a notional nominative form if they appeared on the book in an oblique case.

Two means of initial recording were compared: photography of the titlepage and direct filling in of the form by hand. The cost and, to some extent, the accuracy of the methods for recording and providing a good punching document were examined. In certain cases, titlepage images were marked up before punching so that they could be used as if the information were set out on a form.

The information was intended to provide either a rough catalogue entry or the means of matching. It was chiefly traditional: title, date, place of publication, etc. An exception to tradition was the recording of the date in the form in which it appeared on the book, without regularization of Roman to Arabic (this was later done by algorithm). A further exception was the inclusion of an item of information known as the 'fingerprint'; this went some way towards providing the 'points' for discrimination required by analytical bibliographers, since it consisted of eighteen characters taken in pairs from the ends of lines, three lines to each of three determined pages. It provided a virtually unique short identifier for the work from which it was taken and in combination with the text of the date, proved a powerful and robust means of matching.

Since the fingerprint could only be used in those cases where it had already been recorded, two other types of matching were tried to deal with the one case of matching an entry from an existing catalogue with another such entry, and with the other case of matching a record established from a book with a catalogue entry.

An index number of proximity of match was computed on the basis of occurrence of words in the two titles being compared, weight being given to number of words matched, the order in which they appeared and the lengths of strings which they spanned. A different approach was along the lines of the University of Chicago 'search-code' but in a form closer to that adopted at Grenoble, and resulted in a short, fifteen character, item for comparison, constructed from date, title, author, edition and place of publication. The former method required more machine work and more complicated files than the latter, for a less certain matching result, while the latter proved to be little inferior to the fingerprint in matching potential.

All computer operations have been carried out on the Cambridge *Titan* computer; the programmer has used a terminal in her own home for program development and testing. All programs, at the moment, are in *Titan* machine code (*IIT*). A long term difficulty may well be the reprogramming required for another machine. Input has been from paper tape, in three codes, which are converted to a special internal code related to the normal Atlas one. Accents, special characters and non-Roman alphabets have been coded and entered without difficulty.

When all the evidence gained from this Project has been evaluated, it will be possible to suggest the magnitude of the task of constructing a full union catalogue for these libraries, the best combination of recording and matching methods to be used, and some cost guidelines from which both the duration of the project and the number of staff required can be estimated. The wider important of the Project may well be the establishment, for general use, of a fairly cheap and efficient means of matching catalogue entries by computer, thus permitting both the extension of this union catalogue to embrace other libraries and the construction of union catalogues for other libraries.

Library Automation in Trinity College, Dublin: A Progress Report

A. TUCKER

The Trinity College *MARC*-based acquisitions and cataloguing system, which has been operational since December 1969, was designed to utilize *BNB*-generated *MARC* records in a practical context for the control and augmentation of the processing of copyright accessions, and in an experimental context for the provision of an *SDI* service to the academic and administrative staff of the College, and to a small number of outside individuals and institutions.

Analysis of the Library's acquisitions and cataloguing operations indicated that the introduction of a *MARC*-oriented system was both feasible and attractive, largely because of two unusual situations obtaining in the *TCD* Library. The first is the fact that the copyright accounts for something over 80% of Trinity's total accessions. Thus the development of a machine-readable catalogue for current acquisitions requires an acceptably small amount of data conversion, and provides, in the short term, the prospect of a file capable of machine manipulation representing a heavily used area of the collection—the thought of converting the Library's card catalogue, which contains mainly post-1962 acquisitions, is considerably less daunting than that of a complete retrospective conversion project—on which a number of functional and experimental projects could be based.

The second is a purely fortuitous solution to the problem of timeliness which several libraries have found to be troublesome in their attempts to use *MARC*. A weekly *MARC* tape normally arrives at *TCD* four days after leaving the *BNB*; but, left to the tender mercies of *BNB* (who use copies destined for *TCD* as the source for cataloguing), the several casually co-ordinated arms of a transport company, shipping and dock strikes, and the Irish Customs, a shipment of books arrives rarely less than four, and sometimes as long as seven, weeks after the *MARC* tape to which it numerically corresponds. As a result of this, better than 97% of the contents of a copyright shipment are located on the first pass through the matching list used to check in these materials; a recent examination of the twenty-five titles (out of shipments totalling nearly 1200 items) not found on the

matching list disclosed that six were in Irish, decreasing the likelihood of their appearing in *MARC* or *BNB*.

Underlying the system design at *TCD* was the intention of mini-
mizing, to the extent allowed by local cataloguing practice and by
the acceptability of *MARC* records, the amount of manual intervention required in the incorporation of these records into the *TCD*
system. For various reasons this minimization must be viewed as a
diachronic process, tending toward an ultimate, possibly non-zero,
limit. General factors contributing to this include differences in
cataloguing practice between *TCD* and *BNB*, particularly as regards
certain classes of pseudonymous authors; and an unsatisfactory level
of confidence in the *BNB*'s ability to produce *MARC* records to the
same standard of accuracy as those in *BNB* itself. This latter should
be resolved, in one way or the other, when fully coincident production
of *BNB* and *MARC* is achieved in 1971, while the former may be
subject to compromise dependent on analysis of the relative benefit
resulting from divergent practice in comparison to the cost of maintaining that practice.

On a more specific level, certain aspects of local processing are not,
in their present state, completely amenable to algorithmic handling.
It is not possible, for instance, to predict with any accuracy the
number or type of catalogue cards which a given item will require,
and there is considerable variation in the form and content of cards
depending on their destination among the Library's twenty-one
public and internal catalogues. Similarly, book disposition and shelf-
mark allocation is in many cases quite unpredictable, there being
not less than ten different shelving systems in use; it seems unlikely
that this aspect will soon be freed from the need for human intervention.

A broader design principle, the practical rewards of which will—
hopefully—be reaped as the system is extended, involves the development of modular additions, based on the central *MARC–TCD* processing system, to deal with other technical processes; the original
system contains, for example, interfaces for the inclusion of locally-
generated *MARC*-format records, and for ordering procedures for
non-copyright accessions.

The system currently provides control of anticipated and actual
copyright monograph accessions, insofar as these are covered by
MARC, and provides the Accessions Librarian with notification
when items appear to be sufficiently overdue to warrant a possible

claim. It produces weekly lists of current copyright receipts, before the materials have been catalogued, in toto for use by Library staff, and under the control of interest profiles for more than 220 *SDI* recipients. For each book received it prints a cataloguing work sheet, containing those data from the relevant *MARC* record directly required by the cataloguer, as well as various system-generated data and control fields. These work sheets, having been edited by the cataloguers, are used to update the *MARC* records from which they were produced, and the updated records, after being used by the catalogue card program, become part of the tape 'catalogue'. With the addition of locally-created records representing non-copyright accessions, the weekly file of catalogued materials is used to produce lists of catalogued accessions of the same type as those for uncatalogued copyright materials; *SDI* recipients have a choice between the two types of list.

Direct consequences of the system include increased control over copyright intake; a decrease in overall throughput time for the same material, from receipt to availability of a public catalogue record; orientation of Library staff in the regular use of a machine-centred system, and the apparent dissolution of their very natural initial fears thereof; an increase in the immediacy of the Library's usefulness to at least a small number of *SDI* users; and the development of a considerable body of technical experience, both on the Library and computer side, on which the work of the future can be built.

Computers in British Public Libraries

C. D. BATTY

'A library may be considered from two very different points of view—
as a workshop or as a museum ... the former commends itself to the
practical turn of mind characteristic of the present day; common
sense urges that mechanical ingenuity, which has done so much in
other directions, should be employed in making the acquisition of
knowledge less cumbrous and less tedious.' Thus John Willis Clark,
once Registrar of the University of Cambridge, in his Rede Lecture
of 1894. It is an interesting and even a wry comment on the development of library science, that this seventy-six year old exhortation
rings as urgently now as it did then.

Unfortunately for libraries in the computer age (but perhaps inevitably) the successive generations of computers have been accompanied by successive generations of attitude. Monolithic first-generation thinking was based on the assumption that the only legitimate
and justifiable use for these new and expensive machines was high
level scientific research backed by heavy governmental or institu-
tional funding. Second generation thinking allowed limited and
inconvenient access to minority users but typically refused to take the
minority use entirely seriously. Third generation thinking is more
hospitable, though perhaps only from a livelier sense of the economic
advantages of group participation.

In the last ten or fifteen years libraries of all kinds have realized
the potential of the computer for handling their administrative and
bibliographic records and transactions. Special and academic
libraries, naturally more research oriented, have probably contributed more to the development of library mechanization and
automation, notably in the United States of America, where, for example, *INTREX* (Overhage and Harman, 1965), the *MARC I* pilot

project (Avram, 1968), and the *Bell-Rel* system (Kennedy, 1968) of Bell Telephone are at once more extensive and more experimental than much work in the public library field. But we should remember that public libraries have different contexts and problems, and the uses they make of computers, though not perhaps as adventurous as experiments of the kind just mentioned, are often more realistic and more pragmatic.

In Great Britain the amalgamation of the Metropolitan boroughs of London provoked a similar need. Public library systems in this country are not generally so large as inevitably to suggest that computerization would be an advantage—or at least they did not in terms of second-generation computer thinking. But many of the amalgamated boroughs now had to produce usable, probably union, catalogues from several sources, different perhaps in physical format, depth and content and style, and in the system of technical processing, and this realization led inevitably to the consideration of the computer production of catalogues. Libraries like Holborn (Davies, 1960) before amalgamation had experience of data processing equipment in routine operations and it was natural for the systems they became part of to play a leading role in the new developments. Much has been said about the 'computerized catalogues' of Camden (Maidment, 1965 and 1968; Cataloguing by Computer, 1966; Johnson, 1966), Barnet (Cataloguing by Computer, 1966; Johnson, 1966; Meakin, 1965), and Greenwich (Johnson, 1966; Howard, 1967), though with notable exceptions little has been written that is specifically explanatory. One reason for this is that basically the operation was comparatively simple: catalogue entries were keypunched into machine-readable form and successively added to a growing master file (subject to appropriate diagnostic programs) and later sorted and printed out by the few, principal filing elements of a conventional catalogue. Similar problems and a similar simplicity occurred in the catalogue of plays produced as a pilot project for catalogue computerization in Dorset County Library (Carter, 1968). Unfortunately the very severe limitations of the computer (which seems to have regarded even simple alpha sorting as nearly impossible) only emphasize the difficulties faced a year or two later by the London boroughs.

Camden's union catalogue (Maidment, 1965 and 1968) included all adult lending books, both fiction and non-fiction, but excluded musical scores. Author lists appeared fortnightly, superseding their immediate predecessors and a cumulated classified list appeared every four months with an alphabetical subject index based on chain procedure. Because of the accepted limitation of 40 characters per author, 80 characters per title and ten characters per class number, the entries frequently had to be abbreviated manually or simply truncated. At the same time Camden moved towards a greater acceptance of standardization: elimination of nearly all local modifications of the Dewey Decimal Classification and acceptance of BNB placings, except where they clash with the 16th edition of Dewey adopted at amalgamation. Branches were indicated by a code to allow future manipulation and revision.

Barnet (Meakin, 1965) offered a situation of extreme catalogue confusion on amalgamation: a union dictionary sheaf catalogue; a union classified sheaf catalogue of a larger size; a BNB-based classified card catalogue; an author-only card catalogue supplemented by union classified duplicated lists; and different editions of Dewey were in use. In addition to the problems of integration, the provision of conventional catalogues for seventeen libraries would have meant the enormous maintenance cost of catalogues containing a total of 5,000,000 entries. Because the authority's computer facilities were inadequate Barnet had to use an outside firm and the consequent cost as well as the limitations of available machines and programs dictated not only an even more severely restricted entry than Camden's but also the initial acceptance only of adult non-fiction, with provision for the future inclusion of fiction and children's books. The catalogue comprised four-monthly cumulations in author and classified order, with an alphabetical subject index, supplemented by fortnightly author-only lists. In both Camden and Barnet the computer printout was reproduced by microfilm and high speed electrostatic printing; in Camden the cumulations were bound, but in Barnet they were kept in specially designed loose leaf binders.

Greenwich (Howard, 1967) had a similar, if less complex problem of the integration of catalogues, and found a similar solution. Their catalogue, which included all lending and reference non-fiction, differed mainly in the timing of production: annual author and classified catalogues were supplemented by cumulating monthly lists, which in turn were supplemented by non-cumulating duplicated weekly accessions lists. In Southwark (Johnson, 1966) the Greenwich pattern was adopted, except for the more ambitious provision of monthly cumulated catalogues. Both libraries preferred reiterated printout to microfilm/electrostatic printing.

Commercial enterprises had used computers for inventory control for years and the only significant differences between their work and that of the London boroughs are the context of use and the nature of the information handled, which was almost totally alphabetic and less susceptible to fixed field format. But these differences are more significant than at first appears. For almost the first time public libraries were equated with other departments for use of expensive facilities, even though the initial decision was probably based on second-generation thinking. And in spite of the decision of most London boroughs to adopt for the most part a very restricted fixed-field format for the catalogue entry, the first steps had been taken towards serious consideration of the problem of handling bibliographic data of indeterminate length, and the development of the variable field formats used in the *MARC* record, previously much neglected by mathematically oriented computer scientists.

Encouraging though this may sound it should be realized that the operation was limited to the *production* of printed catalogues, and vital though the computer might have been in handling the quantity of data, in system terms it was acting as little more than a large filing cabinet and typewriter. Little attempt was made to utilize the catalogue entry as a unit record of bibliographic information which could be used in other stages of library processing. This caveat manifests itself at two levels: in the design of a format to handle bibliographic data in machine-readable form; and in the overall attitude towards library automation. This is not the place to rehearse yet again the differing views on instant as opposed to gradual automation. Suffice it that however different the implementation might be, the end is approximately the same and therefore the overall planning objectives should be the same (Davies, 1965). But it should be stressed that anything less than an overall view can lead to mechanization rather than automation. Mechanization represents a difference only in degree; substituting a machine for a human being is no more than using a bigger hammer to crack a (possibly) bigger nut. Automation represents a difference in kind; it aims at the most sensible use of machine and human being in their proper capacities.

The next stage of computer use moved closer towards an integration of library services. West Sussex, following a pattern represented by university libraries like Newcastle upon Tyne and Southampton, proposed to use the county authority's computer to control both issue system and cataloguing (Davie, 1966), based on the same data and with possible extensions in one direction into other technical processes, and in another direction into the integration of several public departments: libraries, health, and education. Unfortunately West Sussex found that their ideas were in advance of computer capability at the time, and after a change of heart and a change of plan (though apparently with no change of ultimate intention) they chose to separate the two functions of issue and cataloguing (Bearman, 1968), and although both systems use the computer, the issue system relied on an independent peripheral data processing unit at the counter that relies on independent input media for books and produces computer-readable punched paper tape (Wilson, 1969).

This equipment, produced almost as an *ad hoc* solution to West Sussex's problems comprises at a basic level a set of three card readers: two acting as a charge station and one as a discharge station, and a logic unit with a controlling and diagnostic function. The two charge station readers accept prepunched borrowers' and book cards respectively and (retaining the borrower's card until all his book cards have been processed) records the issue on paper tape. The discharge station reader accepts book cards to record the return. The tapes are fed into the computer to update the previous issue record and the returned book numbers cancel the corresponding charges. A later development includes an on-line terminal to allow reservations to be checked against the master file (Kimber, 1968). The system proved so obviously economical that other libraries, like Brighton (Allen, 1969), Camden (Camden, 1970; Maidment, 1966), and Lancashire County, have been encouraged to consider its adoption. This in turn has affected and perhaps inhibited their early development of an overall integrated system based on a computer. It is true that ultimately these libraries may use a computer for all operations involving bibliographical information, incorporating the currently separate issue system, but at present their thinking is inevitably encouraged towards a gradual and separately developed mechanization program.

The third and latest stage in the use of computers has come with *MARC* (MAchine Readable Cataloguing) (Coward, 1968). Although much of the design and the application has been the concern of national and academic libraries, public libraries have already played a significant role in both the *MARC I* pilot project in the United States (Avram, 1968) and the *UK MARC* project in Great Britain. *UK MARC* has so far involved public libraries on two levels. Most significantly the agency responsible for the development of a machine-readable bibliographic format in this country has been the British National Bibliography (Coward, 1967; British National Bibliography, 1968, 1969a). It is true that the choice was inevitable; in the dissemination of catalogue information in a published form suitable for individual library use the British National Bibliography rather than the British Museum is the counterpart of the Library of Congress. But the *BNB* is also more closely attuned to the demands and activities of public libraries in this country than those of academic libraries. The production of *MARC* by *BNB* may well therefore encourage public libraries to consider automation much more seriously than public libraries in other countries. The inhibiting factors are the lack of appropriate software for the dismaying variety of machines owned by local authorities and the consequent disproportionate expense for even the largest single authorities of implementing an automated system based on *MARC* tapes. It is also possible that the general assumption, based on a misconception arising from the Camden-Barnet-Greenwich experiences, of *MARC* as a source only for printed catalogues with only a limited coverage of a library's intake (Hall, 1969) has prevented public librarians from seeing the many advantages implicit in the automation of the bibliographic record, and from considering the desirability of co-operation.

Birmingham Public Libraries (Birmingham libraries joint research on British *MARC*, 1969; Cayless and Kimber, 1969; Duchesne, 1969, and elsewhere in this volume; Hall, 1969; Use of *BNB MARC* tapes in a group of Birmingham libraries, 1968) have already co-operated with the two local university libraries, of Aston University and Birmingham University, to exploit *MARC* tapes in a joint venture. The first phase of the project has concentrated on cataloguing only, and has included a study of catalogue compatibility with a view to an agreed standard approximating very closely to the *Anglo-American Cataloguing Rules*, 1967 as used by *BNB* for the *MARC* tapes. The project intends to go on to consider the use of the same data for other elements of processing: to supplement machine-readable pre-publication data used for ordering, for acquisition, for on-demand production of special reading lists. The project also includes a study of the incorporation of serials records for the constituent libraries. This is to date the most ambitious and fundamental application of computers in public libraries in Britain, though it probably still does not reach the sophistication of some work in academic libraries both here and in the United States. It is, however, as much public library application has been, very much in keeping with John Willis Clark's view of the library as a workshop quoted at the start of this paper, not only in his sense of the word but also in another way entirely: as the very practical laboratory in which new methods are tried, using 'that mechanical ingenuity, which has done so much in other directions . . . making the acquisition of knowledge less cumbrous and less tedious'.

Work in Progress in the Book Trade*

D. WHITAKER and J. BLACKWELL

For a trade not usually thought of first when new developments are discussed, the use of computers in publishing is surprisingly widespread. Book Centre, which warehouses, invoices and dispatches for some seventy publishers, has employed a computer for ten years, and is now on its third machine, an *IBM* 360/50. The Book Centre is also involved in developing some very advanced projects on a trade-wide base and the chief among these is discussed later. Longman, O.U.P., Nelson, Thames & Hudson, Jonathan Cape, Cassell, Hodder & Stoughton, Collins, to mention only a few publishers, are amongst those who employ computers. Either they own these themselves, or they employ the bureau facilities of the Book Centre, or one of the several other bureaux that specialize in work for publishers. It is estimated that some 80% by value of books are invoiced by computer.

Publishers use computers for the production of invoices, picking notes, despatch notes, and labels; for statements, customers' accounts, and credit control; for internal accounts, royalties, stock control, stock low warning, sales analysis, and salesmen's commissions; and in some systems they also indicate the method of despatch and cost.

Mr. J. Y. Huws Davies of Oxford University Press said at a conference held in Oxford in September of 1969: 'The computer slid into publishing to solve *distribution* problems. But its use is now going much further, and, for instance, managing editors are now getting

---

* While the present volume was in the press, copies of this paper were circulated as background material to a weekend seminar organised by the University Booksellers Group of the Booksellers Association in conjunction with the Bath University of Technology Centre for Adult Education; and it was subsequently published in *The Bookseller*, November 28th, 1970, pp. 2472–2479.

from the computer recommendations for re-binding, or re-printing of titles'. He stressed that these were recommendations only, no publisher had any intention of letting the computer decide these things all by itself. Additionally the machinery was proving to be an invaluable management tool so that, for example, four days after the end of each quarter the Oxford computer produces statistics for all of their 18,000 lines—which are split into 20 different management categories—showing a gross profit and royalty. When the accountants agree a formula for overheads it is expected that the computer will produce *net* profit figures equally quickly. The computer's speeding up of administrative routines for publishers—cutting to days processes that previously took months—is enabling them to increase prices at the right time, rather than two years too late, which pleases them. Librarians may view this aspect somewhat differently.

At Oxford again—theirs is probably the most efficiently used machine in the business—the computer is used for mailing purposes in areas not yet covered by University Mailing Services or the Book Development Council mailing schemes. The programmes are identical with those used by U.M.S. and B.D.C. Simulation jobs are also being undertaken, one of these being to work out the effect of additional discounts on Oxford's profits. They are also experimenting with computer typesetting, and hope that their 1971 complete catalogue will be computer set.

The latest development at Oxford—which follows the example of Baker & Taylor, the large American library suppliers—is the installation of visual terminals. Under the old system—which is currently in use in almost all other publishing houses—orders were edited for sense, and, crucially, for the addition of the account number of the bookseller who originated the order, and the *SBN* of the titles that are on the order itself. This is a time-consuming process. The introduction of visual terminals at Oxford abolishes this part of the exercise and orders go straight to the terminal operators without preliminary editing. The operators key in the first four characters of the bookseller's name, and of the town in which he operates. The computer consults its account file and throws up the full name and address of the bookseller concerned, together with his credit rating, on the screen in front of the operator. If the eight characters keyed in are insufficient for a unique hit the computer throws up the alternatives on to the screen in front of the operator. The operator selects the correct account. Next she keyboards the first few characters of the title that appears on the order form, and of the name of the author if this also appears. The computer displays on the screen the title that matches these characters. If no unique hit is possible the computer throws up on to the screen all the possible alternatives, and the operator must make a selection from the fuller information contained on the order form. Oxford University Press have found that they get a unique hit fourteen out of fifteen times. The fifteenth time the operator has to use a small amount of intelligence which, anyway, is no bad thing. It does tend to keep the operators interested.

W. H. Smith are no longer wholesalers in the accepted sense of the term, but they are still very large suppliers in that they centrally warehouse for several hundred branches, and have a permanent title stock of well over thirty thousand. W.H.S. use their computer in ways very similar to a publisher, but with the additional task of accounting for the customer. In this instance the customer is wholly owned, i.e. the W.H.S. branch. This extra job is particularly interesting in that one machine is dealing with aspects of accounts involving main supplier (publisher), wholesaler (warehouse at Swindon), and retailer (the W.H.S. branch).

The statistics of the W.H.S. operation are: 700 owned outlets that may be termed bookshops; 15,000 newspaper outlets which sell some books; a warehouse title stock of some 35,000 titles with a value of £4 million at any one time, with 5000 titles only of this 35,000 total satisfying 75% of the demand.

Among W.H.S. future plans are a system for the automatic replenishment of basic lines of branch stock: for instance, titles within a series of which the whole range is always available, perennial best sellers, standard reference works, and so forth; the institution of an ordering system whereby branches will supply *SBNs* for Swindon stock (branches have catalogues that show all titles available from Swindon, and the catalogues include the *SBN* with other details of the book): the introduction of document readers as well as visual terminals because, while Smiths are very interested in the introduction of these latter machines, they believe that with 75% of demand at any time concentrating on 5000 titles only visual terminals are not the only answer, and for very fast moving lines order entry via document readers has a great deal to commend it; what is called 'cash till analysis' whereby the computer analyses paper tape produced by the cash tills that shows the quantity, the amount of money taken, and the item number of the goods sold; and a computer-based ordering and payment system for main suppliers.

Just as Smiths led the demand for an *SBN* system—which was subsequently taken up on a scale far greater than they envisaged when they began their campaign—they will probably lead the demand for some kind of tear-off slip or card to be carried in books which, by the addition of quantity and standard account number, can become an ordering document acceptable to an *OCR* device. Perhaps in the same way that *SBNs* were quickly exploited by the library world this new suggestion may also be of interest as the inclusion of *OCR* symbols on, perhaps, the back flap of a book, could be of help in the automatic recording of loans.

Very little use of computers is made by booksellers, although Thin's of Edinburgh have employed one for several years. They use it for the production of orders for publishers and of invoices for their own customers. Most of their books are ordered through the computer. All the main publishers have had a number allocated to them by Thin's. A title description is entered into the computer, together with the publisher's number on which the computer sorts, and then prints out orders to all the publishers from whom books have been ordered during the course of the day. When the books arrive the computer, by means of a reference number it has allocated to the order, locates the customer who has asked for the book and prints out an invoice made out to that customer. If the book fails to arrive after a given period, a reminder to the publisher is produced by the computer.

Books that are supplied from Thin's stock—some 40% to 50% of any order—are invoiced manually, and the basic details of the invoice are supplied to the computer so that the customer's account is debited. The computer is used to control some 40,000 accounts. It provides monthly statements, and prints out chasers on overdue accounts.

Basically the computer is used as a sorting device, but it also does certain operations automatically which mean that Thin's do not have to bother with them: reminding publishers, chasing slow payers, and so forth. The computer is not used for stock control, and it is interesting to note that it has no basic file. Thin's are particularly interested in the Book Centre plans (see below) to provide access to a title availability file that can be interrogated from a distance by booksellers using visual terminals. Thin's believe that this could substantially reduce the time for passage of orders, and it would be extremely useful to be able to know immediately if titles are available.

The Woolston Book Company have engaged consultants to see if it would be a viable exercise for them to begin to use a computer, either their own or a bureau, and there is no doubt that other library suppliers are similarly engaged, but the writer has no details.

The Greater London Council Educational Supply Department is scarcely a bookseller, and not a wholesaler in that no stock is held, but they are still a supplier of books to 3,000 schools and colleges. They do their book order processing by computer, and the West Riding of Yorkshire, Kent, and Essex Educational Authorities are expected to follow the pioneering of the G.L.C. very shortly. The G.L.C. computer is provided with a bank of information that contains publishers' names and addresses, title descriptions which include *SBN*, published price and the discount given by the publisher to G.L.C., and availability statement, i.e. re-binding, o.p., etc. Schools are provided with catalogues by publishers—there is a serious updating problem here, and not all schools find it easy to obtain the catalogues and the *SBN* information—and supply to G.L.C. their orders on standard forms which contain the school's account number, the *SBN* of the title required, quantity and so on. Entry into the computer is by paper tape which contains the school's account number, quantity and *SBN*. The machine is programmed to sort and collate the orders by publisher, and produce twice weekly for each publisher a summary of total G.L.C. requirements in *SBN* sequence. The output quotes a short description of the title as well as the *SBN*, although internal processing is by number only.

Publishers, including those not using computer, find that the G.L.C. computer orders are much easier to handle because there are only two large orders per week instead of—as previously—many small ones each day. On average schools order some 5000 titles per day from the G.L.C., and these titles come from several hundred publishers.

Deliveries at the G.L.C. Southfields Depot run to about 160 publishers' parcels per day, averaging twenty titles in each parcel. The G.L.C. distribution service operates on a weekly basis, so, when the computer has been advised of receipt of titles, it produces one delivery note per week for each of the G.L.C. 'customers' which summarizes all books or reports which have been received during the week. The delivery note which accompanies the books to the customer gives the *SBN*, a short title description, the quantity, published price, the value and the special G.L.C. discount so the schools have an up-to-date statement of the expenditure which they have incurred.

It should perhaps be added that the G.L.C. is one of the eight educational authorities that traditionally buy direct from publishers and receive a discount.

Two main snags in the system are the difficulty that schools have in obtaining *SBN* information, although this is getting better and better as publishers make *SBNs* more widely known; and the other snag is the updating of the G.L.C.'s own main file. Book Centre and some other publishers now supply updating material in magnetic tape form, but this does not solve the whole problem. G.L.C. and Whitakers are investigating it jointly in the expectation that one source of updating material will be more efficient than the hundreds now in use.

Standard Book Numbering, or *International* Standard Book Numbering as it should now more correctly be called, is still 'work in progress' because, while all current output is numbered, and the numbers are easily obtained from the British National Bibliography, or Whitaker publications, backlist numbers are not so immediately accessible. The Whitaker book lists are now computer held, and pages are produced by computer-controlled phototypesetting. The *BNB* goes live with a similar system in 1971. The Whitaker systems were designed by the *BNB*, and the programmes were written by them under contract to ensure total compatibility.

So far as Whitaker's are concerned 'work in progress' is the conversion of the *British Books In Print* card index file to a machine held file, and the numbering of this. When the *British Books In Print* file is fully converted to a computer base, when it has been fully numbered, and when material from the *Books of the Month & Books to Come* and *The Bookseller* files—which are already computer held—are added to it, there are all the essentials of what is beginning to be called an 'availability' file: a machine held record of what books are currently available, at what price and from which publisher. Such a file, centrally produced and maintained, but copies of which can be readily available, is a *sine qua non* of effective computer-based order processing operations. Creation and even maintenance of files of the size of this one—basically 250,000 records added to at the rate of 32,000 per year and with some 22,000 deletions each year, and 14,000 price changes—is uneconomic for the individual user. Educational authorities, library bodies and the Book Centre have already expressed an interest in having copies of the main file and a weekly updating service. Others have begun to investigate the possibility of access to the file itself or to one of the copies held elsewhere. The file and the updating service is expected to be available in 1971.

The projected Book Centre use of the file is of particular interest. They intend to take the total file and to make it even larger so that, for instance, a title such as 'Penguin Atlas of Medieval History' by McEvedy could be called up on visual display terminals by inputting only an approximation of the title. It will be appreciated that orders are not always accurate. Thus perhaps:

'Penguin Medieval History Atlas', 'McEvedy's Medieval History Atlas', 'Atlas of Medieval History', 'Medieval History Atlas', 'McEvedy's Atlas', 'McEvedy's Medieval History', and so forth.

If the input was 'Penguin History' the visual terminal would throw up all the various alternatives that were available under this brief description, and the operator would either select one from further information available, for instance price and author, or if this was not possible return a list of the options to the source of the order.

A file of this nature would be vast, but so are the uses to which Book Centre are planning to put it. They plan to hold a file for all books available in Great Britain which will be amended and updated on a daily basis. Ultimately they hope to add to it details of U.S. books and those from other countries as well. Book Centre aims to attract from the majority of booksellers and library suppliers *all* of their orders. They want to put an end to constant research by booksellers and the sending off of numerous orders to hundreds of different publishers. The Book Centre plan would be for all orders to be received at their offices and these would go to the visual terminal operators who would key in the standard account number, quantity, and a brief description of the title. Everything, in fact, that Oxford University Press do at this moment. But while Oxford are operating a system for their own books only, Book Centre would expect to operate it for the books of all publishers.

The central computer complex that they plan consists of two computers, a large file store, eighty visual display terminals, paper tape readers and punches, card readers and punches, and magnetic tape. Of the two computers the larger would be used for order entry purposes through the display terminals and the smaller for invoice preparation, order preparation etc. If the larger computer were out of action, then the smaller one would take on the order entry function temporarily, so that there would be no delay in order entry.

The larger file store would contain two files:

1. A file of books in print. The initial source for this information would be the Whitaker book lists.

and 2. A file of titles of publishers who wish to have the central computer produce invoices. This file would be kept up-to-date by the publisher direct to the computer in much the same way that the Book Centre file is maintained at the present time. This file would be used only for publisher's invoicing.

The bookseller would send all his orders to the central computer without necessarily concerning himself with the publisher or the supplier. The order could be in several forms:

1. Existing order forms, or even a photographic copy of the customer's order for the bookseller if this were legible. The order would contain as much detail as is immediately known to the bookseller. The computer centre would, through the display screens, interrogate the central file and take three courses of action

   (a) Store the order ready to place with the supplier.
   (b) Return the order to the bookseller as not traceable.
   (c) Report to the bookseller the alternatives available according to the information given.

2. If the bookseller had his own computer he could send the order in automatic form, either card, paper tape, or magnetic tape. This input would contain the *SBN* and the central computer would simply store the order ready to place with the supplier.

and 3. Cards, paper tape or magnetic tape supplied to the bookseller by his customer, i.e. library or educational authority.

At the end of each day the central computer would have compiled orders for all customers using the service for all publishers. The orders would then be forwarded to the publishers in various ways: either printed out on standard order forms, or in magnetic tape form, or in paper tape form, or punched card, depending upon the requirements of the publisher concerned, and his willingness to pay for any of the more sophisticated methods that would save trouble and expense in his own warehouse.

Future developments would be the placing of visual terminals on the premises of the larger bookshops, and direct on-line communication from the central computer to the smaller computers of individual publishers. Larger booksellers might well have several terminals on their premises, and their own printer controlled by the central computer.

It is expected that the existence of this large bank of book information will be of interest to other organizations than bookshops. Such a data bank is a pre-requisite of any computer based ordering system, but a bank of this size is extremely expensive to handle and needs a large through-put to be economic. But access to such a file by remote terminals, in association with on-line printers, might, in some circumstances, solve the economic problem for library suppliers, and perhaps educational authorities, and even some specialist libraries.

But quite apart from possible direct use of the Book Centre facilities by a few specialist organisations, the work is of obvious interest to all libraries. If one substitutes libraries for booksellers as the order generators, and booksellers and library suppliers for publishers as the recipients of orders, the whole Book Centre system could stand in a library context. Whether the library and educational world will duplicate the Book Centre plans, or make use of the Book Centre project itself in some as yet unidentified way, or will devise some other system altogether, remains to be seen.

Saul Steinberg, Chairman and Chief Executive Officer of Leasco Data Processing Equipment Corporation, made some interesting remarks at the recent Data Decade Conference. While he may have come slightly unstuck in his excursions into publishing, he has been notably successful when he has stuck to his last, and is as likely to be right as anyone. He said: 'In order to create systems that are complete and effective, even greater investment in software will be made in the 70's; complexity and completeness of these systems will be beyond the reach of the individual firm: even the largest and most powerful chain. Sooner or later users with common requirements will share the high cost of development. . . .' The Book Centre plans have in them the beginnings of a net-work project. This sort of thing is vastly expensive, but an obviously desirable objective.

It may well be that the size of the files required by the book trade and library world to satisfy its information and order processing demands and the size of the central processors needed effectively to cope with their requirements both in information supply and acquisitions, and the cost of system design and programming to ensure that information is readily and *economically* available, and orders are processed speedily and at lowest cost, will bring librarianship and bookselling and publishing closer together, at least where computing is concerned.

SECTION II

Methods and Techniques

The Computer/Library Interface: an Introduction
by E. D. Barraclough, J. D. Dews and J. M. Smethurst

An Introduction to Computing Methods for
Library Information Processing
by N. S. M. Cox

Systems Analysis in Libraries: the Role of
Management
by F. Robinson

The Computer/Library Interface: an Introduction

E. D. BARRACLOUGH, J. D. DEWS and
J. M. SMETHURST

The purpose of this paper is to attempt an analysis of the environment within which computers may be used in libraries and to identify some of the difficulties which are encountered. It is well to realize that we are proposing to use computers for purposes for which they were not originally intended, and that this inevitably means that such use of the computer will be rather cumbersome. The range of problems to which computers are being applied is already wide and increasing rapidly, in all walks of life, but current progress in the design of computers does not lead us to believe that the environment will change radically in the next few years. It remains an unfortunate fact that the present, and the next, generation of computers are designed essentially for scientific and commercial use, and the processing of bibliographical records is a somewhat peripheral activity.

There are three aspects of the computer environment which we should consider. Firstly the actual equipment (hardware); as with any other equipment, its capabilities and limitations must be appreciated in order to make reasonable use of it. Next there are the programs (normally provided by the manufacturer) which enable the user to put the machine into service and without which it is completely inert, referred to as software. Finally there are the programs created by the user himself in order to solve his particular problems or perform work useful to him. The ease with which he can do this depends very much on the characteristics of the hardware and software.

The use of this term computer is somewhat misleading in that it implies a single machine, and that machines bearing the same name are similar in size and capability. In fact a computing configuration is a collection of devices: one or more linked central processors, surrounded by a variety of peripheral devices for input, output and intermediate storage. The particular configuration installed is chosen to support the overall pattern of activities.

The name of a machine, therefore, conveys very little about the equipment a particular centre may have, and hence what work it can perform, but is merely a guide to the speed and type of the central unit, which performs simple arithmetic and logical functions. It is in terms of very simple operations that the processing capability of the computer is assessed.

For scientific and commercial work, the ability to perform, say, a million additions per second is a useful facility, especially when the numbers to be added are each stored in a single identifiable location. The processing of alphabetic strings of characters, however, inevitably results in considerable loss of speed, when each location contains an equal number of characters which must be packed and unpacked by means of logical comparisons. The computer which can add two numbers in a few millionths of a second might take 1000 times as long to select a particular group of characters from a string. The main differences in the functional capability of computers for our purposes are the speed and facility with which such operations as this can be performed.

Probably the most critical consideration from the library point of view is the quantity of data which can be stored, and the speed with which it may be accessed. As might be expected, there is a direct relationship between access speed and cost. The core storage of the central processor, in which operations may be performed on the data, provides an access time of 1 microsecond or less, but costs approximately 100 pence* per character, so for economic as well as practical reasons it is not usual to keep data in this kind of storage unless it is being operated upon, but to keep it in some form of back-up storage medium.

Normally this background storage is used for holding data which is transferred to the fast store in 'blocks' when required for processing and subsequently returned to the cheaper and slower store. The quality of this back up storage is measured by the speed with which data may be transferred between it and the core store. Generally speaking, the shorter the access time, the more expensive the storage will be.

* In this paper, 'pence' imply £.s.d.

Backing storage is of two main types: random access devices (in which all the data is equally accessible), such as discs and drums, and linear access devices, such as magnetic tapes. Drum stores are usually permanently attached to the computer, whereas some discs and magnetic tapes can be interchanged, thus making it possible to store any amount of data away from the computer with the inconveniences of possible delay during processing caused by the necessity of operator intervention to select and load the disc or tape. Once mounted, discs give the possibility of very rapid access to the data. A typical large disc unit could contain over 200 million characters; the cost of allowing the store to be immediately accessible is about 0·12 pence per character which drops 0·002 pence per character for storage away from the computer. Magnetic tape is much cheaper, at about 0·0002 pence per character, but with the disadvantage that the data may only be accessed sequentially, and where the difference in access time between the first and the last character may be upwards of five minutes. Clearly magnetic tape is not suitable for storing files to which immediate access is required (as when a reader uses a card catalogue) but it is quite adequate for work in which most of the records in a file require some processing and which can be carried out in the order of the records in the file.

The availability and cost of storage media are therefore of prime importance in determining the types of operation which are possible. For the operation itself, the means of converting data for input, and the type and quality of output, become dominant considerations, the latter particularly in its effect on relationships with users of the library. For scientific and most commercial work the important characters are the digits 0–9 with perhaps the symbols '.' '+' ',' '−'. The attitude of the scientific user to alphabetic characters is aptly expressed in the *KDF9 Usercode Programming Manual* where it states 'on *occasions* it is useful to be able to set up characters for use when headings or comments . . . are required *with* results on output'.* Typographical quality in these situations clearly plays a very secondary role. In general, large quantities of output are required for short periods of time so that speed is the main consideration. In defence of the scientist one should however note the large numbers of mathematical tables that have been set using computers and associated composing machines, though once more the bulk of this has been pure numerical printing.

* The italics are ours.

For library work (a catalogue for example) the output may be required for constant use by a large number of people, and may be required as a permanent record, in which case typographical quality becomes very much more important. In the present stage of computer technology our needs cannot easily be met. Computer typesetting (in which output from the computer on, say, magnetic tape can be fed to a composing machine) is advancing rapidly (though the equipment is expensive) and can now match the ordinary computer printer in speed (2000+ characters a second).

With the scientific and commercial machine where the characters required are limited to the upper case alphabet, the numbers 0–9, and a few punctuation and mathematical symbols, the number of characters available for output on a line printer may be as few as 55. In view of the developments in computer typesetting this might be regarded as a temporary restriction, if it were possible to input the data in a form which would make the distinctions necessary to achieve adequate output when the technology advances, but here also there are severe restrictions. The number of distinct character codes available on card punches is almost as restrictive as for line printer output. Paper tape typewriters are more flexible and allow about 128 symbols, which at least gives the possibility of using upper and lower case; this may be adequate for the majority of English titles, if fitted with an appropriate keyboard, but the character set required by the average academic library will be considerably larger than this for adequate representation of the data.

Before leaving the subject of hardware, the recent development of the on-line typewriter must be mentioned. A typewriter connected to the computer, so that data typed on it may be entered directly into the store, offers great possibilities for libraries, especially as the ability to use several of these simultaneously reduces the cost for each of them. Data may also be transferred from the computer to such typewriters, which enables them to be used as very slow output devices. Even with multiple access the cost is likely to be high in comparison with the scale of costs to which libraries are accustomed, and it will be necessary to give careful consideration to the most economic way of using such devices—but the possibilities, however, are of great interest.

These, then, are some of the limitations of the hardware which must be set against the attractive advantages of great speed and accuracy in the processing of large amounts of data. However, the ability to use the hardware efficiently depends very much on the software provided with the computing system. It is quite possible to develop one's own special-purpose software but the magnitude of the task should rule this out for the individual library. IBM are said to have spent 400 man-years developing software for their 360 system. Although this is a general system, a special-purpose system might be developed more quickly, especially if parts of the general system were used where they were appropriate; however this is not a task to be undertaken lightly. Nevertheless time spent providing basic facilities for use in bibliographical work is time well spent, if those providing the programming effort are well informed about library problems and the functions required are well defined.

The main concern of the user in the matter of software will be the variety and kind of 'compilers' available. These are programs which translate other programs, written in a commonly used programming language, into the basic order code of the particular machine. It is quite possible to write programs directly in the basic machine code, and there are advantages of flexibility and efficiency in so doing, but it requires more effort and skill, and usually takes longer, than using a 'high-level' language.* The *ALGOL* statement

$$\text{`m:=y} \uparrow 2 + 4 \times Z \uparrow 3;\text{'}$$

(Laver, 1967, p. 35) provides a good example of an expression that may be written in such a language. To achieve the same result in *KDF9* Usercode would require many instructions and several assumptions about the form of the numbers. For example if the values y and z are less than 1 we would write:

Yo ; DUP; × ;
Y1 ; DUP; DUP; × ; × ; SHA + 2 ;
+ ; = Y2 ;

but if the x and y were whole numbers the coding would be quite different.

The use of a high level language results in some loss of efficiency which may be perfectly acceptable compared with the saving of programming time for a single operation; for a frequently-run production job, however, considerations of efficiency alone may dictate that the program be written in machine code.

* A high level language can in outline be described as a device for making the computing system appear to the programmer–user as though its hardware were designed especially to tackle his type of problem.

Programming languages are usually developed with the performance of a particular class of operations in mind, and the compiler writer will naturally try to optimize the efficient performance of these operations to the exclusion of others. As with the hardware, the needs of scientific and commercial work have dominated design, with the result that the commonly used languages (and therefore the compilers provided by manufacturers) are cumbersome and more or less inefficient to use for handling linguistic data for bibliographical work. *ALGOL* and *FORTRAN* for example are designed mainly for mathematical and scientific work, whereas *COBOL* is useful for commercial work. *PL/1* is intended for use in both mathematical and commercial work. Although all these languages can be, and have been, used for bibliographical work, the resulting programs are necessarily less efficient than they could be, if written in machine code. (It may be of interest to note that the Symplegades Research Group at the University of Newcastle upon Tyne has for some time been developing an experimental high-level-language environment for library and other information processing activities.)

In library operations therefore, if we are not prepared to develop special software, we are in the position of cumulating the inefficiencies of program language with the unsuitability of hardware. This is not to say the operation is not worthwhile, but merely to point out that the benefits, for us, of the computer are somewhat reduced, in the present state of the art.

Having discussed the computer environment, we may now turn to the library to see in what respects it can be improved by the use of the computer.

Library records are, at present, stored in random access devices known as catalogues or files. Access time is usually found to be faster when these devices are of the codex form, than when they consist of cards in drawers, though the card form is significantly easier to amend. The means of locating a particular entry is by an ordering device which follows a well-known convention, such as the order of the alphabet or the decimal digits. This ordering device enables the file to carry retrievable information. For example, it is impossible without great difficulty to find a particular card from a large file in random order, but when they are in a known order, a card may be retrieved by that part of the data which is ordered, e.g. author's name in an author catalogue. The kind of information which can be retrieved depends on the order adopted for the file, and the part of the record which is used for filing. This is well known to librarians. Advantage is taken of the ability to insert duplicate copies of the record in a file, each ordered by a different part of the data, but the physical growth of files, as well as the cost of creating duplicate entries, set limits to the extent to which this may be done.

The manual creation and maintenance of these files is time-consuming, costly, and subject to error: the copying, sorting, amending and merging of files of records is work which would seem to be well suited to the capabilities of the computer, and we are therefore encouraged to hope for some improvement in library file-handling by its use. However, although it is easy to do by computer some things which it is difficult to do manually, the converse is also true.

The requirements for library records are:

1. Ease of access to any part of the file. Direct access is possible to a manual file, so long as the approach is via the part of the data used for filing; otherwise it is difficult or impossible. The same is true of a computer file held in direct access storage, though it is possible to have several different filing orders in the same file. In a serial file, if it is properly constructed, there is little difference in the search time whichever part of the record is required;

2. Ease of maintenance and updating. In the manual file the unit is the single *record*, and the time taken for updating depends directly on the number of amendments. For the computer the unit is the *file*, and it takes almost the same time to amend one record as it does to amend every record on the file;

3. Ease of expansion. This is not difficult in either situation, subject to certain physical conditions, though the expansion of a direct access file is a non-trivial operation;

4. Rearrangement of the file, either from random order to a known order, or from one known order to another. This is very difficult in the manual situation and rarely contemplated except after catastrophic error; it is time consuming (relative to other processing) for the computer, but of an order which can readily be contemplated. When more than one order is required in the manual situation, it is customary to maintain separate files. With the computer, different orders may be generated from one file, though it may be desirable to maintain the generated files once they are created;

5. Reproduction of the files. Rarely considered for manual operations, though this is fast and cheap for the computer;

6. Visual display. The manual file is always available for consultation. The computer file must either be printed or must be held in direct access storage for consultation from a typewriter or visual display terminal. Both these methods of access are relatively expensive;

and 7. Multiple entry, at different places in the file. Kept to the minimum
necessary in the manual operation, because of time, cost and space
considerations, but for the computer, duplication of a master record is easy
and fast, though it can be expensive.*

There is, however, a significant difference between a manual
record and an equivalent computer record. The data on a catalogue
card for example, is heavily loaded with information (that is, it can
be interpreted by the human mind and lead to action on its part,
even if this is only an increase in knowledge). The computer record
contains the same *data,* but the *information* it contains must be explicitly put there by human beings, at the input stage, and the computer
must be instructed on the action it must take. Ordinary 'common
sense' involves many logical discriminations, some of them referring
to factors external to the data under consideration, and it is not
possible, in the present stage of development, to take account of all
these factors in a program. Hence the description of the computer as
a 'totally obedient moron'.

In time programming techniques may develop to the stage where
the computer will recognize that the character strings

SHAW, George Bernard
SHAW, Bernard
SHAW, G   B
SHAW, [George] Bernard
G.B.S.

refer to the same author and are equivalent, but are distinct from
SHAW, Bernard as the author of a book on Lasers; but this time is
not yet. In the meantime, every unit of data by which we need to
discriminate must be marked and identified in soem way so that the
computer can recognize it and the action to be taken can be defined.
A character string which is to be matched with another and treated
as identical must *be* identical, unless the program can apply some
rule to make the equivalence judgement.

Some fairly complex rules have been developed to ensure that
some degree of consistency is maintained in library catalogues, but
these have relied very heavily on the ability of the human mind to
associate different things and 'see' when they are equivalent, so that
a comparatively high degree of inconsistency is tolerable in a manual
catalogue. In fact some of the inconsistency, as for example the
introduction of classified sequences in an alphabetical catalogue,

* See, however Bregzis (1967).

may improve its usefulness.* A great deal of research needs to be done before the computer can approach the recognition processes of the human mind, but as an interim measure, the careful incorporation of appropriate information into the data should enable us to make considerable progress towards the production of tools similar to, but more effective than our present ones. If the computer cannot recognize equivalences, it can at least show up inconsistencies, and thereby improve our knowledge of what equivalences need to be made (Jolliffe, 1968).

We have mentioned access time in connection with hardware and noted the direct relationship between time and cost. We were then thinking in terms of the hardware itself, and talking of microseconds, but we must also consider access time from the library point of view, where the times are of a different order altogether—hours and days rather than microseconds. Hardware time affects cost only, whereas library access time affects the efficiency of the library itself: from this point of view it is of no significance whether a job takes 30 seconds or 30 minutes or 30 hours, if it takes three days to get the job to the machine and the result returned. Clearly this kind of access time must be taken into account in the design of the library system, bearing in mind the relative costs. Batch processing with an unguaranteed turn-round time may be quite adequate for the processing of some of the library's files (as for example the printing of a catalogue of a special collection) and will be the cheapest form of service. For the loan files, where it is necessary to know where a particular book is at any time, a guaranteed daily turn-round may be too slow, and direct turn-round time will be different for every file in the library, and it will be necessary to consider activity on each on a cost-benefit basis.

In considering this, one point which must be noted is that all the library's computerized data files may be stored away from the library—perhaps miles away—and will be not available for casual amendment or consultation. Consultation will not be, of the file itself, but of the last printout—on which, of course, manuscript amendments may and will be made. But this operation has no effect on the files, for the amendment of which specific instructions must be punched onto paper tape or card. A library which is likely to make extensive use of the computer would be well advised to have its own

* Sorting by computer is a purely mechanical process, whereas the filing order of the library catalogue is highly sophisticated. For an indication of the problems and limitations see Hines and Harris (1966).

data preparation equipment, but even so it will probably be necessary to accumulate manuscript amendments which are cumulated until they can be punched. Mistakes can be quite costly, resulting for example in a job having to be run again, or even in a file having to be regenerated completely. Careful back-up arrangements are necessary, such as the preservation of the originals of all amendments made since a particular file was last generated. A further problem clearly arises when the library will be relying perhaps for the first time on another department to service its records; restrictions may well be imposed upon access simply by the demands made upon the computing service by other users. A library cannot rely on 'burn-up' time being available for its processing. Costs may well rise simply because of convenience considerations—in this case they would at least be the cost of running the computer as shown in the appendix to this paper.

We have drawn attention to the disadvantages resulting from limited character sets. These can be overcome to some extent at the input stage by appropriate coding. The depression of a key on the keyboard of a tape-punching typewriter or a card punch produces a pattern of holes on paper tape or card, and we are almost in a position to say 'This means what we say it means' regardless of the character the key represents. The same applies to combinations of codes. We can say for example that ' $B' means '?'; however this is likely to present difficulties in proofreading, depending also on the level of sophistication of the output device on which the hard copy is generated. To achieve high accuracy in proofreading requires that a minimum of the intellectual effort of the proofreader should be devoted to transforming the character which he sees into the form with which he is familiar; for example, proofreading Russian printed in mnemonic form in Roman characters is likely in itself to give rise to proofing errors. Furthermore, if the association between the printed form and the form familiar to the user is difficult, the effectiveness of the entire system may be dangerously reduced. The situation where only a librarian is able to use a complex catalogue is probably only too familiar to us.

From the point of view of input, a restricted character set requiring the punching of mnemonic forms may sufficiently increase the number of keystrokes to make a significant difference to the cost of data preparation both in terms of the number of keystrokes and the necessity for the keyboard operator to make the necessary association.

It is believed that better keyboard performance is obtained if the operator understands at least in outline what is being punched. (A counter example to this has been offered by Dolby* who pointed out that a particularly intractable class of errors in the punching of a dictionary was eventually attributed to the association of the words in error to sexual connotations by the operator.)

In what we have said so far we have concentrated, perhaps unduly, on the problems for the library of using a computer, but before we pass to the probable advantages, we would like to draw attention to the main implication of what we have been saying, which is the prime factor on which successful use of the computer will rest. This is that in order to promote a successful and useful interface between the computer and library environments, the most important consideration must be the achievement of the right balance between the tasks that can be performed by the machine and these which *must* be performed by human beings. The difference in speed between the two is enormous, and very careful thought will be necessary, by librarians, to ensure that changes are made in the way the library system is arranged so that this imbalance is minimized, and that the interaction between people and the machine is such that neither causes gross inefficiencies in the work of the other. Computer people give a lot of thought to ensuring that their resources are used efficiently; so do librarians, though they have not the means of measuring the results so accurately. It may be that the optimum balance between the two environments means some loss of efficiency in one or both of them, but it is the overall result which is important; to optimize this requires not only a constant dialogue between systems analysts, programmers and librarians, but also a thorough training or retraining of the members of the library staff, particularly the relatively junior members who would provide the interface.

One further factor we should take into consideration is the problem of scale. A lot of the work that has been done in the bibliographical field has been of a research nature and inevitably has been limited to relatively small quantities of data. It is dangerous to assume that the techniques that work for these small data collections can be applied to large quantities of data. For example it is trivial to sort the information that can be held on one magnetic tape (about 30,000 300-character records) but to sort 10 times that number requires a completely different approach; this is equally true in the

* J. L. Dolby, Private Communication.

library field where the filing rules for a small library would be entirely inadequate for the British Museum Catalogue.

In the face of all these problems, we may well wish to consider whether the use of the computer is worthwhile, and what advantages there can be to offset the problems. We do not regard any of the problems as incapable of solution, either by technological improvement in hardware or improvements in programming techniques—both these fields are advancing rapidly—so long as appropriate resources are devoted to their solution. Even in the present state of the art however:

1. we can contemplate handling much larger quantities of data, with little more effort than it takes to handle present amounts, once the system change has been planned correctly;

2. we can increase the effectiveness of our bibliographic tools, even in their present form—the required data is already there (titles, publishers, dates of publication, etc.) all of which represent information which is under-utilized at present. (How many University libraries can present a reader with a list of 18th-century Spanish books in their stock for example?) (Cox, Dews, and Dolby, 1966, p. 79);

3. we can achieve much firmer control of our system by maintaining the statistical and management information, which can be collected with ease as a by-product of computer operations. Even 'raw' this data will enable us to base decisions on better knowledge of what is happening in the system, but the application of statistical techniques (by employing the computer in its traditional role) will enable us to improve this still further, at a minimal cost;

4. higher levels of consistency and accuracy will be possible—perhaps mandatory;

5. the existence of files in machine-readable form gives the possibility of speeding up the research and experimentation necessary for the advancement of techniques of subject analysis and retrieval, which are the particular metier of libraries. Machines will not *solve* these problems, which are intellectual, but they may *help* us to solve them. Their tenacity alone is a commendable advantage here;

and 6. the possibilities of improvements in co-operation between libraries will be much greater when machine-readable data is available, and compatibility problems have been overcome.*

We have tried to stress the importance of library staff becoming aware of the facilities available to them on the computer, and in the short term, the need for computer people to understand the complexity and requirements of library operations. In the long term it is essential that library staff are capable of initiating and managing

* See also the papers by Coward.

their own computer functions. We believe that the best method of initiation into computer systems is by gaining experience on a small scale with the assistance of computer centre staff.

The problems that will inevitably arise in tackling a system transition of this magnitude can only be solved by individual librarians assimilating an additional body of professional knowledge and pooling this information. The cost of the operation may be high but the benefits could be considerable.

APPENDIX—COSTS AND CAPABILITY OF TYPICAL SYSTEMS
Capability

The capability of a system in this context refers solely to the hardware. An attempt has been made to assess this in terms of library function, taking as examples:

(a) Order system
(b) Production of printed catalogues
(c) On-line catalogue and issue system

Most computers have the capacity to tackle (a), as it involves serial files and updating processes only. Capability (b) necessitates sorting into several filing orders and so requires more storage; (c) needs on-line access to large files and therefore random access store.

Systems

The computing systems are assessed by their ability to perform the listed library tasks, and the cost of sorting 10,000 records averaging 300 characters each is given.

A KDF9, 16K × 48 bit core 4 tape drives
B 1905E 32K × 24 bit core 4 tapes drives 2 discs × 4 million 6 terminals
C 360/67 512K bytes core 2 tape drives 8 discs × 29 million 17 terminals

System	Task capability	Sorting time (10,000 records) Minutes	Cost/hour (£)	Estimated Commercial Charge/hour (£)
A	a, b	12	15	100
B	a, b	12	12	75
C	a, b, c	3	25	270

Note 1. Cost/hour is running cost excluding amortization of capital cost.
2. Commercial charge would probably include some programming assistance.

N.U.M.A.C.* SYSTEM, AUGUST 1968

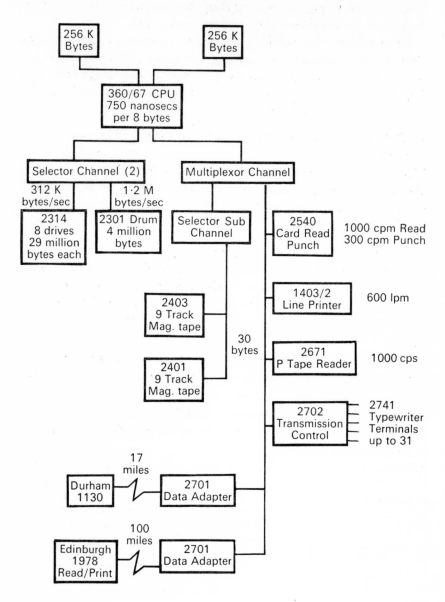

*Northumbrian Universities Multiple Access Computer

Figure 1 The IBM 360/67 Computer at present installed in Newcastle with links to Durham and Edinburgh.

```
1; A; Withals/John/f.1556→
1; REV; Evans/Lewis/f.1574→
1; CONTIN; Fleming/Abraham/1552£-1607→
1; D; Dudley/Robert/1532£-1588/Earl of Leicester→
2; L; [A] Shorte dictionarie in Latine and English,
verie profitable for yong beginners. Compiled
at the first by John Withals,
afterwards revised and increased... by Lewis Evans.
And nowe lastlie augmented... by Abraham
Fleming....→
4; I; Printed at London by Thomas Purfoote, 1586→
4; PR; 1586/E/L/Purfoote/Thomas/ /snr.→
6; 4to→
7; 19→
8; L,T/E→
10; D→
11; <4 A-O8 P4→
12; pp.[240]→
14; c.1586/C/BT/Centrepiece,Ker XXX→
15; c.1586/E/O→
16; 33→
17; PR; Bainbrigg/Reginald/ /H.M. Appleby G.S. 1580-1606→
20; 1→
20; 17;25881→
20; 21;151→
20; 506→
20; 503;T33→
20; 505;C2→
23; NUL/BAI/ /1586-WIT→
```

1.	RECORD CARD – RARE BOOKS			
Desc.	Surname	Forenames	Dates	Epithets
A	Withals	John	f.1556	
REV	Evans	Lewis	f.1574	
CONTIN	Fleming	Abraham.	1552?-1607	
D	Dudley	Robert	1532?-1588	Earl of Leicester

2F.		2A.	

2L.
[A] Shorte dictionarie in Latine and English, verie profitable for yong beginners.
Compiled at the first by John Withals, afterwards revised and increased... by Lewis
Evans. And nowe lastlie augmented... by Abraham Fleming....

3.

4. Printed at London by Thomas Purfoote, 1586

Desc.	Date	Country	Place	Name
PR	1586	E	L	Purfoote/ Thomas/ /snr.

5.	6. 4to	7. 19	8. L,T/E	9.	10. D

11. π⁴ A-O⁸ P⁴

12. pp. [240]

13.

Figure 2. Illustrating the use of specific codes and the structuring of a complex catalogue entry to permit machine manipulation of the record.

Note: the code used at label 11.

Example taken from C. J. Hunt 'The computer production of catalogues of old books' in Cox and Grose (1967).

G

THE **CHINESE**   THEIR HISTORY & CULTURE
THE **CHINESE**   THEIR HISTORY & CULTURE.
THE **CHINESE**   THEIR HISTORY AND CULTURE
THE **CHINESE**   THEIR HISTORY AND CULTURE.
THE **CHINESE** THEIR HISTORY & CULTURE
THE **CHINESE** THEIR HISTORY & CULTURE.
THE **CHINESE** THEIR HISTORY AND CULTURE
THE **CHINESE** THEIR HISTORY AND CULTURE.
THE CHINESE.   THEIR HISTORY & CULTURE
THE CHINESE.   THEIR HISTORY & CULTURE.
THE CHINESE.   THEIR HISTORY AND CULTURE
THE CHINESE.   THEIR HISTORY AND CULTURE.
THE CHINESE. THEIR HISTORY & CULTURE
THE CHINESE. THEIR HISTORY & CULTURE.
THE CHINESE. THEIR HISTORY AND CULTURE
THE CHINESE. THEIR HISTORY AND CULTURE.
THE CHINESE;   THEIR HISTORY & CULTURE
THE CHINESE;   THEIR HISTORY & CULTURE.
THE CHINESE;   THEIR HISTORY AND CULTURE
THE CHINESE;   THEIR HISTORY AND CULTURE.
THE CHINESE; THEIR HISTORY & CULTURE
THE CHINESE; THEIR HISTORY & CULTURE.
THE CHINESE; THEIR HISTORY AND CULTURE
THE CHINESE; THEIR HISTORY AND CULTURE.
THE CHINESE,   THEIR HISTORY & CULTURE
THE CHINESE,   THEIR HISTORY & CULTURE.
THE CHINESE,   THEIR HISTORY AND CULTURE
THE CHINESE,   THEIR HISTORY AND CULTURE.
THE CHINESE, THEIR HISTORY & CULTURE
THE CHINESE, THEIR HISTORY & CULTURE.
THE CHINESE, THEIR HISTORY AND CULTURE
THE CHINESE, THEIR HISTORY AND CULTURE.
THE CHINESE: THEIR HISTORY & CULTURE
THE CHINESE: THEIR HISTORY & CULTURE.
THE CHINESE: THEIR HISTORY AND CULTURE
THE CHINESE: THEIR HISTORY AND CULTURE.
THE CHINESE: THEIR HISTORY & CULTURE
THE CHINESE: THEIR HISTORY & CULTURE.
THE CHINESE: THEIR HISTORY AND CULTURE
THE CHINESE: THEIR HISTORY AND CULTURE.

Figure 3. Example taken from Richmond, Phyllis A. 'Note on updating and searching computerized catalogues'. *Library Resources and Technical Services*, 10, No. 2, Spring 1966, pp. 155-160.

In an ordinary card catalogue these would file as one entry. Unless the program can apply some rule to recognize these character strings as equivalences, they will file as forty entries in a machine sorted file.

" "O IDENT 1/1	HEADING 2/1	LOCATION 3/1	TITLE 4/1	SIZE 11/1
13666 T8F		519.4%	RENEWAL THEORY.X	SM.8VO
13662 M2F	COX, DAVID ROXBEE AND LEWIS	519.9	THE STATISTICAL ANALYSIS	8I.
13692 M8E		MATHS	THE STATISTICAL ANALYSIS	9I.
13704 T2E	COX, DAVID ROXBEE AND WALTE	519.4	QUEUES.X	SM.8VO
13716 T8F		COMP.	QUEUES.X	SM.8VO
13728 T8E		MATHS.	QUEUES.X	SM.8VO
13738 M2E	COX, DAVID ROXBEE AND MILLE	519.4	THE THEORY OF STOCHASTIC	9I.
13752 T1E	COX, DONALD D.	PATTER	BOULDER (COLORADO). BIOL	E8HT
13760 M1E	COX, DOROTHY HANNAH	QUARTO	THE GREEK AND ROMAN POTT	12I.
13773 T1F	COX, E...M.	TOWN P	A HISTORY OF GARDENING I	
13781 M1E	COX, EVAN HILLHOUSE METHVEN	581.95	PLANT-HUNTING IN CHINA I	9I.
13790 T2E	COX, E.v. AND OTHERS	K.C.P.	THE ROLE OF CASTLE.S IN	LA.8VO
13803 T1E	COX, FD.ARD GODFREY	016.91	A REFERENCE GUIDE TO THE	LA.8VO
13821 T1E	COX, ED.ARD WILLIAM	159.96	A MONOGRAPH ON SLEEP AND	8VO.
13829 T1E	COX, FD.ARD WILLIAM SERJEA.	343.09	REPORT OF CASES IN CRIMI	8VO.
13882 T2E	COX, FD.ARD WILLIAM AND OTH	CUPROA	REPORTS OF COUNTY COURT	8VO.
13899 T2E	COX, ED.ARD WILLIAM AND HEM	CUPBOA	REGISTRATION APPEAL CASE	FROM L
13912 E1E	COX, ED.I.		CHANGING AIMS IN RELIGIO	K8
13920 T8E		STORE	PRACTICAL OBSERVATIONS O	PP. 12
13928 H1F	COX, ED.I. MARION (TRANSL.)	G.X841	THE DABATE BETWEEN FOLLY	PP. XX
13939 E1E	COX, ED IN		SIXTH FORM RELIGION. A S	K8N
13948 T1E	COX, EPIC VINCENT	ST. EN	THE MEGALOBLASTIC ANAEMI	LA.8VO
13955 T1E	COX, ER.ST GORDON	BOX 54	AGRICULTURE AND SOME OF	LA.8VO
13966 T1E	COX, EVAN HILLHOUSE METHVEN	TOWN P	WILD GARDENING.	SM.8VO
13975 T2E	COX, EVA. HILLHOUSE METHUEN	TOWN P	MODERN TREES.X	8VO.
13984 T1E	COX, F.A.	4245.9	A HISTORY OF THE JANEWAY	
13990 H1E	COX, GARFIELD V.	380.12	AN APPRAISAL OF AMERICAN	PP. VI
13999 T1E	COX, GEORGE J.	L701	ART, FOR AMATEURS AND ST	PP. XX
14006 T8F		408.92	A GRAMMAR AND COMMENTARY	
14014 T8E		APT SC	ART, FOR AMATEURS AND ST	PP. XX
1402! T1E	COX, G..	CLASSI	THE GREEKS AND THE PERSI	PP. XX
14030 H1E	COX, SI GEORGE W. BART.	291.13	AN INTRODUCTION TO THE S	PP. XV
14038 T1E	COX, GLADYS M.	612.63	CLINICAL CONTRACEPTION.X	PP. X,
14046 T1F	COX, GLF NELSO. AND FLOEI.	MECH.	FLUID MECHANICS.X	LA.8VO
14057 T1E	COX, H. BARTLE	ARCHIT	ANGE-JACQUES GABRIEL (16	PP. 32
14067 T1E	COX, H.L.	629.13	PRELIMINARY NOTE ON THE	4TO.
14080 T2E	COX, HARTING AN. GERALD WIL	STORE	COURSING AND FALCONRY.XC	8VO.
14092 H1E	COX, HAROLD	230.4	ECONOMIC LIBERTY.	PP. VI
14099 H8F		385	THE FAILURE OF STATE RAI	PAMPH.
14106 T2E	COX, HAROLD AND JOH E. CHA	010.94	THE HOUSE OF LONGMAN, WI	PP. £V
14116 H8F		STORE	THE HOUSE OF LONGMAN, 17	PP. £V
14125 I	1300			
14126 I	1004A.1300CO.EN			
14127 H1E	COX, HAROLD	312	THE PROBLEM OF POPULATIO	PP. 19
14133 T1E	COX, HAROLD LESLIE	620.11	THE BUCKLING OF PLATES A	LA.8VO
14142 M8F		CIVIL	THE DESIGN OF STRUCTURES	9I
14150 T1E	COX, SIR HARLOD ROXBEE (ED.	621.43	GAS TURBINE PRINCIPLES A	8VO.
14156 T8E		MECH.	GAS TURBINE PRINCIPLES A	8VO.
14163 T1E	COX, HE RY EDWARD	543.1	THE CHEMICAL ANALYSIS OF	8VO.
14173 T8F		ADVISE	THE CHEMICAL ANALYSIS OF	

Figure 4. To illustrate the incongruities of filing in a manually maintained catalogue file. This example is from the Name Catalogue of the University Library, Newcastle, and shows the standard of filing which is acceptable but undesirable in a manual system. It is one example of the sort of situation which has been brought to light by the University of Newcastle upon Tyne Catalogue Computerization Project.

```
OVAC BULLETIN
    NO. 1-, 1960-, LO.
    NO. 1-, APR, 1960-, (LACKS: NO. 2), LD: NW.
    NO. 2-, OCT, 1960-, CA.
    NO. 3-, MAR, 1961-, RE: SO.
    NO. 4-, OCT, 1961-, (INCOMPLETE), OX.
    NO. 9-, APR, 1964-, HL.
```
Example 1

```
OVERSEA EDUCATION
    1-34, 1929-63, LO.
    1-34, 1929-1963, (1 INCOMPLETE), RE.
    1-34, 1929-63 (2, 3, AND 11 INCOMPLETE), HL.
    4, NO. 4, JULY, 1933: 5, NO. 1, OCT, 1933: 6, NOS.
        2-4, 1935: 7, NOS. 1-3, 1935-36: 8, NO. 2 - 12,
        NO. 1, 1937-1940: 14, NO. 2, JAN, 1943: 15, NO.
        1, OCT, 1943: 16, NO. 2 - 34, 1945-63, BH.
    5, NO. 1, OCT, 1933: 9, NO. 1, OCT, 1937: 10, NO.
        3, APR, 1939: 13, NO. 4 - 18, JULY, 1942 -
        JULY, 1947, (LACKS: 14, NO. 1, OCT, 1942): 26,
        NO. 4 - 34, JAN, 1955 - 1963, NW.
    18-34, OCT, 1946 - 1963, (LACKS: 18, NO. 2: 23,
        NOS. 3-4), BR.
    19, NO. 1, OCT, 1947: 20, NO. 2 - 34, JAN, 1949 -
        1963, LC.
    20, NO. 3 - 34, APR, 1949 - 1963, LD: NO.
    25-34, 1953-63, AB.
    25, NOS. 1-2: 26-34, 1952-63, CA.
    26 - 34, APR, 1954 - 63, EX.
    27 - 34, 1956 - 63, MA.
    27, NO. 4 - 34, JAN, 1956-1963, SH.
    28, NO. 2 - 34, JULY, 1956 - 1963, SO.
    33, NO. 2 - 34, NO. 4, JULY, 1961 - JAN, 1963, OX.
    %CEASED PUBLICATION, JAN, 1963%.
```

Example 2

OVAC BULLETIN
No. 1-, 1960-. LO.
No. 1-, Apr. 1960-, (*Lacks*: no. 2). LD: NW.
No. 2-, Oct. 1960-. CA.
No. 3-, Mar. 1961-, RE: SO.
No. 4-, Oct. 1961-, (*Incomplete*), OX.
No. 9-, Apr. 1964-. HL.

OVERSEA EDUCATION
[*Ceased publication Jan* 1963]
1-34, 1929-63. LO.
1-34, 1929-1963, (1 *incomplete*). RE.
1-34, 1929-63 (2, 3, and 11 *incomplete*). HL.
4, no. 4, July, 1933: 5, no. 1, Oct, 1933: 6, nos. 2-4, 1935: 7, nos. 1-3,
    1935-36: 8, no. 2 - 12, no. 1, 1937-1940: 14, no. 2, Jan, 1943: 15,
    no. 1, Oct, 1943: 16. no. 2 - 34, 1945-63, BH.
5, no. 1, Oct, 1933: 9, no. 1, Oct, 1937: 10, no. 3, Apr, 1939: 13, no. 4
    - 18, July, 1942 - July, 1947, (*Lacks*: 14, no. 1, Oct, 1942): 26, no.
    4 - 34, Jan, 1955 - 1963. NW.
14-, no. 1, Oct, 1942-, 33, no. 4, Jan, 1963, (*Lacks*: 17, no. 4, July,
    1946), KE.
18-34, Oct, 1946 - 1963, (*Lacks*: 18, no. 2: 23, nos. 3-4), BR.
19, no. 1, Oct, 1947: 20, no. 2 - 34, Jan, 1949 - 1963, LC.
20, no. 3 - 34, Apr, 1949 - 1963, LD: NO.
25-34, 1953-63. AB.
25, nos. 1-2: 26-34, 1952-63, CA.
26 - 34, Apr, 1954 - 63, EX.
27 - 34, 1956 - 63, MA.
27, no. 4 - 34, Jan, 1956-1963, SH.
28, no. 2 - 34, July, 1956 - 1963, SO.
33, no. 2 - 34, no. 4, July, 1961 - Jan, 1963, OX.

Figure 5. Illustration of the difference in quality of reproduction between line printer output and Monophoto output. Note the use of '%' to represent square brackets on 'ceased publication' statements.

Examples are taken from 'The Union List of Periodicals held in Institute of Education Libraries'.

Example 1 is from the 1966 edition photo-litho production from line printer output.

Example 2 from the 1968 edition, computer typeset.

Both examples are printed at 55% of their original size.

```
583
===
UTLOOK (NATIONAL COAL BOARD) 237
CCCCCC BCCCCCCCC CCCC CCCCCB ===
      1, NO. 8-, 1948-, LO. 386
                        UU  ===
583
===
UTLOOK FOR THE BLIND. SEE NEW OUTLOOK FOR THE BLIND
CCCCCC CCC CCC CCCCCB CBB CCC CCCCCCC CCC CCC CCCCC
  577
   ===
583
===
UTRE-MER  462
CCCCBCCC   ===
      1929-37, LO. 445
                  UU  ===

583
===
VAC BULLETIN. 428
CCC CCCCCCCC ===
      NO. 1-, 1960-, LO. 401
      U                UU  ===
      NO. 1-, APR, 1960-, (LACKS: NO. 2), LC: NW. 190
      U      U              JIIII       UU  UU  ===
      NO. 2-, OCT, 1960-, CA. 361
      U      U              UU  ===
      NO. 3-, MAR, 1961-, RE: SO. 319
      U      U              UU  UU  ===
      NO. 4-, OCT, 1961-, (INCOMPLETE), OX. 254
      U      U              JIIIIIIIII  UU  ===
      NO. 9-, APR, 1964-, HL. 358
      U      U              UU  ===

583
===
VERSFA EDUCATION  374
CCCCCC CCCCCCCCC ===
              =CEASED PUBLICATION, JAN, 1963= 273
              (JIIIII IIIIIIIIIIII JIII IIII) ===
      1-34, 1929-63, LO. 401
                        UU  ===
      1-34, 1929-1963, (1 INCOMPLETE), RE. 264
                        IIIIIIIIII  UU  ===
      1-34, 1929-63 (2, 3, AND 11 INCOMPLETE), HL. 202
                        IIIIIIIIII  UU  ===
      4, NO. 4, JULY, 1933: 5, NO. 1, OCT, 1933: 6, NOS. 2-4, 1935: 7, NOS. 1-3,
                                    U
      1935-36: 8,  0. 2 - 12, NO. 1, 1937-1940: 14, NO. 2, JAN, 1943: 15,
                                                          U
      NO. 1, OCT, 1943: 16, NO. 2 - 34, 1945-63, BH. 153
                                                  UU  ===
      5, NO. 1, OCT, 1933: 9, NO. 1, OCT, 1937: 10, NO. 3, APR, 1939: 13, NO. 4
      U                  U                      U
      - 18, JULY, 1942 - JULY, 1947, (LACKS: 14, NO. 1, OCT, 1942): 26, NO.
      U                  U              JIIII          U
      4 - 34, JAN, 1955 - 1963, NW. 278
      U                          UU  ===
      14-, 0. 1, OCT, 1942-, 33, NO. 4, JAN, 1963, (LACKS: 17, NO.
```

Figure 6. To illustrate the difficulties of proofing coded computer output where the output device only has a limited character set. This example is proof copy output from the University of Newcastle upon Tyne Computer Typesetting Research Project's composition program used for the production of the most recent issue of the *Union List of Periodicals in Institutes of Education Libraries*.

```
BTISORT2/02
MAGNETIC TAPE
→
FETCH C1 E2 TO R10
J1R12=1
J2R12=2
J3R12=3
J4R12=4
J5R12=5
J6R12=6
J7R12=7
6)7)FINISH
2)STRING[*4*.2p*3]
SET CURRENT FORMAT 0.2/0.2
BTI OUTPUT C1E1
STRING[*4*2ph*3]
SET CURRENT FORMAT 0.1/0.0
OUTPUT C1E3
FINISH
1)STRING[*4*2pd*3]
SET CURRENT FORMAT 0.0/0.0
BTI OUTPUT C1E1
STRING[*5*21*3See*2r*3*5]
BTI OUTPUT C1E3
FINISH
4)STRING[*4*2pd*3]
SET CURRENT FORMAT 0.0/0.0
BTI OUTPUT C1E3
STRING[*5*21*3See*2r*3*5]
BTI OUTPUT C1E1
FINISH
3)STRING[*4*2p*3]
SET CURRENT FORMAT 0.0/0.0
BTI OUTPUT C1E3
STRING[*2pl*3*5*21*3Related Headings:*2r*3*2pm*3]
BTI OUTPUT C1E1
FINISH
5)STRING[*4*2p*3]
SET CURRENT FORMAT 0.0/0.0
 BTI OUTPUT C1E1
STRING[*2pl*3*5*21*3See*2r*3*2pm*3]
BTI OUTPUT C1E3
FINISH
→
```

Figure 7. An example of the pilot version of the Newcastle File Handling System A code. This example was used to photocompose galley proofs of the British Technology Index.

An Introduction to Computing Methods for Library Information Processing

N. S. M. COX

The previous paper, by Barraclough, Dews and Smethurst, introduces the problems associated with the application of computing systems to library activities. This paper draws attention to recent advances in computing techniques which have, as yet, not been fully exploited in this field.

Computing traditions have been heavily conditioned by the pressures applied to the whole field of automatic computation. The original electronic computers (and, incidentally, Babbage's 'engine') were developed for numerical computation; from this computing languages were developed to facilitate the use of these machines. It soon became clear that computers were economically viable for commercial financial administration and, what is more, purchase could be justified for the improvements provided by about 20% utilization of the computing system. This gave rise to cheap commercial computer-time in some organisations and management pressures to make use of this resource. At about the same time University computing systems were being evolved, mainly to serve the requirements for complex numerical calculation. Thus the scene was set for the development of the whole range of activities which have followed.

These developments can be grouped into a number of rather vague categories:

1 Language processors

Much attention has been given in the last decade to the development of 'logical' computing facilities—the development of high-level computer languages such as *COBOL, ALGOL, FORTRAN, PL/1,*

93

and so on, the formal language in which the programmer states his processing requirements. This is then processed by another computer program (the *compiler* or *interpreter*) which organizes the computing system to carry out the required actions. A very wide range of language processors exist today and much progress has been made in the development of formal computer languages to meet both the general and the highly specific requirements of different groups of users. Many advances have also been made in methods of compiler construction.

2. *Applications packages*

The types of activity for which applications packages have been developed are now almost innumerable, ranging from concordance packages handling Greek New Testament texts to on-line airline reservation systems. The main difference between a *language processor* and an *applications package* is in the flexibility and generality of the language (the *parameters*) which defines the processes to be carried out and the complexity of the separate units of activity which may occur.

The boundary between language processor and applications package is not always clear. For example, in the sorting system of the Newcastle File Handling System (Cox and Dews, 1967: page 15), the steering tape, which provides the parameters which define the files which are to be sorted and the method of comparison of the keys, contains statements in 'clear language', allows tests to be made and the key value determined on the basis of the result of these tests.

Perhaps the most important difference is the specificity of function of the program. The sorting package, mentioned above, is used only for the application of a single process (sorting) to a narrow range of files, whereas a high-level language generally provides a system with in which the process itself is defined by the statements in the language.

3. *Operating systems*

Nearly all computers require, in addition to the hardware, a permanent resident computer program generally called the *operating system, director* or *supervisor* which, in the early stages of the evolution of computing systems, fulfilled certain minimum requirements, permitting the computing system to detect illegal activities in the users' programs (such as attempting to access non-existent storage, 're-wind' a typewriter or interrogate a magnetic tape drive). In addition, monitoring facilities were sometimes included, preventing users from occupying the system for more than their allocated time, recording the accounting information associated with each process undertaken and reporting, to the computer operator, changes in system state. In the last decade, particularly recently, considerable changes have occurred in this area, due to advances in *storage organization, multi-programming, multi-processing* and *time-sharing.**

Present-day operating systems not only monitor processes for illegal activities and accounting, but are also capable of providing a wide range of services to the user for the management of data and for interactive processing.

4. Storage form, organization and management

When the main emphasis was on numerical computation, the problems of data input were trivial in comparison with those of process. The data required by the process was rigorously pre-defined —it is relatively easy to define the range of data states corresponding to a numerical value—and furthermore, for commercial financial administration with a pre-defined process, such as sales analysis, payroll processing, etc., the data states could also rigorously be defined. Access to this data, however, became more and more difficult the larger the data base (the 'size' of the total data) became. A need arose for large random-access data storage devices as the processes to be undertaken could not be conveniently formulated in terms of serial (record by record) access to the data base. As the number of times which the data had to be passed through the process section of the computing system increased, the proportion of time for which the major part of the system was standing idle also increased and there thus arose a considerable problem in attempting to attain 'system balance'—that is the relative utilization of the various parts of the system compared with the range and proportion with different process and input/output requirements which the system had to handle. In particular, although input and output peripheral devices became faster, capable of handling more characters per second, the

* *Multi-programming* is the ability of present-day computing systems to execute processes for a number of different users concurrently. *Multi-processing* is the ability to build computing systems which contain more than one processing unit. *Time-sharing* is the ability to produce systems at which many users may operate computer terminals, located remotely from the main computing installation, and request activity in the computing system depending on the response by the system, to the users, for the previous activity.

processing capability of main processors became proportionately faster still. Thus, unless something was done to alleviate this disparity, the main processor would have had to spend a large part of its 'working' life waiting for input or output peripherals to complete their preceding operations. One of the main methods currently employed to overcome this difficulty is for the operating system to intercept input and output operations to and from a user's program and arrange to store the input and output in intermediate storage so that this either can be output by the system later at its convenience or the users' program can be prevented from beginning operation until all the data for the process is available in intermediate storage. These modern computing systems require large quantities of intermediate storage both for 'spooling' (the independent input and output of data) and for random access to data. In addition, for reasons of cost, those parts of the operating system which are only occasionally used are located in this intermediate storage and called into the main storage by the resident part of the operating system when they are required. Also it is customary to have available a wide range of applications packages, language processors and an extensive library of routines (parts of programs which can be called for by the language processors) and these too are generally maintained permanently in the intermediate storage. In general, most data is obtained for the user's program by a request to the operating system from the user's program and there is therefore a need for a complex organization and data structure so that the operating system can access any of this data as and when it is required. This is discussed below.

4.1. Storage form

The conventional forms of storage available in modern computing systems include high-speed core storage from which a few bytes of storage can be accessed in about $\frac{3}{4}$–2 microseconds, magnetic disc storage from which blocks of storage can be accessed in about 75 milliseconds, magnetic card file storage from which blocks of storage can be accessed in about 200 milliseconds and magnetic tape files which can only be accessed serially at up to 80,000 characters per second—this may mean that the record at the far end of a magnetic tape might take up to 5 minutes to access. The following table gives access rates and storage costs for a range of storage media.

Storage Medium	Approximate Access Time	Approximate Cost of Storage per character		Storage Capacity (characters)
		*	†	
Fast core store	c. 0·75 micro-seconds	10s.		
Slow core store	c. 6 micro-seconds		2s. 6d.	
Magnetic drum	c. 9 milli-seconds		6d.	4×10^6
Magnetic disc (dismountable)	c. 75 milli-seconds‡	0·002d.	0·1d.	3×10^7
Magnetic card file	c. 200 milli-seconds	0·013d.	0·5d.	4×10^8
Magnetic tape	a few milli-seconds up to 5 minutes	0·0002d.	0·12d.	2×10^7

* excluding the cost of the peripheral device on which the date resides.
† including the cost of the peripheral device on which the data is assumed to be permanently resident.
‡ Making allowance for the movement of the device to locate (on average) the required block.

4.2. *Storage organization and data management*

With large quantities of data in a complex computing system, it is generally necessary to provide, within the framework of the operating system, facilities for the storage of a variety of types of data base (the *storage organization*) and a number of access facilities to this data (the *data management facilities*). For example it should be possible to organize records so that they can be accessed serially with data management facilities to obtain the 'next' record in main storage although the physical records may be stored together in groups (blocked) and although the system loads further blocks of records into main storage in anticipation of their being required. Similarly facilities can be provided for such serial access with, in addition, the access to records in terms of a 'name' or 'key' identifying the record. Further sophistication is clearly possible and many complex information systems use access to data through logical networks. Developments are in hand to provide this sort of facility for large scale general data bases.

5. *Hardware*

As has been mentioned earlier, considerable improvements have been made in the speed and flexibility of computers. The 'price per unit computation' is generally decreasing. The range of types of peripheral devices has been growing, including graphical display units, graph plotters, marked sense card readers, optical character recognition equipment, computer typesetting devices and so on. Experience is growing in the ways in which such devices may be utilized within computing systems and, furthermore, with increasing utilization their speed and reliability is also increasing. It would seem that future advances in peripheral hardware capability are of more relevance than those advances likely in central computing systems. Perhaps the most interesting feature in this latter area are increased channel 'intelligence', the development of computing and data transmission networks and, in some respects, the evolution of the 'baby' computer, the central processor of which costs less than £10,000.

6. *User requirements*

Some of the most fruitful developments in computer-based information handling systems stem from the development of a more detailed understanding and better formalism of user requirements. Ten years ago, for example, it was thought that citation retrieval, information services (fact retrieval), library housekeeping, computer based printing and even automatic language translation were almost within the 'state of the art'. The same could be said of all these fields today! However, the real development which has taken place has been, from the experience gained in a wide range of attempted applications, to expose the potential fields of application to a much more careful scrutiny, with respect to conventional practices and their justification. This has shown the need for a much more careful analysis of the existing or proposed system than had previously been considered necessary, and the need for the design of much more complex systems to admit the necessary 'quirks' of such systems.

It is interesting to note that many of the more sophisticated rules—the necessary exception conditions—have been evolved because the information handling systems have almost exclusively been designed to provide service to humans, as their end product. The problems generally seem to arise in *either* producing results which 'seem' right to the human rather than being 'logically correct' *or* in producing results which will permit the human user to attain his required goal, despite his incomplete information on or understanding of the product which he uses.

An outstanding example of this is the *British Technology Index* in which the technologist, seeking citations to relevant work, should need only to know the order in which the letters occur in the alphabet, the technical terms relevant to his own field and the ability to distinguish, both from the form and typography of the index entries, whether he is reading a cross-reference or a citation to a work.

Other examples are legion; the authority files associated with library catalogues, telephone directories, and so on: the proportion of words in a dictionary which are deliberately mis-filed: the inability, so far, to produce 'perfect' hyphenation or to translate, by computer, from English to Russian to a satisfactory level, despite the umpteen million dollars spent on research in this field.

It is at least heartening that, even though many of these problems still defy solutions adequate to the needs of some potential applications, the understanding of the technical feasibility in these areas has now become sufficiently precise for it to be unlikely that expensive mistakes will occur, provided that such experience is properly taken into account.

7. *Methods*

Many of the notable achievements in this field have been successful due to the ruthlessness with which the objectives of the project were defined. This is discussed elsewhere in this volume (pp. 181–194). It is worth noting that where the methods selected were effective they were so, in attempting to meet the limited goals of each project, by taking advantage of any well established formal principles which were relevant but in the main rigorously and pragmatically developing methods specific to the functions required by that project only. The methods developed under these circumstances are generally masked by the detail of the specific requirements of the single project. One of the main themes behind the activities of the Symplegades Research Group at the University of Newcastle upon Tyne has been the attempt to develop application-independent facilities for various components of the total 'information processing function'. This has culminated, so far, in the design of an experimental general purpose information handling system—the 'Newcastle file handling system—Phase 1' (Cox and Dews, 1967; Cox, 1970,*a*). The design of a possible 'production' version of this system is in hand.

Many of the processes for which computers have been used have required a fairly simple or a well-controlled data base—numerical values, wage rates, parts numbers and so on—however, free-form language text has rather more complex and less well defined information properties. Language text is not usually, in any meaningful sense, 'well-defined'. Attempts at formalization of such information, such as the creation of bibliographical records, book indexes, dictionaries and so on illustrate this from the complexity of the rules for their creation, control and arrangement and the anomalies which still exist in such files of records despite the detailed rules.

In attempting to provide computer systems for the processing of this kind of information, it is important to recognise that not only is one concerned with a very large and often extremely complex data base but, due to the lack of formalism in the natural language parts of the data base, also one is concerned with very complex processes which must be applied to this data base to give meaningful results.

The review of 'landmarks' of information processing in this field by Balmforth, Grose and Jeffreys (*see* Section I) shows that many obstacles exist and some of them have been successfully circumvented. However, most of the computing activity has been at a 'machine-code' level or in a computer language better suited to other kinds of application. It is clear that a substantial body of experience and methodology has grown up in the field of computer science. It would seem to be timely to exploit these methods and techniques in the field under consideration.

Systems Analysis in Libraries: the Role of Management

F. ROBINSON

There seems to be a strong view that systems analysis is a subject that can be discussed with a special relationship to particular interests. This is not true. One can properly discuss systems design in a particular field; a number of papers of this type are presented elsewhere in this volume. These are the papers on British *MARC* (Coward), and on the state of progress of computer applications (Cox). It is also possible to discuss problems or situations met during particular studies and these can be concerned with library systems. The value of knowing 'how I climbed Everest' is however limited unless one intends to adopt the same objective and the same route. It may be useful, when planning to climb K3 to know the climbing techniques used to overcome the conditions met on Everest and to be able to identify similar conditions elsewhere. Knowing the location of the ice fields on Everest will be less useful. In the same way descriptions of library studies, the situations in which they were made and the solutions applied are often extremely interesting. They are of limited value in planning studies in other libraries and are not descriptions of systems analysis.

This paper presents systems analysis in that way. The role of the systems analyst will not vary significantly when studying warehousing methods or library routines. It is his job to study an existing system in such a way as to be able to design the most efficient replacement system. The conditions may differ—the objectives of the unit being studied could be tremendously different—but the problems to be them recognized and techniques used to overcome might well be the same in both cases. This should not be taken to indicate indifference. The initial study of any new project will include a study of the problem area. This gives a general impression of library organization, traditions and practices, which serves as a background to the detailed study the analyst carries out and, as this progresses, so his knowledge increases. The knowledge gained by analysts in particular areas of operation explains why many become specialists in the study of those areas. However, many analysts move from problem to problem successfully and they are able to do this because the essential qualities for analysis are patient investigation and careful design.

The analyst, therefore, has two basically simple things to do: first to find out what happens now, and then to work out how to do it better. This is difficult when the situation being studied is complex and techniques have been developed to assist in both the analysis and the design of systems. The techniques range from the apparently obvious (e.g. interviewing) to the apparently obscure (e.g. decision tables). He also has knowledge of ways in which things can be done to help him in designing the replacement system. Nowadays this includes knowledge of computers and methods of using them, but if this is the analyst's only expertise he will almost certainly produce stiff, unworkable, clerical systems.

There is a temptation to discuss techniques, and computer system design only. It is at least as important to consider the impact of system analysis on libraries and particularly on the library management.

To do this is really to take a close look at the role of the 'user' department in the development of a new system. It is sometimes thought that the role is a passive one, but this is clearly not so. Library management must play a part in the following aspects of a project:

> 1. Selecting the application;
> 2. Determining the objectives;
> 3. Project estimating and planning;
> 4. Studying the proposals made and specifications developed;
> and 5. Controlling the project.

Each of these warrants separate treatment.

Selecting the application: In considering library operations the number of possible project areas is rather more limited than is the case in an industrial or commercial organization. Nevertheless, it is probable that at any given time there will be a number of operation areas that merit study, ranging from the redesign of commercial operations to research studies in bibliography. Assuming that resources are limited there are various factors which must be taken into account in selecting applications, and these are detailed below. More important, there are two approaches to the selection process.

The first approach is to make the selection only when resources become available to work on a project. At that time the potential projects are studied and the most suitable (based probably on the factors discussed below) chosen. This assumes that the choice is made by the management. It is possible for this prerogative to be lost either with or without the consent of management. If this has happened without consent (e.g. by an approach from a particular library section to the analyst staff) it calls for some control of the process. If management has abdicated its responsibility by allowing others (possibly analysts) to select applications for development, it is unlikely that the choice will be made with all the interests of the library in mind. Even if the choice is made by management, this method of selection has major drawbacks since it affords little time to study all the aspects of all the potential projects, and in particular because it is difficult to see the future pattern of development.

The second approach is based on the need to study this pattern and must involve management. It requires all potential applications to be studied as a special, but preferably continuous, exercise. This produces a long-term plan for the development of the library system. This plan should be continuously amended as conditions change and as projects are completed. Therefore when resources become available they can be allocated to the most appropriate project in the plan. A long-term plan is probably the only way in which an integrated library system can be achieved.

No matter which approach is used (and there may be libraries where the first is appropriate) the factors which govern the choice of application are still important. These factors will vary principally with the objectives of the library, and include:

1. *Cost savings—the basic economic considerations:*
   Projects are chosen on the savings they make in the cost of running the library;
2. *Services improvement:*
   The benefits of improvement to the service provided to library users are intangible and the choice between alternatives in this area will be difficult. It can be based on the number of users of the various services but this may exclude improvements which could lead to heavier usage of a particular section and also projects in important minor activities. The assessments of benefits will take notice of the numbers of users of the various services, any

H

potential for increasing the use following the improvements, and the needs of minor, important activities. In this field the work of the Durham University PEBUL (*Project for the Evaluation of the Benefits of University Libraries*) team must be mentioned (Hawgood and Morley, 1969).

3. *Long-term research:*
As a matter of policy it may be decided that research offers considerable potential advantages and that some resources should be devoted to it. This is even more intangible than improvements to service. The alternative is of course to allow other people to do the work or to obtain external finance. Money will not necessarily provide all the resources needed; it will not provide, for instance, more library management time;

and 4. *External circumstances:*
Changes in external circumstances (e.g. building changes) can make it important to replace certain systems which would not otherwise warrant attention.

Balancing these factors against the resources available either now or in the future is the only satisfactory way either to develop a long-term plan or select a project for immediate develoment. Anaysis is a necessary part in the process of proposing solutions and weighing alternatives. Systems analysts can usefully be employed to help library management in this problem.

Determining the objectives: Clear definition of objectives is an essential preliminary to the development of a project and is also important in the setting of a long-term plan. Without this clear definition it is unlikely that either the system or the plan will be satisfactory. This is obvious—the best system will not be appreciated if it is doing the wrong things. It is possible to exaggerate this for at a routine level the objectives may be so clear that the trap is avoided, but when one thinks of cataloguing, user services and other fundamental activities, the possibility of providing good answers to the wrong questions is fairly high.

A good analyst will try to avoid this happening. He can however be thwarted by the members of the library staff with whom he discusses the problem. The analyst will be looking for the network affected by the system under study and will consider for what purposes the information which it generates is being used. He will also be looking for external factors influencing the network. This cannot however be done by the analyst in isolation. The library management must be clearly involved, and the staff made aware of the importance of the job.

The main hurdle for library management is an over-confiden

assumption that the objectives are obvious. This may be so in the routine operations, as has already been discussed, but in the more abstruse areas of the library it is probable that the effects of tradition, academic variations and changes in staff procedures will have obscured the original objectives without identifying any new ones.

In library catalogues, for instance, the effects of changes in standards and practice over the years will make the definition of the objectives of the cataloguing service difficult. Many of the changes will be associated with changes in staff and some will have been made because of changing conditions. Whatever the causes, the effect of change without planning is to obscure the purposes of the work.

The task of defining objectives has the advantage that it allows management to consider whether the current objectives should be retained. It may be easier to define existing objectives but this carries the risk that the needs of some small but important areas may be overlooked.

Whether one is defining current or setting future objectives, it is essential to:

1. look at the objectives of the total organization;
2. determine how the particular unit contributes to the total;
3. define the internal objectives of the particular unit;
and 4. consider any effects outside either the unit or the total organization.

For example, a library may be attached to a research organization and have its main functions determined by that fact. It will have some internal objectives principally in the maintenance of records for future use and could well have some external links with other research libraries. The purpose and nature of all these will need to be closely investigated. At present the objectives of many libraries are ill-defined, particularly in academic institutions. Because of this, and because the definitions are fundamental in systems development, library management must be prepared to play a leading part in the study.

Project estimating and planning: Estimates must be prepared for the cost of developing and operating the replacement system. Operating cost estimates should be considered with the proposals to which they apply and may be an important factor in the final acceptance of a proposal. Estimates of the costs of developing the system should be considered at the same time and library management should insist on these being realistic, since failure to produce good estimates of development costs can be a major cause of dissatisfaction. In computer systems many of the estimates will be difficult to challenge. In those parts of the project linked more closely with the library however the estimates should be studied carefully to ensure that they are realistic. This is particularly relevant in such things as the conversion of existing records and catalogues into computer-usable form.

Costs are easier to assess, but rather less important in non-computer systems. This applies also to project planning; in non-computer systems planning is directed mainly to a smooth change-over from the old to the new. One aspect which will require planning is the change to records and files which may be necessary in a new non-computer system. In computer systems the complex process of development and the more prolonged period over which it takes place make planning essential.

Library management must be involved in this planning. The planning target is of course the implementation date. The major stages preceding this are:

> Systems Analysis and Design,
> Programming and Testing
and Trials and Parallel Running.

Some elements in the planning and performance of each phase will require effort by the library.

In the analysis and design stage it is important for the eventual success of the project that the existing system is properly studied and management should ensure that the planning makes adequate provision for this. In particular the study will need the active participation of at least some member of the management and the plan cannot be achieved if this time is not made available. In this stage plans will probably be prepared for the conversion of the major files. This is vital to the success of the overall plan and management will be in a good position to help in both the planning and performance of the work.

If project objectives have not already been decided, analyst time must be allowed for them to be finalized before the design of the replacement starts.

Planning of programming and testing is obviously a matter for the computer specialists. The library management may be able to assist by ensuring that plans for the preparation of test data are realistic. During this stage the selection and training of staff for their new or revised duties will also be proceeding. Once again it is important to make staff available and this requires forethought. It is usually made more difficult by the need for work to be done on converting the system files and additional staffing should be provided if possible.

The planning of trials and implementation is a complex matter and many decisions will be taken as the stage develops. As the work depends on the needs of the new system it cannot be planned until the design stage is complete. Again there is a strong need for additional staff to be available because of the possible need for parallel running and for the checking of results.

It should be remembered that planning is an essential preliminary to estimating and that the accuracy of both will be improved as work on the project proceeds. This indicates that firm implementation dates should not be fixed before the project starts, and that management should retain the right to cancel the work if costs are escalating.

A major responsibility of management, which must be considered during planning, is for the well-being of the staff concerned in the system changes. This is affected in several ways. The staff may feel that their future is affected by the system, and that their skills which have been valuable for years may no longer be required. In many cases this will not be so and management must make this clear to avoid unrest and lack of interest in the scheme. In those cases where staff redundancy is inevitable this fact must be made clear and steps taken to minimize the personal disturbance this causes. Lack of interest will adversely affect any timetables made and this factor can be easily avoided by a little forethought.

The need for staff involvement in the project goes deeper than this however. It is important to remember that much of the knowledge of the existing system and of the needs it fulfils is held by the staff operating it. It is the analyst's job to find out about the existing system and this means close contact with the staff. Management can help by making it clear that the knowledge and opinions of the people will be respected and taken into account when the new system is designed. Management must also help in assessing what training is necessary to fit people for their changed duties. This, in particular, needs careful planning.

Studying proposals and specifications: As the project develops the analysts will submit to the library management various proposals for and specifications of the new system. The proper consideration of these is the responsibility of library management. Failure to do so will mean that the management cannot be sure that the proposals meet their requirements and this could lead to an unsatisfactory system. Proposals will probably be submitted at the end of the feasibility study and when the new system has been designed.

The first of these documents is a system proposal or feasibility report, following a survey of the operations area to determine the practicability of the application. The system proposal contains a summary of the existing procedures, a statement of the information seen to be required and a proposal for the replacement system with notes on any alternatives considered. The document is a proposal for further work to be done. It cannot be a complete design based on full analysis as detailed work cannot have been done. Management should look at the proposal in this light. In respect of the existing system the document will show whether the analyst has discovered the facts and this should be verified either by the management or by the library staff. Errors of detail are not so important as misinterpretation of the general structure. Failure to appreciate the basis of the existing system makes any proposals meaningless.

Library management must ensure that the information requirements are identified correctly. The information requirements are to some extent an expression of the system's objectives, insofar as these can be stated as information stored or reported. In projects such as book ordering systems they will include the routine reports. Such a project will tend to have three levels of information requirements. At the lowest level these will include the orders and the lists for checking receipts. The intermediate level might have summaries of books ordered on a particular day, possibly by university departments or library sections, so that the ordering supervision can check that allocations are correct.

At the highest level the system might summarize current order levels, include budget checks, and numbers of books on order by class with cumulative figures of holdings. The interpretation of the requirements at the highest level is the most difficult. This difficulty is also apparent when considering systems dealing with library services such as cataloguing. It is up to the library management to ensure that the analyst's interpretation of these requirements is valid.

Finally, the proposed system must be examined to ensure that it satisfies these requirements and appears likely to be satisfactory in operation. It is often difficult to comment on the operation of the computer element of the proposal (this difficulty is discussed more fully below) and this often prevents users from commenting on the non-computer operations. As the latter most affect the library it is important that these parts of the proposal are studied for simplicity, effectiveness and practicability.

Acceptance of the system proposal (and its associated cost estimates) is authorization for full system analysis and design to be carried out. At this point the outline design has been accepted. This will be completed and possibly amended in the light of the full analysis. If the scheme is significantly amended a revised proposal should be submitted. Normally the amendments are slight and eventually the system will be fully designed and a complete specification submitted to the library management.

The detailed system specification of a major project is a considerable document. It will contain layouts of all the reports, notes on procedure in the library, recommendations for organization and full estimates. Clearly by this time a lot of work has been done and heavy costs incurred. While rejection is a serious step this fact should not deter the library management from giving the specification a very close examination. This is the first time that the full system has been available for study and a detailed specification deserves the study. In practice senior library staff are unlikely to be concerned with checking detail but should delegate this to the supervisors of the functions concerned. Library management should ensure that the principles agreed during the preparation and discussion of the system proposed have been implemented in the specification. The supervisors must ensure that the functions currently carried out manually are adequately covered in the specification. Satisfactory answers to omissions must be obtained from the analysts; these should have been discussed during the design period.

Finally, the library management must decide whether or not the system specified is acceptable. Discussion is inevitable and valuable but eventually this must come to an end with a decision to proceed or cancel. This decision can only be taken by the management.

There is one final chance for the management of the library to examine the project formally before it is implemented. This comes when the trials of the new system have been completed and some form of parallel or pilot running has been carried out. These final tests of the system will inevitably bring to light minor faults. There may be a fair number of these errors; the causes may be programming, design or inadequate specification of requirements by the library staff.

Such errors are unlikely to invalidate the basic principles. If they do management has to decide whether to write off the whole project or to re-start at the beginning 'sadder and wiser men'. This is an extremely serious decision and the need for it reflects badly on the organization and control of the project. In practice a more serious risk is that the number of errors leads the management to believe that the principles are wrong. This belief is likely to be fed by those who tend to exaggerate the effect of the errors. It is important that management take a balanced view of this, weighing the probable optimism of the project team against the possible pessimism of the people who are to operate the new system.

In most cases the worst that need be decided is whether the operational date of the project should be deferred. If the problems are likely to cause delay of more than one to two months, then suspension of parallel running may be necessary. This might also be necessary if the nature of the errors is making the operation impossible. If suspension is not considered necessary the extension of the trials will probably be beneficial in the long run by getting the staff fully conversant with the new system.

These are the three major check points during the development of a project. After some months of operational running the system must be checked against the specification. This audit of the system will be reported to the management and should include suggestion for corrections and amendments.

Controlling the project: It is usual for the leader of a project team to be a systems analyst. He should, if possible, be supported by a member of the library staff seconded full time to the project. The team must report and be responsible to senior management. It has been the usual practice for this higher contact level to be the management of the computer department. This has the advantage in that the technical aspects of the job are more readily appreciated. Nevertheless one of the most important factors in a computer development is the involvement of library management. If there is a feeling in the library that the development is something which 'they' are doing, involvement is unlikely to occur.

There are two alternative ways of tackling this problem. The first is to have a steering committee consisting of management members of both departments to which the team reports progress. If this is to be the only control the meetings will need to be fairly frequent. It is better to have the team report to the chairman of the committee whose responsibility it is to call meetings if necessary but who is authorized to manage the project in normal circumstances. The chairman of the committee will normally be the manager of the computer systems department but there is no reason why he should not be a library manager.

This leads to the second method of tackling the problem; namely to make the team report to the management of the library with functional responsibility to the computer department. This will clearly lead to active involvement in the project. It has however the disadvantage that library management may get too deeply drawn into the technical computer aspects, and at the implementation date, be too involved in overall project matters to concentrate on the situation in the library itself.

The steering committee approach has much to offer. Properly used it will ensure that both sides are aware of the views and problems of the other and can build up a relationship between the management to match the close links that the project team should be establishing at the operational level.

Summary: This paper has discussed some particular aspects of system development which affect library management. There is one outstanding moral: the development of a new system for a major library operation is going to affect library management. The impact will be greater if management do not interest themselves from the very beginning of the job. Ideally this interest should start with the production of a plan for future library system development but it must not be delayed beyond the time of the system survey. Early involvement will not guarantee a trouble-free development but will help to achieve this and will also do much to ensure that the operational system is what the library wanted.

SECTION III

Centralized Services

Centralized Services for University Librarians

A. E. JEFFREYS

Centralized processing has long been urged on librarians as a panacea to combat the increasing costs of maintaining systems of increasing complexity but decreasing efficiency. Unfortunately there is no clear definition of precisely what is implied by 'centralized processing'. To some this is almost synonymous with 'centralized cataloguing' but to others it has implications for a wider range of activities in which libraries are engaged—ordering, accessioning, cataloguing, classification, circulation control, as well as the co-ordination of services between different libraries.

The application of computer techniques to library operations is forcing librarians to a more careful and detailed analysis of what it is they are proposing to automate and why. It may well be that the most valuable function of the computer for librarians is its power as a catalyst. Line (1968) has said that 'we must not automate what we do not understand'. Our starting point must not be 'we have computers, how can we use them' but 'what are our functions and can computers help us to perform them?'.

Line makes an initial assumption that 'the function of the university library is to bring together information or knowledge on the one hand and human beings on the other'. Cox (p. 184) gives a more precise elaboration under five heads:

1. control—including ordering, accessioning, cataloguing, circulation and stock-taking;
2. archive—building up the necessary collections;
3. service—professional guidance and assistance to users;
4. co-operation—the need to link with and contribute to the local and national network of library resources;

and 5. research and development—the library staff's activity in perfecting the techniques of librarianship.

But, as Line (1968) points out, there is an enormous gap: 'we are hampered in designing a library as an information system by an almost total ignorance of the needs of the user'. Librarians may be at least fairly certain that some of their users want the following:

1. a specific book (or other item) (this includes the regular scanning of periodicals to keep up to date in a particular subject);
2. a specific piece of information;

and 3. some less than specific information (This may turn out to be something fairly precise or fairly vague).

But this by no means exhausts the needs of library users; some may want a quiet place to work (or rest?) or somewhere to meet their friends.

The provision of some of the specific needs may be confidently anticipated by librarians—for example, set textbooks for undergraduates, as recommended by the departments concerned, and certain standard reference books and abstracts services. But beyond this there is less certainty: the librarian attempts to provide a wide range of peripheral material and too often has no firm criteria to establish more precisely what is implied by 'peripheral material'. Such material may be acquired more or less haphazard, for example, as donations, or it may be acquired as the result of a specific request.

(We do not here intend to deal with two related but separate problems:

1. the difficulty of determining how many copies of particular titles are to be obtained and the practical limitation on buying very many copies because of shortage of money;

and 2. the difficulty of deciding the items which cannot be bought (often periodicals), again because of shortage of money.)

There are at least two parameters of library use which must be established with more precision before a library can improve its services:

1. frequency of use of books;

and 2. delay tolerated in having books available for use.

These two are, of course, interrelated: a particular professor may insist that he can tolerate a delay of no more than 15 minutes in having made available to him an item which has not otherwise been used for the last ten years. The two factors are thus flexible and subject to change.

A good case can be made out for storing lesser-used material in some cheaper form of storage, away from the main library, to which readers are not normally permitted access. Such a store could be used to serve a number of libraries. Several American university libraries already use this type of storage (see for example Ash (1963) and Fussler and Simon (1969)); it is less common, although not un-known, in Great Britain (see, for example, the Parry Report paras. 397ff.) In a paper elsewhere in this volume (pp. 146–178), Cox has made suggestions for costing this approach.

There is the difficulty of identifying the little-used material suitable for storage; here again American experience can be used as a guide. The University of Chicago (Fussler and Simon, 1969) concluded that past usage was the most reliable guide to future use; failing this there are other parameters—for example, age, subject field and language. Loan records are normally not easily manipulated to give the required information about extent of use (computerized circulation systems provide an exception) and there is the difficulty of recording or at any rate, calculating, the use of items within the library which are not loaned.

The practice and undoubted value of browsing is often cited as a factor militating against any systematic weeding of lesser-used material from open access stacks. But little is known about browsing. It is merely aimless wandering through the book stack? Or is it carried out according to some (conscious or unconscious) plan? Do some kinds of library users browse more than others? There is at least one immediate difference between the browser and the systematic searcher through bibliographies: the former has his material immediately to hand, the latter has only references to the material (perhaps abstracts as well) and will probably find that he has immediate access to only a minority of these references (the smaller library is unlikely to have anything like all the items; in the larger library the access time will inevitably be greater, and in any library some of the items will be in use by other readers and so away from the shelves).

The difficulties of identifying little-used material relate to the working of the library system within itself. Other problems arise from external factors, for example, the extent of storage accommodation available and its distance from the main collection.

There is little firm data available on the delays tolerated by users in having books made available to them. Some users will demand that certain items must be immediately available to them. Some such users will have set up their own departmental libraries in order to have this standard of service available. Others will be content if the majority of the material they need (the '80% rule' has been put forward as a working proposition) is available within say 12 hours (or whatever delay the standard of service provided by their own library has led them to expect as 'reasonable'). For the remaining 20% of the material a longer delay must be expected. This proportion may be a rationalization of traditional services (Trueswell (1969) draws a parallel between book loans in libraries and business inventory holdings). One may however hazard a guess that in view of the 'information explosion' (more is being published and it becomes increasingly expensive per unit to make it available) the ratio is not likely to get better and thus the delays in getting material to the user will be greater. The 80% here represents the material possessed by the library itself (which may be on its shelves or on loan): the remaining 20% has to be obtained from elsewhere—for example, via the inter-library loan network.

More detailed costing is necessary to throw light on a related problem: is it cheaper to buy an item or to borrow it from another source? The item itself will always be a variable but more data could be made available to remove some of the guesswork, used at present. A third possibility may occasionally be preferred: to transport the user to the book (a practice already followed by some libraries within a couple of hours journey of Boston Spa).

There is one type of material that users traditionally expect to be immediately available: newly published books. 'Newly published' is itself susceptible of no clear definition, since publishers are perpetually optimistic about the date a new book actually becomes available to the public. Delays which are accepted with older material are intolerable for yesterday's new book. This may be due to some deep-seated desire to get at what is new with the least possible delay. An inverse square law appears to operate here and the oldest material of all (e.g. incunabula, which often cannot be bought at all) is rarely brought to the user; the user has to go to it.

CENTRALIZED CATALOGUING

'At the present time, if a specially valuable book is published it finds its way to at least a thousand different libraries, in all of which it must be catalogued. One of the highest-salaried officers of each of these thousand libraries must take this book and examine it for the scores of points that only a cataloguer can appreciate the necessity of looking up. Then the title must be copied and revised. Perhaps half a day is spent in preparing a satisfactory note to append for the benefit of readers. And all this work is repeated to a certain extent in each of the thousand libraries! Can libraries complain if practical business-men call this extravagance?' So wrote Melvil Dewey in 1877 in an article on co-operative cataloguing. His sentiments have been re-peated many times since. Leonard (1968) quotes Dewey's words in the introduction to his bibliography of co-operative and centralized cataloguing and processing. This is mainly restricted to American material, covers the period 1850–1867 and includes over 950 items.

The Library of Congress (*LC*) has sold copies of its catalogue cards since 1901. In the first nine months *LC* sold cards to 212 libraries for cash sales of nearly $4000. It was very soon receiving copy for print-ing catalogue cards for titles it did not have itself and so the centra-lized cataloguing service became a co-operative venture.

In 1942 the first volumes of the *Library of Congress catalog of printed cards* appeared making *LC* catalogue cards available in book form. This catalogue was extended to include cataloguing copy from other libraries and is currently published as the *National Union Catalog*.

Two criticisms of the *LC* catalogue card distribution service have been made from its beginnings:

    1. delay in supplying cards;
and 2. inadequacy of coverage.

It was reported in 1928 (*Library journal*, vol. 53, p. 592, July 1928) that from 20% to 75% of the annual accessions of American college and university libraries were not covered by *LC* printed cards and co-operative cataloguing was extended in an attempt to reduce this gap. In 1965 a study of cataloguing in nine large university libraries, carried out by the Association of Research Libraries, showed that these libraries were cataloguing only some 50% of their acquisitions with cards or proofsheets from *LC*. This was the same result as a similar study carried out in the same nine libraries in 1952.

These two surveys helped to pave the way for the U.S. Higher Education Act of 1965 which, in its Title II C, charged the Library of Congress with:

    1. 'acquiring, so far as possible, all library materials currently published throughout the world which are of value to scholarship;
and 2. providing catalog information for these materials promptly after receipt.'

I

In order to assist in implementing the 1965 Act a number of large research libraries receive a depository set of *LC* catalogue cards and check their foreign orders against it. Copies of their orders are then sent to *LC* for items not in the depository cards for *LC* to buy for its own collections and subsequently catalogue.

Kochen and Segur (1970) have argued that cataloguing costs would be cut if *LC* did as much as possible of all the original cataloguing required by U.S. libraries. But this attempt by *LC* to achieve world-wide coverage can be criticized as Utopian and impractical: it might be more realistic to rely on other national bibliographic centres (e.g. *BNB* and *Deutsche Nationalbibliographie*) to cover their own areas and then to supply *LC* with the relevant bibliographic data (*BNB* have been sending catalogue data to *LC* since 1966 (*see* Wells, 1968)). The *LC* card distribution service is at any rate showing the strains of the heavy demands made upon it. In January 1970 subscribers were told that the service had 'deteriorated greatly during recent months' (*Catalogue and Index*, No. 18, April 1970). Essentially the problem stems from the lack of stock to fulfil incoming orders. The card stock has become depleted because of high sales in 1967 and 1968, (63 million cards were sold in 1966 and 78 million in 1968) and through lack of storage space for housing current cards and previously catalogued cards. Cards were in stock for less than 50% of the titles currently ordered. However measures are under way for a 'massive reprinting and restocking project' and *LC* is confident that the situation will shortly improve.

The British National Bibliography (*BNB*) has been selling catalogue cards, printed from entries in its weekly booklist, since 1956, i.e. for less than 25 years. The Library of Congress has been issuing catalogue cards for nearly 70 years. Since libraries are on the whole conservative institutions and slow to change established traditions it is hardly surprising that *BNB* cards have not won the same degree of acceptance in Britain accorded to *LC* cards in America. The results of a survey published by Lewis in 1967 showed that over three-quarters of the cards sold went to public libraries and that 'no university library was using *BNB* cards on any scale for cataloguing purposes.'

This non-use of *BNB* cards does not imply a rejection of the *BNB* as a whole. Lewis concludes: 'The alternative to reliance on cards is so frequently a reliance on the cataloguing data supplied by the published *BNB* booklists as to give no grounds for doubting that the centralized services supplied by this organization are likely to become more and more essential for the efficient compilation of catalogues of all kinds, so long as the British National Bibliography continues to remain aware of current problems in organizing and administering bibliographical and cataloguing departments in libraries'.

An important difference between the *BNB* and *LC* is of course that the former supplies cataloguing data only for current British publications whereas the *LC* current intake includes both current and older material from a wide range of countries.

Wells (1968) includes this factor in listing the possible reasons for the non-use of *BNB* cards. Other criticisms of the cards noted by Wells include:

1. the method of ordering, which involves searching the *BNB* lists for the card order number, is time consuming and involves a wasteful matching procedure;
2. The quality of reproduction is not high*;
3. Incompatibility with already established cataloguing rules;

and 4. The cataloguing information is incomplete in that a *BNB* card does not give tracings for added entries or subject headings.

CO-OPERATIVE PROCESSING

In the United States regional processing centres serving groups of mainly public libraries began to appear in the late 1950's and a list of over 60 of these centres was published in 1966 (Vann, S. *et al.*, 1966). The processing carried out by these centres covers all or some of the following activities:

ordering;
accessioning;
cataloguing;
classification;
pasting in book and spine labels, book pockets, etc.

Doubt has been thrown on the view that central processing of this kind does in fact reduce costs (e.g. Clapp, 1967) if only because there are no firm data available on the costs of original cataloguing etc.

---

* Recent changes of procedure, consequent upon automation of *BNB's* internal operations, have caused a marked improvement in the quality of reproduction of *BNB* Cards.

Others claim that 'processing centres have successfully accomplished the purposes for which they were organized:

> elimination of unnecessary duplication of work;
> released time for librarians;
> uniformity of catalog data and processed books;
> savings on the cost of books.' (Duchac, 1967).

The same writer also notes difficulties which have arisen: different policies about the permitted length of Dewey numbers; the use of different subject headings; different policies and practices in analytical cataloguing; different amounts of detail in descriptive cataloguing; differences in the size of book pockets, and differences in the size and position of labels pasted on and/or within books.

A recent feasibility study of centralized book processing for nine academic libraries in Colorado (Leonard, 1969) first studied present processes and then concluded that a centralized book-processing centre would reduce the unit cost of acquiring and processing volumes. Library staff now engaged in technical processing would be transferred to public service duties. The processing centre proposed should be able to reduce the time a user must wait before new books are available. The greatest savings in time would occur when the processing centre was able to purchase from a supplier who had built up his bookstock to meet the needs of academic libraries. A processing centre would also enable the participating libraries to make better use of cataloguers with special language qualifications.

It seems hard to doubt that with sufficient prior thought libraries could make effective use of this type of centralized (or rather regionalized) processing to free their higher level staff from much of the routines of ordering and cataloguing. Such staff would then be able to devote more time to direct reader service (i.e. to a job with an end in itself, not a means to an end). This will improve the level of the library's service; it will not necessarily save money as such. Uniformity of practice appears to be a basic criterion of success for centralized processing.

MARC PROJECTS

One of the aims of the *MARC* Project is the distribution of catalogue data from a central source in machine-readable form. (Readers are referred elsewhere for an account of the project, for example, see the short bibliography in Jeffreys and Wilson (1970)). The *MARC* format represents an attempt to formulate a standard set of rules for structuring bibliographic records in machine-readable form and as such has been widely accepted in America and Britain. It is at present under active consideration in a number of countries in continental Europe.

However, the cost-effectiveness of *MARC* as part of a local cataloguing system has yet to be demonstrated. It may well be cheaper (and better?) for individual libraries to do their own cataloguing locally (though here again cf. Cox's paper on p. 146). But this is not to deny the wholly beneficial effects of the *MARC* Project in persuading libraries to consider more closely the implications of using standardized techniques.

CATALOGUING IN SOURCE

The basic idea of cataloguing in source is that a full catalogue entry should be printed in the book itself. In 1958 the Library of Congress carried out an experiment to test the feasibility of doing this. Catalogue entries were printed in 1203 books produced by 157 American publishers. The subsequent report (Library of Congress, Processing Department, 1960) concluded that cataloguing in source was not feasible from three points of view:

1. Publishers complained that sending proof copy to *LC* and incorporating the catalogue entry afterwards held up the publication of the book and increased its cost. (300 publishers were invited to take part in the experiment; 244 accepted and only 157 actually participated.)

2. *LC* did the cataloguing from final page proofs. By giving priority treatment to the books in the experiment, *LC*'s processing time was reduced from several weeks to one day. For *LC* to catalogue all books in source within one day would prohibitively increase costs;

and 3. Users complained that more than half of all the catalogue entries printed in the books contained differences from the actual state of affairs as presented by the book itself, and so had to be corrected. These differences came from changes made after the proofs had been catalogued; changes in pagination, illustrations and size were especially frequent. The users concluded that in order to be successful, cataloguing-in-source data must be accurate and all the users participating in the experiment said that they preferred the present *LC* card arrangements.

The user group's conclusions were undoubtedly conditioned by what they had come to expect from an *LC* catalogue card. Since 1960 more attention has been paid to what catalogue users needed from a catalogue entry rather than what they have been conditioned to expect. (It is for example doubtful if users of catalogues which serve primarily as finding lists need information about pagination, illustrations and size.) The news in early 1970 that *LC* is investigating the possibility of a resumption of the cataloguing in source programme is therefore particularly welcome (Association of Research Libraries, 1970). Discussions with the American Book Publishers Council suggested that the situation has changed since the 1958 experiment and that a sufficient number of publishers are now prepared to co-operate in a modified programme. It is suggested that cataloguing-in-source would supply the intellectual data elements (e.g. main and added entries, *LC* and *DC* class numbers, *LC* subject headings and cross reference structure), leaving individual libraries to supply non-intellectual elements (title, place, publisher and date of publication, and collation). Such non-intellectual elements could be supplied by non-professional clerical labour. Such a system would enable the intellectual data elements to be supplied from galleys rather than from final page proofs.

Cataloguing in source has two important advantages over cataloguing data centrally distributed in machine-readable form:

1. it comes with the book to which it relates and obviates the need for any matching process of data with the book;

and 2. Unlike data on magnetic tape it is immediately readable to the human eye.

TOWARDS STANDARDIZATION

The Anglo-American Cataloguing Rules (*AACR*), British text, (1967) have been adopted by the British National Bibliography for the production of its weekly and other lists and are, of course, used in the UK *MARC* Project. The Library of Congress has been less positive in adopting these new rules and it is to be hoped that it will abandon its policy of 'superimposition' in favour of the full adoption of at least the American text of *AACR*. ('Superimposition' implies the use of the new code for newly established headings but carrying on with the old code for existing headings).

The UK *MARC* format and the use of the Anglo-American Cataloguing Rules are thus closely interconnected. More recently there has been the separate but related development of a Standard Bibliographic Description. A Working Party on the Standard Bibliographic Description (*SBD*) was set up by the International Meeting of Cataloguing Experts in August 1969. The purpose of the *SBD* is to provide rules for the form and order of the elements in the descriptive part of a bibliographic entry, and to act as a standard for the making of the descriptive part of the definitive national record of a book as produced by the national cataloguing agency of the country. It is intended that this definitive national record should serve as the basis for catalogues and other listings within the country and also for the international exchange of bibliographic data.

The International Standard Book Number is another example of a standard practice which, after acceptance by the majority of British and American publishers, is now extending its area of agreement to continental Europe. Owing its inception to the efforts of a group of British publishers and conceived quite apart from purely bibliographic purposes it has since been incorporated into the *MARC* format.

CONCLUSIONS

Before any significant progress can be made in the centralized provision of services to libraries a clearer idea must be obtained of what services a library should provide. This in itself requires that libraries should have more data on their users' needs.

There would seem to be a possible danger in over-centralization; a single mammoth centre might become choked by its very size and complexity. A co-ordinated system of centres divided by region or function might be more practical.

Nevertheless, whatever centralized services are to be provided, it is clear that libraries must adopt more precisely defined and standardized practices and techniques than is their present custom if these centralized services are to be successful. An analogy may be drawn from electronic engineering: a wide range of standard components, energized through a co-ordinated network of electrical power, is available to build a vast number of different devices, from crystal sets to computers (May, 1954).

The Capabilities of the British *MARC* Record Service in terms of the Academic Library*

R. E. COWARD

INTRODUCTION

The British *MARC* Record Service is a centralized cataloguing service for libraries in a machine-readable form. It has particular significance in the context of academic libraries because, unlike existing services, it is designed to meet their requirements, and because generally speaking such libraries have suitable computers to hand for utilizing *MARC*. However with very few exceptions they have no experience in using either the computer or centralized cataloguing. This paper presents, as a basis for discussion at the seminar, some thoughts on the following topics:

1. Why academic libraries have not, in the past, made use of centralized cataloguing services;
2. Why they will be under pressure to change their policy in the future;
3. What changes will result in the library and the service;

and 4. How the library should introduce *MARC* into the system.

THE NEED FOR *MARC*

Academic libraries can hardly be unaware that they are having to run very fast indeed to keep up with the pace of development in their libraries. They are in the middle of a revolution which is changing the relationship between the universities and technological development in industry. Universities are now expected to play a positive role in applied technology and their research staff, who often have

---

* This is included in its orginal form and should be read in conjunction with the next paper also by Richard Coward and the following one by Nigel Cox where some performance figures are given.

industrial experience, expect and need the kind of expensive information service that sophisticated current awareness systems can provide. While research teams are demanding information at one end of the scale the student is being encouraged to seek it out himself at the other end. Add to this the long term problem of the information explosion and we have reached the point at which material can hardly be produced or stored in the traditional printed form. There are already bibliographic guides to magnetic tape information services and I wonder how long it will be before we have a machine-readable bibliography of machine-readable bibliographies. The academic library is weighed down with a vast range of bibliographic guides and as these proliferate in machine-readable form its users will expect to be provided with the facilities to use them. If they don't get these facilities through the library they will assuredly get them through their own departments. In spite of this, we all know from personal experience that the academic library functions primarily as an immediate information store. Above all its users want information on the spot, not a reference to information elsewhere. Why else should we be providing vast and expensive collections of books and periodicals at the centre of our new universities? Almost the only method a library has to display its range of material is through its catalogue and under these circumstances I would view with the greatest suspicion any suggestion that academic libraries are over-cataloguing their collections although it is fairly obvious that the traditional emphasis on bibliographic description is a hangover from the past. It is also clear that cataloguing techniques developed during a more leisurely age are breaking down.

Although *MARC* is designed as a cataloguing service its use in the library cannot be entirely separated from other administrative operations. In most libraries the cataloguing operation is very closely linked with the purchasing operation and to a lesser extent with the circulation system. Although I believe it is possible, perhaps desirable, to automate these three operations at decent intervals the system design should cover all three from the start. Every academic library in the country sees a steady growth in the use made of its stock and in the amount of interlending that takes place between itself and other libraries. Circulation systems cost money and they take up a lot of valuable space. Organized in a traditional manner they become more inefficient as they become larger because large files with constant activity are expensive and difficult to maintain. In the final analysis this is also true of machine files but it will be a long time before this factor becomes significant. In practical terms a circulation file is a small machine file.

The circulation file need not carry catalogue data to carry out its primary function, unless an accession number is considered to be catalogue data. Essentially it is a simple stock location system. However, for a percentage of items—reservations, overdues, etc.—it is necessary to be able to link catalogue data with circulation data. Just how this link should be effected is a critical problem in the design of automated circulation systems. So far not enough attention has been given to it.

Cataloguing and circulation control are big problems. Purchasing systems are perhaps less of a problem. This is because the amount of material and the number of records involved is small. I have yet to come across a library that did not have its purchasing under control. We would be poor managers if we could not purchase at most a few hundred items per week without using a computer. The question is whether the computer can be used to provide a more efficient system and how the *MARC* service should be fitted into this system. This is an awkward moment to ask such a question because both *MARC* and the Standard Book Numbering system are only just established. While it is relatively easy to design a cataloguing system which uses a *MARC* record when it is available, it is less easy to set up an acquisitions system on the same basis and there is less advantage at this stage in obtaining data from a *MARC* tape. Not much data is wanted unless the purchase record is handled as a cataloguing record. Although there has been a tendency in the past to treat the order file as a catalogue file I doubt if this is the best approach in an automated system. While it takes several weeks as it does at present in most academic libraries to complete the cataloguing operation there is some point in trying to link purchasing and cataloguing but if catalogue data is available at electronic speed when a book actually arrives there is very little point in trying to pre-catalogue. Of course if the printed *BNB* or a *MARC* printout was an important primary book selection tool in the library a different situation would exist.

THE BOUNDARIES OF *MARC*

The novelty of a machine-readable cataloguing service must not blind us to the fact that the medium is not the message. The *MARC* system must be considered first and foremost as a centralized cataloguing service. With this in mind it is worth while taking a brief look at the use made of centralized cataloguing academic libraries in the United Kingdom and the United States. It is quite clear from the figures we have that centralized or co-operative cataloguing is a way of life in the United States. The Library of Congress sells some 63 million cards per year (Davison, 1967) and a roughly equivalent number are produced by a vast variety of commercial and co-operative agencies. Nevertheless they whole system is constantly under attack because libraries find that a considerable proportion of their intake is not covered by a cataloguing service. They are not inclined to sit back and bemoan the fact. I don't know how much pressure or influence has to be brought to bear on the United States Congress to raise the sum of $19 million (Dix, 1967) over three years to support centralized cataloguing but I cannot imagine similar pressure being brought to bear by libraries and research institutes in this country to develop and maintain a comprehensive cataloguing service. Unless there is a change of attitude the *MARC* Service will ultimately have to be self-supporting. The boundaries of *MARC* are in the last analysis economic.

In spite of financial limitations the *BNB* has developed as a successful cataloguing agency for one group of libraries in this country. 40% of our public libraries buy catalogue cards and the vast majority use the weekly service as a cataloguing and acquisitions tool. Yet *BNB* as an aid to cataloguing has almost totally failed to penetrate the university and college library. Only ten libraries in a group of perhaps 200 which fall into this class purchase *BNB* cards and the great majority make very little use of *BNB* as a provider of cataloguing information. So far university libraries have not seen fit to use centralized cataloguing services and there is no reason to think that mounting a centralized service on a strip of magnetic tape will alter this situation unless we can establish why these libraries have not used centralized cataloguing in the past and do something about it.

THE NEED FOR CHANGE

The reason for this almost total failure to provide a service for university libraries is fairly obvious. I would not go so far as to say that university libraries were ignored when the centralized services were set up in 1949 but as the service was literally being run on credit there was no alternative but to try and supply a recognizable and reasonably homogeneous market. The public libraries were such a market. Their intake in those days was very largely covered by a listing of books with British imprints and a great majority used some variation of Dewey for shelf location and in their card catalogues. Catalogue entries were generally fashioned on the old 1908 *A.A. Code* standards. In short, although it would be ludicrous to suggest that recognizable standards existed, there was at least the basis of standardization to work on. But what of the universities? Well, they were certainly there but in a sense they were nearly invisible. As Dr. Parry said last year in a paper given at the L.A. Conference (Parry, 1968) 'Up to the early '50s universities were there and were known to be there, but like the Society of Antiquaries or the General Medical Council, they were allowed to pursue their harmless activity unmolested'. Those were the days! Universities and university libraries have since become powerful—and rather more aware that they cannot continue to ignore the outside world. The expansion has been so rapid and over such a brief period of time that I do not think that university libraries have yet fully appreciated either their combined power to command services or their responsibility to continually question their function and practices. To balance Dr. Parry's remark I would like to quote a comment made in a recent *BNB*-sponsored research report by Peter Lewis of Queen's University, Belfast*: 'For what it is worth, an outstanding impression gained during the course of the enquiry (into the use of *BNB*) was that there was certainly one category of subscriber ripe for the development of systems dependent on the regular use of *BNB* services—namely the university libraries whose present utilization of the service is derisorily small, in view of their very large interest in the bibliographic organization of current literature—an interest which is at least equal to that of the public libraries, even if the latter are more numerous. There are signs . . . that a long overdue expansion of interest in the national bibliographical services is gathering in this area; and that if continued it may transform the university library from amongst the least to amongst the most significant users of *BNB* bibliographical services in their various forms.'

THE SERVICE REQUIREMENTS OF ACADEMIC LIBRARIES

BNB is profoundly concerned to extend its services to meet the requirements of academic libraries and the *MARC* experiment offers

* Unpublished research report.

both parties a chance to plan together a service for the 1970s and beyond. This is a vitally important operation because the requirements of academic libraries today are a pretty good guide to the requirements of all libraries tomorrow. Universities need bibliographic services covering past and present publications. They are concerned or should be, as much with periodical literature as monographic literature and their intake is international. This is quite a challenge and I would like to say right away that there is absolutely no possibility of meeting all of these requirements until we develop a new type of bibliographic superstructure in this country. It is possible for *BNB* with considerable government support to set up the *MARC* project and it will be possible for us to continue to provide a *MARC* service at an economic price as a technological spin-off from a computer-produced *BNB* indefinitely into the future but the service has been designed on the assumption that by the time the special development period is over plans will exist on paper at least, for an organization capable of maintaining the very comprehensive service that should surely grow out of our first early efforts.

The *BNB MARC* service is based on five principles:

1. It must form part of an international exchange system;
2. It must offer total flexibility in use;
3. It must be compatible with a wide variety of machine systems;
4. It must provide a certain and efficient search factor for data;

and 5. It must accept satisfactory standards where they exist and adopt new standards when they are prepared.

The first three of these principles involve system design. The last two involve data content and it is particularly with reference to the standards involved that I want to examine the service requirements of academic libraries. Briefly, I see the situation like this. The academic libraries are ready to think seriously about the use of centralized cataloguing. This will involve also accepting basic cataloguing standards. It is *BNB*'s responsibility to offer these standards and it is the library's responsibility to accept them. I have heard far too often in academic libraries the remark: 'We cannot accept *BNB* cataloguing'. From now on this is the same as saying that a standard code is unacceptable as a basis for local cataloguing. *BNB* cataloguing is now Anglo-American Code cataloguing. The argument that local cataloguing is necessary to fit circumstances is hardly supported by an examination of academic library catalogues. By and large local cataloguing fits the past—an amalgamation of out of date codes and

the peculiar idiosyncrasies of chief cataloguers long since departed—
though their influence lingers on. The basic dilemma of university
libraries is that the past tends to be pretty permanent both on the
shelf and in the catalogue. There is no easy answer to this dilemma
except perhaps the divided catalogue and I do not see this as the
evil it is sometimes made out to be. Divided catalogues can be based
on a firm dateline—everything published after 1970 say, will appear
in the computer book catalogue—everything before 1970, in the card
catalogue. So many enquiries are concerned with current material
only that this division may well serve the general interest better than
a single file system. On balance it would seem that libraries should
resist any attempt to merge the old with the new by making adapta-
tions in both directions. Typical of this approach in cataloguing is a
decision on one hand to adopt entries under pseudonyms and shifting
local entries from real names as they occur, but on the other hand
deciding that the entry of corporate publications under name instead
of place would be too much of a good thing. This kind of approach
will just involve you in all the chaos of recataloguing with few of the
benefits of standardization. The benefits are not just local benefits.
Why should we cheerfully expect our users to adapt themselves to an
unfamiliar catalogue situation in every library? Why should our
interlending systems accept the appalling inefficiency caused by
requests couched in a bewildering variety of types of heading? How
can we expect central government support until it is clear from our
actions that we are prepared to modernize our system and to create
the environment in which it is at least possible to offer an efficient
centralized service?

THE DESIGN OF *MARC*

I have already said that the system design of *MARC* was based on
five principles. The first and most important was its international
basis. To achieve this we need international agreement on machine
format, character codes and data content. More has been achieved
in this direction than could reasonably be anticipated at such an
early stage although perhaps if anything is to be done at all it must
be done at an early stage. The world's first *MARC* projects mounted
by Library of Congress and *BNB* have a common machine format,
and a common character set. We have failed to achieve complete
agreement on a standard set of data within the record. This is partly
due to the fact that British libraries and American libraries have

naturally evolved along somewhat different lines and partly due to the fact that the Library of Congress have made the fatal mistake of trying to be compatible with the past on the *MARC* record as well as in their own catalogue. The Library of Congress have perhaps for sound internal reasons adopted the policy of superimposition in their catalogue. Roughly speaking this means that when an existing heading is in their catalogue then the new entry is inserted under this heading even though the Anglo-American code would call for another heading. We feel rather strongly that there was absolutely no reason why this policy of superimposition should be carried into the *MARC* system. It is in terms of *MARC* quite indefensible and I am sure they will come to appreciate this. There is, of course, no reason why *MARC* records issued by great libraries should not carry any amount of special information required by that library system. There is an enormous amount of elbow room in the exchange format for just this kind of requirement. However, we will go on arguing that shared cataloguing must mean standard cataloguing and hope that our voice will be heard. In the meantime *BNB* will investigate the possibility of modifying Library of Congress records where necessary to bring them into line with Anglo-American standards.

The second principle was that of total flexibility in use. I have emphasized the necessity of standardization but this need not, in fact should not, extend to fixing the amount of information in a local record or the complexity of the local cataloguing system. The *MARC* record is so organized that a library can design virtually any set of printed catalogues or any machine-based retrieval system that meets its local needs. This has been done by a process of record analysis and data identification. A *MARC* record consists of a series of defined data elements and the essence of any *MARC* user program will be the selection of the data elements required by the local system and the addition of purely local data. I have already suggested that it should not except under special circumstances involve the modification of the data itself.

The third principle of the *MARC* service is that it must be compatible with a wide variety of machine systems. The apparent determination of computer manufacturers to collaborate only when forced to do so by governments have made this much more difficult to achieve than it should have been. The *MARC* record is constructed in an 8 bit character orientated machine. It has to be used in 6 bit word orientated machines. Everything is different. An *ICT* machine cannot read an *IBM* tape and a *KDF9* machine cannot read an *ICT* tape. As a result the *MARC* service must supply three tape standards and issue exchange records in a character form which is not really convenient to anybody. The major part of the effort that has gone into *MARC* user programs so far has been concentrated on these problems. They have been resolved by the efforts of *ICL* and *IBM* and by individual *KDF9* users but a lot of valuable time and energy which could have been directed to genuine systems programming has been involved. Moreover these three machines are so different that it is difficult to believe that any common systems development will be possible. The problems we have faced in the last few months are essentially short term but it is disturbing to realize that a massive duplication of effort, particularly programming effort, will follow as a result of this basic machine incompatibility.

The fourth principle of the *MARC* service is that the record must contain a key by which a user can identify and select the data he wants. This is a problem that affects the whole book trade—not just libraries interested in computer systems. The solution is the standard book number system. In 1969 it is hoped that standard book numbers will be supplied with every entry appearing in *BNB*. The United States publishers have adopted the system and a concerted and successful effort has been made to make the system completely international. I don't think there is anything that can now stop the universal adoption of standard book numbering in the 1970s. A new set of initials (*ISBN*) is already being used. This should have a profound effect on ordering, accessioning and interloan systems in libraries and any systems analysis and design work should take this factor into account.

THE CONTENT OF *MARC*

In order to assess the capability of *MARC* in academic libraries a detailed picture of the contents of the record is required. A tabulation of the *MARC* record fields with an analysis into data elements has been published (British National Bibliography, 1968). The record offers a standard catalogue entry with a complete set of references required for that entry plus a range of classification numbers and subject headings. The intention is to provide with the record all of the data needed to fit the record into a catalogue system. There is no authority file needed to establish catalogue cross-references. They are listed with each entry. I am satisfied that this cataloguing packet is superior to any that is offered today in machine or manual systems and it would be well worth while purchasing a copy of the exchange tape simply to print out catalogue data for use in the local manual system.

The subject data to be supplied with the record is extensive but as yet incomplete. At the time of writing a *BNB* class number and a standard *DC 17th ed.* number is provided. An exhaustive analysis of *LC* classification and subject heading practice is under way and we will start adding classification numbers early in 1969. To achieve this we are setting up a multi-system file at *BNB*. All class numbers are constructed from a basic subject analysis. Ultimately this file will provide a complete conversion kit from one scheme to another so if you are contemplating switching we may be able to provide you with a machine-readable translation file in 1971 or thereabouts.

The decision to include Library of Congress classification numbers and subject headings in the *MARC* file was taken because a significant proportion of academic libraries use these schemes and because the *LC MARC* records carry this information. However the *LC* classification is more a complicated shelf location device than a classification system. In this respect it is no different from the *DC 17th ed.* number. These classification numbers are supplied to meet the system requirements of libraries. Except in a very crude way they do not meet the information retrieval requirements of the library and certainly not of a machine-readable file. This is a very long term problem and although the practical implications of some recent work carried out under the auspices of the Classification Research Group are being investigated at the *MARC* office, it is clear that we are a very long way indeed from being able to provide a sophisticated information retrieval system in *MARC*. However we can and will provide a set of subject descriptors with each *MARC* record using controlled language terms. These will be in addition to the 'Library of Congress' type subject headings. We are at present investigating a system whereby the set of subject descriptors can be organized so that index entries applicable to any of the classification numbers associated with the entry can be constructed.

THE APPLICATIONS OF *MARC* IN ACADEMIC LIBRARIES

The academic library is, like all libraries that are not merely repositories of books, a system for information transfer. It so happens

K

that the requirements of the academic library tend to be fairly complex. While some level of automation will be the only way of meeting system requirements in the fairly near future the design and running of a fully automated system will necessarily be elaborate.

However any automated system will essentially consist of two loops of information. There will be a flow of information between document source agencies and the library in one loop. This is the function of the traditional order and accessioning section. Once a library has got hold of information in the form of books, periodicals, films, tape, records, etc., it has to construct a retrieval system, traditionally in the form of a card catalogue. The internal loop is used by readers and librarians to locate information in the system. Constructing this loop is traditionally the function of the cataloguing department. In both areas the bibliographic record is the information carrier. I cannot see this changing for some time although a system in which one loop carries only an *SBN* and the other carries free text can be imagined. However the first automated systems in university libraries will certainly be concerned with producing familiar looking book orders on one hand and traditional looking catalogues on the other. In fact, as the catalogues will almost certainly be book catalogues they may look even more traditional than our card catalogues. It is a pity that we are forced to use our computers as printers in this fashion, but booksellers are not yet ready to receive orders on magnetic tape. Nor can I see the catalogue being replaced with a bank of cathode ray tubes linked to an on-line information store for a few years.

Clearly an academic librarian contemplating some degree of automation in the acquisitions and cataloguing area must consider very carefully the utility of the *MARC* record service. Unfortunately for him, he must judge its utility not as it is—a scarcely launched experimental project—but as it will be in about three years time because that is when his own system will be operational. What will happen to *MARC* during that period will depend largely on the capacity built into the *MARC* system and to the degree on which he and his colleagues in other academic libraries are prepared to agree on common objectives and common requirements. It is my belief that the *MARC* service has an unlimited capacity built into it and that the next three years will see a rapid extension of *MARC* services. I also believe that the standard book numbering system will enable central cataloguing agencies to reduce the problem of late recording from a major deterrent to a minor irritant. As from the beginning of 1969 *BNB* will have advance notice of all material in this country issued with Standard Book Numbers and by and large this covers the vast amount of monograph material which is demanded more or less on publication in libraries.

So we can look forward to a service which could provide a very large percentage of the cataloguing data required in academic libraries when it is wanted. Exactly how this will be provided it is difficult to predict. We do not anticipate issuing reels of tape week in and week out indefinitely. There will certainly be technological developments which will enable libraries to link up on-line to a central store to collect a file of records perhaps once a week. There may be regional data banks combining the functions of a regional catalogue, a data reservoir, and a *MARC* service. Whatever pattern emerges however the library operation will begin with the build up of a file of orders containing international standard book numbers. This file will be matched against a *MARC* file either locally or centrally. When there is a match the catalogue record is transferred to the local system.

To make this a feasible proposition the percentage of matches must be above a certain figure. I suspect this percentage is actually quite low as the cost of local cataloguing is already high and even if your system were established in 1969 there would probably be an economic trade-off in using *MARC*. In order to gain full benefit from an increasing hit rate however the local file structure must be very carefully planned. You can take as much or as little of the *MARC* record as you like but it will be very difficult to push it into a rigid framework. So the first requirement is a flexible local format and this implies also flexibility in your various printouts. Printing load is not conditioned by whether one or half a dozen lines are permitted per entry but on the average length of the set of data elements you require in your local record.

THE INTRODUCTION OF *MARC*

It is not my intention in this paper to present anything resembling an automated system design for libraries using *MARC*. This operation takes several months in each library. I am concerned with the use of *MARC* during this period. The problem is not simply one of introducing automation. The library has also got to introduce centralized cataloguing. It is essential that the cataloguing department is given the opportunity to become completely familiar with the *MARC* record and the *A.A. Code*. The problem is to do this with a minimum of data processing effort.

I suggest starting by planning to hold a *MARC* file built up from the weekly tapes supplied by *BNB*. The file should simply consist of *MARC* records in the form they are issued. No alterations, no additions, no deletions. The amount of data processing effort required is minimal—merge routines will probably be available. It is important that the whole record is held. Not only is it much easier but it is far too early to make any decisions about what might or might not be wanted. The length of the file will not be a serious consideration for many months.

The objective of the operation is to link up a copy of the *MARC* record with the book when it is forwarded to the cataloguing department for handling in the manual system. This may seem to be a very small step indeed towards automation. In fact it has practically nothing to do with automation but a great deal to do with centralized cataloguing and that is what the system change is really about. Nevertheless the mere presence of a *MARC* tape in the computer section will involve that department and make the system design discussions more meaningful.

Incoming books can be linked with the *MARC* record file through one of three control numbers. About 70% of British books carry *SBN*s and a high proportion of American books carry *LC* card numbers. *SBN*s for most of the remaining British books can be found in *BNB* or *The Bookseller*. Prepare a file of these numbers on punched card or paper tape and run it against the cumulated *MARC* file taking a printout of matched entries. This operation will produce valuable catalogue data and vital statistical information. It is important to know exactly how much material is available in *MARC* when you want it. Try holding unmatched numbers for two or three weeks before discarding them. If the present cataloguing operation takes four weeks or so on average if would be worth finding out whether the data became available during that period.

The catalogue department will now have a *MARC* record supplied with a proportion of each intake. How useful this will be depends on the local cataloguing practices. As the record contains a standard entry together with *BNB* and *LC* classification numbers and a complete set of references and cross-references it would be odd if it were not useful. The operation will certainly give the cataloguing team the opportunity to become fully conversant with *MARC* cataloguing standards. With any luck it will ease the load of work in the department. Perhaps an edited version of the printout will serve as copy for the catalogue card typing.

This preliminary operation should extend over several months as system design work goes forward. At the heart of the system design will be a decision on the data set required for the local system. Programming work on extracting this from the *MARC* data set will be done before this decision is made—the operation of selecting fields and subfields is a general one irrespective of the actual fields finally selected. When the data set is fixed it can then be tested against the *MARC* file by printing out records for the cataloguing department which contains only these fields. Once again it is advisable to arrange a fairly extensive check. The automatic selection of fields from a record can result in some unforeseen situations.

Beyond this point the local system really begins to take shape. The data set extracted from the *MARC* file must be transferred to a local file. Once this is defined the experimental and testing phase is virtually over. The whole operation up to this stage has not involved much data processing and very little system design but it has provided an excellent environment for testing preliminary assumptions, for giving computer staff and library staff a sense of familiarity with *MARC* and introducing under favourable circumstances the concept of centralized cataloguing.

The British *MARC* Record Service: An Evaluation of the Present Position and Prospects for the Future

R. E. COWARD

INTRODUCTION

The development of the British *MARC* Project during its so-called 'experimental' phase has been a classic example of defining objectives, preparing a system design and developing an operational system within a projected time schedule and budget. It is impossible to regard this operation as experimental and it is equally impossible to evaluate it except perhaps as a case study in how or how not to carry through a major project. The objective was to reach a point where experiments could begin. Apart from work being done in an extremely small group of libraries most of which have been acting as detached parts of the main project, the real experimental work and the evaluation will not begin until 1971. In this second phase, as in the first, detailed planning is necessary, but at the same time the project must be responsive to feedback from a real network of users without losing sight of the fact that the first *MARC* users are unlikely to be typical *MARC* users. The tactical adjustments made to rectify mistakes—some of which are already obvious—must be made in the context of a long term strategy. The purpose of this paper is to look again at the fundamental decisions which were taken three years ago in the light of subsequent events and to look forward to the project developments planned for the period 1971–72.

THE *MARC* DECISIONS

1. *To provide a traditional bibliographic description plus special 'search factors'.*

In *MARC* the assumption, and it is little more than this, has been that a traditional bibliographic description is the most appropriate 'document surrogate' in a machine-readable file. The logic behind this decision was that the technique of communication was relatively unimportant. It is possible that by carrying forward a traditional form we are 'marching into the future looking backwards'. It now seems likely that the special search factors provided in the *MARC* record need to be considerably extended so that implicit information such as the fact that a document is a specification is explicitly coded.

2. *To adopt as a basic standard the new Anglo-American code (British Edition).*

This decision was based on a detailed and expert evaluation of the new code. This national code is derived from the only internationally accepted code of cataloguing principles prepared by *IFLA* at the International Conference of Cataloguing Experts, Paris, 1961. The adoption of the code has resulted in a serious level of incompatibility with the Library of Congress data base but there are now signs that this may not be a permanent situation.

3. *To adopt a communications format agreed with the Library of Congress.*

This was a far reaching and controversial decision. After two years of discussion the format, with minor improvements, now exists as a draft International Standards Office document. It is believed that the development of information networks will be materially assisted by the existence of this standard for bibliographic exchange in magnetic tape form. As experience is gained in exchanging records a more fundamental understanding of the properties of communications systems will be acquired and this may lead in turn to the formulation of a more generalized standard applicable to any machine-readable medium and to any type of record.

4. *To make effective use of MARC as quickly as possible.*

This has also been a controversial decision. The more *MARC* is used in a wide variety of situations the sooner its properties can be assessed. The risk is that errors become increasingly expensive to rectify. However it seems a risk that must be taken. After a few months' experience it is now clear that a *MARC* service must meet fairly rigorous standards if it is to be used. It would be easy enough to meet these standards in a small experimental system but the slightest experience of bibliographic systems is enough to convince anyone that size is the essence of the problem. We can only find out if these standards can be met in a total system by attempting a total system. The national bibliography must therefore commit itself to using the *MARC* data base it is preparing in order to establish the real level of accuracy and the real speed of production that can be achieved. These factors are so important that theoretical assumptions would be unacceptable.

These decisions will form the foundation of the British *MARC* Record Service for the next ten years. The next stage (1971–72) will establish the pattern of development.

MARC DEVELOPMENT PLANS

During 1971–72 *MARC* must move decisively into its first utilization phase. The whole purpose behind the project is to provide a master data base for use at international, national and local levels. This is very different from the public image of *MARC* as it is today— a simple distribution of data in bulk as it is created by the central agency. *MARC* is a data base from which services can be provided and in the immediate future the emphasis will be on the production of services in a more or less traditional form. There are strong economic reasons behind this decision. Perhaps the strongest is that the amount of money available for *MARC* development is limited. If the amount that is needed to maintain the data basis is reduced more will be available for supporting the development of local systems. The project development has therefore been planned round three main objectives:

  1. To assist the development of local systems;
  2. To extend the potential value of the service;
and 3. To provide new economic services.

1. *The development of local systems*

The basis of planning is decentralization of effort. This unfortunately cannot be a carefully balanced programme. We have to use what limited data processing experience exists where it exists. In practice four or five centres of development will emerge and financial support will be provided to cover the cost of co-operation. *BNB* will also be directly involved in this area so that its own data processing experience can be utilized. The central team are more favourably placed to prepare general utility programs but it seems certain that these cannot simply be given to a local system. There must be the backup of an educational project to train local librarians in data processing concepts. It will be years before the library schools effectively take over this work and in the meantime some kind of intensive training course will be necessary to educate the middle level librarians who will be responsible for the day to day running of the first generation of computer-based systems.

2. *To extend the potential value of the service*

The major effort in this area must be to get an international system going and to encourage close co-operation between the international network as it develops. The omens are extremely favourable. *BNB* has already been successfully involved in the development of three major international standards, i.e.:

    1. The Standard Communications Format;
    2. The International Standard Book Number;
and 3. The Standard Bibliographic Description.

Big problems remain to be tackled in the next two years. The international *MARC* network must be encouraged to adopt a standard set of cataloguing principles and a standard technique for supplying subject information. It has sometimes been thought that standard *MARC* implementation is also necessary. This is not so. National systems must have the freedom to develop their own special implementations. It will be the task of each national centre to handle incoming records and convert them to a national standard. *BNB* is already using conversion programmes to translate Library of Congress records to a national standard.

The goal of a standard technique for supplying subject information in *MARC* records may seem an impossible task. In fact as long as there is a clear understanding of the purpose of the standard it should be easier to achieve than agreement on the Paris Principles. National practice is not involved at all. All that is needed is a common means of carrying subject information in the international network. Clearly this system must be familiar and already in widespread use. It must also be an adequate working tool for subject retrieval in a machine system. Only one existing scheme meets these requirements and this is fortunately already an international standard. The Universal Decimal Classification is widely used in America, in the

United Kingdom and in Europe. It has retrieval capabilities that are far superior to the Decimal Classification or the Library of Congress Classification. The schedules are issued in English, French and German and it has the solid backing of the Federation Internationale de Documentation. All of this is of vital importance but in the context of an international network the value of *UDC* would be its high conversion factor to other systems. *UDC* numbers can be linked in a thesaurus to Library of Congress or *DC* numbers so that incoming records can have national system equivalents added by machine editing only. The decision to use *UDC* as an international language is too important to be taken without a detailed investigation of its properties. This work should be carried out during 1971–72.

The use of *UDC* in all *MARC* records will also link the *MARC* record service with the considerable amount of work that has been already carried out on handling *UDC* and constructing *UDC* indexes in machine systems. However the fundamental problem of indexing remains. In *MARC* an indexing system is needed that will operate efficiently in the humanities and the sciences and at any depth of analysis. During the last two years a new indexing theory has been developed at *BNB* which has these properties (British National Bibliography, 1969*b*). The *PRECIS* system (*Pre*served *C*ontext *I*ndexing *S*ystem) will be used by *BNB* for its internal indexing requirements in 1971 and it is anticipated that a special two year research project will be undertaken to:

1. test the indexing capabilities of the system;
2. identify the problems associated with constructing a multi-system authority file linking a *PRECIS* statement with a string of different system classification numbers;
3. build up a structured thesaurus;

and 4. develop programs for the automatic production of printed indexes linking a *PRECIS* string to any classified array.

These plans to extend the potential of the *MARC* service form part of the long-term strategy of the project. They will have little effect on the operation of the project during 1971–72 but the results should be ready for use when they are needed.

3. *To provide new cost-effective services*

The existing national bibliography combines a weekly cataloguing service with a cumulative listing. The existence of this service has

over a period of years resulted in considerable changes in local processing operations and any extension of this service would necessarily
affect local plans for utilizing *MARC* data.

During the 1971–72 period *BNB* intends to investigate the potential of micropublication services. In the past few years there has
been rapid development in microfilm technology and many of the
difficulties associated with early microfilm or microform system are
disappearing. The development of direct magnetic tape to microfilm systems offers a technology which may overcome the line-
printer bottleneck inherent in computer cataloguing systems. Microfilm may also be a satisfactory method of providing a visual index to
the very large data base being built up by *BNB*. Consequently *BNB*
has chosen the combined Library of Congress and *BNB* data bank as
a basis for an experimental service. A combined file, with subject,
author and title listings will be produced and during an experimental
period of a year the possibility of a permanent microfilm service will
be assessed.

CONCLUSION

The prospects for the future of the *MARC* service after the next
two year period must be examined within the context of a new
bibliographic service structure in this country. In the previous paper
the statement was made 'The boundaries of *MARC* are in the last
analysis economic'. These boundaries are reached fairly quickly
within the present structure. By 1972 at the latest a new structure
must be designed if the *MARC* project is to continue to develop.

On the Introduction of Machine-processable Centralized Cataloguing Services to Libraries

N. S. M. COX

It is a self-evident truth that centralized cataloguing services must be economic to succeed. It is important, however, to assess the economics of such a service within a framework wider than that of cash flow for unless, for example, account is taken of the quality of the end product the most viable cataloguing might consist of a standard book number, or—by extrapolation—nothing at all. It is therefore perhaps worthwhile to mention some of the general merits and demerits of systems based on centralized machine-processable sources before proceeding to an outline of the criteria which should be taken into account in the assessment of the viability of such a system.

COMPATIBILITY vs. USER SERVICE

One of the claims made by the proponents of machine-processable central cataloguing services is that the effort put into the creation of the catalogue record, although probably greater than at any single institution, should be very much less than the total cumulative effort required for cataloguing separately in each individual institution; furthermore better production control and increased specialization can give rise to a lower error rate and increased definition of information in the record. This is likely to be possible if sufficient care is taken in the planning of the system; however, it is altogether too easy to assume that a highly detailed bibliographical record with low error rate is, *per se*, better than a locally produced intermediate (and possibly indeterminate) quality record. It should be noted that catalogues generally exist as service tools both for user communities and for the administration of the library systems. Libraries are not identical—nor is it clear whether they should be (see, for example: Jolliffe, Line and Robinson, 1967); the communities served by different libraries will necessarily differ. If therefore seems likely that the 'ideal' library will provide services corresponding as closely as possible to the special needs of the community which they serve and the collections of materials which they house whilst, at the same time, maintaining as close a compatibility as possible between the inter-library exchange services and the centralized services available to them. Quite naturally, a conflict arises here, but this conflict is not necessarily satisfactorily resolved by neglecting orientation to user requirements to maximize compatibility.

It is therefore necessary when considering centralized cataloguing services to attempt to establish whether such a service will, in fact, be of greater benefit to the ultimate user—a problem familiar to library management, but often without a clear-cut answer.

FORM OF IN-HOUSE RECORD

As has been mentioned above, in-house records generally contain much less information than is found in centrally produced records such as the *BNB MARC* records, and the forms and contents of machine-processable in-house records will depend on the requirements of the institution, the form and content of the information from the centralized source, and any decisions made with respect to retrospective materials. It is likely that only the necessary information will be extracted from the total centrally produced records due to the cost of storage of such records and the problems associated with rapidity of access to the library files. In addition changes will have to be made to the information in these records to meet the specific filing, display and retrieval requirements, (see, for example, Cox, 1970*b*). Some of these changes will be made entirely by computer algorithm and the only problem here is in the creation of an effective algorithm for this purpose; however it is quite probable that some of the data fields in the record may need 'intellectual modification' in circumstances where no effective algorithm can be devised and where a change in the information content of the record is required. Such changes illustrate the differences between compatibility of information between systems where algorithmic changes are made to *data* and changes in the information content of the record where the new *information* must be presented by a human to the system.

Thus the main in-house catalogue file is assumed in this paper to consist of a set of records corresponding to the bibliographical units in the library each of which contains a sub-set of the data fields provided by the central source, and probably modified both by algorithm and by librarian. It is probable that the standard book number (SBN) can be used to permit access to the full bibliographical description provided by the central source, particularly if the file of data on which the full record resides is maintained as part of the in-house record. It should be noted that these records are not likely to take the form of the present $MARC$ record, even if the data content is roughly compatible. (See, for example, Cox and Davies, 1970a, b, c,).

Two further major problems exist in the use of centralized services —what to do about restrospective material and what to do with new material not covered by the centralized service.

RETROSPECTIVE MATERIAL

The existing accumulated catalogue is likely to be costly to convert to any machine-processable form (see, for example, University of Newcastle upon Tyne, 1968 and 1969; and the report by Jolliffe on Project LOC, elsewhere in this volume), let alone to the standard of the centrally produced record. It may be possible to create a national retrospective catalogue source in machine-processable form, but considerable thought still needs to be given to the desirability of such a source and which materials it should reasonably contain. Even if such a source existed there remains the problem of matching the holdings of an individual library to the centrally produced source file. The cost of such an exercise cannot be less than that given in table 1, in which it is assumed that a bibliographical item can, on average, be identified uniquely by 20 characters and that the entire cost of the operation is the keyboarding of this information. The cost is likely, of course, to be greater than this, particularly if the opportunity is taken to review the bookstock and at the same time to select materials for withdrawal. It is interesting to note that, if space saving and user efficiency are considered, the major argument in favour of a machine-processable source for retrospective materials may well be the cost savings consequent upon the provision of a sufficient level of discrimination in the user's records to implement an efficient (computer-based) withdrawal policy.

TABLE I. Cost per 1000 records of keyboarding a 20-character identifier

Assume	20 characters per record	= 20 characters
plus	20% redundancy for layout, case changes, etc.	= 24 characters
plus	20% excess for correction (alternative is verification 100%)	= 29 characters
	for 1000 records	= 29,000 characters
Assume	keyboarding rate of 6000 key depressions per hour	= 5 hours
	At rate (to include holiday, overheads, equipment, depreciation and maintenance) of 12s. per hour	= £3

If one were to postulate a centrally produced retrospective file in which $(100 - N)\%$ of the 'average' library's material was represented by a corresponding full bibliographical description together with special control information for withdrawal, it is possible to estimate the cost of matching such records with a minimum identification of the library's stock such as is outlined in table I. The costs which might accrue in such an exercise are:

1. *Creation and correction of the identification of the bibliographical units in the library* at, say, three times the cost given in table I, £9 per 1000 records.

2. *Computer processing to select the corresponding master records from the centralized source.* The computer time required to sort the bibliographical identifications into the order of the master records increases exponentially with increase in the number of identifications to be sorted. It is assumed here that 300,000 identifications are matched against a master file of 2 million records (each containing 400 characters), thus giving an approximate cost, per 1000 records, of £0·1 × c, where c is the charge per minute for the use of the central processor of the computer. No charge is made here for the use of computer storage media.

3. *Cost of recataloguing manually the $N\%$ of records which do not occur in the centralized source.* In considering this, it is necessary to deduct the proportion of this $N\%$ which will be withdrawn from the current stock.
   Let the withdrawal policy make provision for six alternative actions in respect of a bibliographical unit:
      (a) it should remain in the current stock;
      (b) it should be withdrawn into reserve storage;

(c) it should be considered (by a 'stock editor') for withdrawal into reserve storage;

(d) it should be withdrawn (and destroyed);

(e) it should be considered (by a 'stock editor') for withdrawal and destruction;

and (f) it should be withdrawn and destroyed if another copy exists in, say, the National Lending Library for Science and Technology (*NLL*) or the National Central Library (*NCL*); otherwise it should be presented to one of these institutions.

Let the percentage of the total existing stock of the library in each of these categories be

pa ... percentage to remain in current stock;

pb ... percentage withdrawn to reserve storage (by fixed set of rules, without the intervention of the stock editor);

pc_1 ... percentage considered for withdrawal to reserve storage by the stock editor, and transferred to reserve stock;

pc_2 ... percentage considered for withdrawal to reserve storage by the stock editor, but retained in the current stock;

pd ... percentage withrawn as destroyed (by fixed set of rules, without the intervention of the stock editor);

pe_1 ... percentage considered for withdrawal and destruction by the stock editor, and destroyed;

pe_2 ... percentage considered for withdrawal and destruction by the stock editor, but retained in reserve storage (for simplicity the proportion of materials retained are all considered as transferred to reserve storage);

pf ... percentage of materials withdrawn and destroyed or sent (at no cost in transportation!) to *NLL* or *NCL*.

Let the cost of full recataloguing for current stock be $£Rf$ per record and the cost of recataloguing materials for reserve storage only be $£Rr$.

Thus, for each 1000 records, of the present stock there are $10N$ records which require manual cataloguing or withdrawal.

Of these, $(pa + pc_2)\%$, require *full* recataloguing;

$(pb + pc_1 + pe_2)\%$, require *reserve* recataloguing;

and $(pd + pe_1 + pf)\%$, do not require recataloguing.

The cost of recataloguing is therefore:

$$\frac{£N}{10}((pa + pc_2) \times Rf + (pb + pc_2 + pe_2) \times Rr)$$

4. *The cost of the application of the 'withdrawal algorithm' to separate the $(100 - N)\%$ of the records, available from the centralized source, into the six categories (a) to (f)*

If one assumes a computer central processor requirement of one second per record then the cost per 1000 records of existing stock will be:

$$£10(100 - N) \times \frac{c}{60} = \frac{£1}{6} \times c \times (100 - N)$$

5. *The cost of the stock editor in sub-dividing categories (c) and (e).* If one assumes that, on average, the editor will make one decision per three minutes, that he is paid £2000 per year, that he effectively works for 30 hours per week and for 46 weeks per year, then the cost, per 1000 records of the present stock, will be:

$$£0 \cdot 73 \times (pc_1 + pc_2 + pe_1 + pe_2)$$

It is further assumed here that the percentage of material withdrawn, etc. will be the same both for materials represented in the centrally produced retrospective bibliographical source and for all other materials.

and 6. *Cost of physical handling of all materials for transfer to reserve stock, withdrawal, etc.* Let this cost be £m per 1000 records moved. The cost, per 1000 records, of present stock, is therefore:

$$\frac{£\,m}{100}(pb + pc_2 + pc_2 + pd + pe_1 + pe_2 + pf)$$

It should be noted that, because a machine-processable data base is being generated, the problems associated with the adjustment of the catalogues (added entries and other tracings) to correspond to any of the decisions taken above are minimal. Thus, if the withdrawal policy is executed in conjunction with the republication of the catalogues, no costs accrue from these adjustments.

From the above, the total cost, per 1000 items of existing stock, for the execution of the withdrawal policy can be summarized as follows:

(i) *fixed cost per 1000 records*

$$£(9 + c(0 \cdot 1 + (100 - N)/6)$$

(ii) *costs attributed to items retained in current stock*

$$£pa \times N \times Rf/10$$

(iii) *costs attributed to items withdrawn (directly) to reserve storage*

$$£pb(N \times Rr/10 + \frac{m}{100})$$

(iv) *costs attributed to items considered for withdrawal to reserve storage and transferred to reserve stock*

$$£pc_1(N \times Rr/10 + \frac{m}{100} + 0 \cdot 73)$$

(v) *costs attributed to items considered for withdrawal to reserve storage, but retained in current stock*

$$£pc_2(N \times Rf/10 + \frac{m}{100} + 0 \cdot 73)$$

(vi) *costs attributed to items withdrawn (directly) and destroyed*

$$£pd \times m/100$$

L

(vii)   *costs attributed to items considered for withdrawal and destruction and destroyed*

$$£pe_1 \times (\frac{m}{100} + 0.73)$$

(viii)   *costs attributed to items considered for withdrawal and destruction but retained in reserve stock*

$$£pe_2 \times (N \times Rr/10 + \frac{m}{100} + 0.73)$$

and (ix)   *costs attributed to items withdrawn and destroyed or sent to NLL or NCL*

$$£pf \times (m/100)$$

The most obvious cost advantage, in considering such a policy, is the savings associated with the capital cost of the buildings in which the items are housed. When a new library is designed, provision is made for the storage of the predicted number of items to be acquired for a number of years. If, by withdrawal, one can reduce the rate of growth of the library, one can claim, as a direct cost saving, the capital value of the space which would otherwise have to be provided to house this stock. Current floor loadings and costs for new library buildings give figures of 20 books per square foot*, with a building cost of £7 per square foot for open-access storage. Thus one can claim a direct cost saving of 7s. per item withdrawn. And, if one assumes a building cost of £6 per square foot and storage of 60 books per square foot for storage in a reserve store, the direct cost saving in respect of materials transferred to reserve storage will be 5s. per item.

Thus, per 1000 items of existing stock, saving will be:

$$£3.5(pd+pe_2+pf)+£2.5(pb+pc_1+pe_2)$$

No doubt those interested will wish to determine the values of these parameters for their own situation; however, table 2 gives some specimen figures showing the cost of conversion of retrospective material making allowance for the saving in space only. From these it can be seen that in circumstances in which 90% of a library's material is represented on the centrally produced source file, 22% of the library's stock is transferred to reserve storage and 16% of the stock is totally withdrawn there is an inherent profit of £0.8 per 1000 items of current stock.

* The University Grants Committee Standard for library buildings gives 60 sq. ft. per 1000 bibliographical units, but this figure is currently being revised. The figure adopted here assumes a 'worst case' and has been calculated by Mr. H. Faulkner Brown, of Williamson, Faulkner Brown and Partners, Architects.

Columns F and G of table 2 represent a hypothetical withdrawal policy for Newcastle University Library. The percentage of materials in each category are shown schematically in figure 1 (page 176).

If the library is prepared to tolerate minimum cataloguing of materials, not covered by the centrally produced file, at the same cost as cataloguing the reserve material ($£0·25$) then row X of table 2 gives the cost in pounds of the extra saving which is added to the overall saving and the result given, in pounds, in row Y.

If one considers, therefore, the hypothetical case (F) for Newcastle University Library, without upgrading the records not represented on the centralized file, there is an overall cost saving of $£62·2$ per 1000 records. The present stock of the library comprizes 300,000 items giving an overall saving of $£18,600$. If the non-centrally-produced records are upgraded, there will be an overall saving of $£5,100$.

It should be noted that no consideration has been given in these costings to the value of the 'improved' catalogue nor has the cost of creation of the centrally produced retrospective catalogue file. If one assumed that 100 libraries would each be prepared to pay $£5000$ for such a service (equivalent to the salary of the chief librarian for less than two years) then $£½$ million would be available to create this file. Furthermore, if this file was created as a by-product of a recataloguing exercise for one or two of the major libraries, the cost of subscribing libraries would be likely to be very much less.

As has been mentioned above, it may be necessary to modify the records, obtained from the central retrospective file, both by algorithm and by the intervention of a cataloguer. This has not been taken into consideration in the costings above.

Consideration should also be given to additional costs and benefits of the new system. The advantages of a machine-processable retrospective catalogue compatible with current systems based on the *MARC* record services are fairly obvious. Not only will the total system be homogeneous, it is likely that a number of the administrative library services, notably circulation systems and ordering and accessioning systems, will be very much more effective. Attention should however be given to changes in running costs of the library system consequent upon the withdrawal policy outlined above. Simon (1967) discusses the advantages and disadvantages of remote storage of lesser-used material and attempts estimates of the dollar value of book use and loss of book use in storage. Jain (1966) shows

TABLE 2. Specimen figures for withdrawal policy costing

Assumes: $m = £10$:   cost of movement of 1000 items
$Rf = £1$:   cost per item of *full* recataloguing
$Rr = £0.25$: cost per item of *reserve* recataloguing
$c = £1$:   cost per minute of computer *CPU* time

		A	B	C	D	E	F	G
Percentage of records not occuring in central source file	N	30	20	10	10	10	10	20
%age selected as current stock	pa	70	70	70	70	60	55	55
% age withdrawn directly to reserve storage	pb	7	7	7	0	12	10	10
% age considered and transferred to reserve	pc_1	4	4	4	0	4	5	5
% age considered for reserve stock but retained in current	pc_2	2	2	2	0	2	5	5
% age withdrawn and destroyed directly	pd	5	5	5	10	0	7	7
% age considered for destruction and destroyed	pe_1	6	6	6	5	8	3	3
% age of dest. kept in reserve storage	pe_2	2	2	2	5	6	5	5
$\% \rightarrow NLL$ or NCL	pf	4	4	4	10	8	10	10
Total cost* ($£$)	—	259·8	186·5	112·6	104·4	110·2	97·8	152·9
Total benefit* ($£$)	—	85	85	85	100	111	115	115
Overall saving* ($£$)	—	−164·8	−101·5	−27·6	−4·4	+0·8	+17·2	−37·9
X	—	162	108	54	52	46	45	90
Y	—	−2·8	+6·5	+26·4	+47·6	+46·8	+62·2	+52·1

* per 1000 items of existing stock.

that in the Purdue library the usage of an item decreases with the age of publication (except in education) and has constructed models for English-language titles. Trueswell (1965) claims that a library's holdings may be reduced by 60–70% and yet satisfy well over 99% of the user requirements.

It may be fairly difficult to establish for the whole collection, let alone for special sub-sets of the collection, the proportion of material of a given age. Few libraries have so far kept accurate records in adequate detail, and crude statistics of accession rate, being subject to violent fluctuations (for example, as a result of unpredictable donations), provide no guidance on the distribution of volumes among subjects or dates of publication.

It is likely, therefore, that an analysis of a sample of the bookstock will be necessary to be able to develop a withdrawal algorithm appropriate to the library and to establish, in the context of the proposed algorithm, the percentage of materials which will fall into each of the relevant categories.

In the light of the figures mentioned above, it is perhaps worth mentioning that present day costs for the publication of a catalogue (say, 500 copies) to a good typographical santdard (Pace, 1970) is about £150 per 1000 *entries*.* It is of course, necessary to determine the average number of tracings from each entry. If one assumes that, on average, there are five entries for each record this gives a cost per 1000 records of £750. This figure can be reduced*; furthermore, it relates to the number of records printed and allowance should be made for the withdrawal rate, as outlined above (see table 3).

CURRENT MATERIALS

In the two previous papers in this collection some aspects of the British *MARC* Record Service are described, and prospects for the future are hinted at. The utilization of such a record service must be assessed by all potential users in terms of objectives of the institutions

* This assumes a 2-column format in 7-point type, each column being approximately 90 m.m. long, with 100 lines per page. The overall size is A4 and it is assumed that there are 7 lines of type per entry with a blank line separating entries. This rough estimate, provided by Mr. S. A. Pace of the Kynoch Press, also assumes a large number of entries (> 50,000) and bound into volumes, each of 1000 pages. The cost could be reduced, for example, if it was considered that 6-point type was acceptable, the cost would be reduced by about 1/6. Similarly, if there were less than seven lines per entry—say, that on average there were four line entries for half the material (name catalogue) and three line entries for the remainder (subject catalogue)—then the costs could be further reduced (see table 3).

TABLE 3. Approximate cost in pounds, per 1000 records of present stock, for printing 500 copies of a large catalogue

	Percentage of original material not included in the printed catalogue (due to withdrawal, etc.)						
	0%	10%	20%	30%	40%	50%	60%
A	750 (620)	675 (555)	600 (495)	525 (435)	450 (370)	375 (310)	300 (245)
B	630 (530)	570 (475)	505 (425)	440 (370)	380 (320)	315 (265)	250 (215)
C	420 (330)	380 (300)	335 (265)	295 (230)	245 (200)	210 (165)	170 (135)
D	350 (280)	315 (250)	280 (225)	245 (195)	210 (170)	175 (145)	140 (120)

Assumes　5 entries per record printed;
　　　　　500 copies printed to best typographical standard*;
　　　　　A4 format, 2 × 90 m.m. columns per page

A.　Printed in 7-point type; 7 lines/entry;
　　blank line between entries†

B.　Printed in 6-point type, 7 lines/entry;
　　blank line between entries†

C.　Printed in 7-point type; half the entries at 4 lines/entry;
　　remainder at 3 lines/entry;
　　blank line between entries†

D.　Printed in 6-point type; half the entries at 4 lines/entry;
　　remainder at 3 lines/entry;
　　blank line between entries†

* It is likely that costs will be greater if, for example, line-printer output is copied.

† Figures for printing without the blank line between entries are given in brackets.

which might need to use such a service. It is perhaps important that such an evaluation should be undertaken, irrespective of whether or not the service is likely to be of use to those institutions in the immediate future.

The *OSTI*-sponsored project, by means of which the British National Bibliography Limited (*BNB*) has been able to create this service on an experimental basis, is likely to give way in the near future to a self-supporting commercial service, commercially defined and controlled by *BNB* or its 'post-Dainton' successor. The formative stages of this project are nearing completion, and emphasis is being given more and more to the exploitation of the services available from such a national cataloguing data base. It is clear that these services must be adjusted in accordance with the terms of the short term and long term market, and it is in this context that evaluation of such a service should be undertaken by all potential users, irrespective of the time scale on which the individual institutions may be planning to use such a centralized service.

As time proceeds there will be an increasing commitment to the form of the record, due to the adjustments in practice which existing users have made, and the considerable investment in computer software which will increase as time elapses. It is highly desirable, therefore, that any institution planning to use the British *MARC* Record Service should assess its viability in terms of the operations of that institution, and thus make available to the central agency detailed information on user requirements. It is only in this way that the services which are or may be provided can be adjusted effectively to meet the requirements of potential users over the next decade.

From the point of view of the user institution, there are a number of obvious potential benefits from the *MARC* Record Service; however, it is clear that these benefits must be considered both in the context of the cost which such benefits will incur and the cost of alternative courses of action.

It may be possible to establish some activities, on a 'stand-alone' basis, for which the *MARC* Record Service may be of some benefit— for example, assistance in the selection of books for ordering or the provision of a limited selective dissemination of information (*SDI*) service. However, most of the long-term benefits of such a service are likely to accrue from a basic reorganization both of the internal administrative operations of the library and of the regional and national library services.

If one considers the parallel between the reprocessing of retro-spective material, described above, and the processing of current materials then one can apply a cost formula to the creation of a homogeneous file of all items accessioned. As it is assumed that no material is withdrawn or destroyed, $pa = 100\%$ and a first approximation to the cost of creation of this file is therefore:

$$\pounds(9 + c(0 \cdot 1 + (100 - N)/6) + 10 \times N \times Rf)$$
per 1000 items accessioned.

However, as the number of items accessioned in any batch is likely to be small compared with the size of the total data base, this formula should be modified in terms of the strategy for the selection of the records from the data base. Curve A in figure 2 shows the relationship between the percentage of 'misses' (N) and cost per 1000 items (with the unmodified formula), assuming that full manual cataloguing costs $\pounds 1$ per item and that computer time costs $\pounds 1$ per minute of central processor time.

These costs do not take into account manual modification of the records from the centralized source. If this is assumed to be equivalent to the cost of *reserve* cataloguing (Rr) then the formula would become

$$\pounds(9 + c(0 \cdot 1 + (100 - N)/6) + 10 \times N \times Rf + (100 - N) \times 10 \times Rr)$$

giving curve B in figure 2 (page 177).

As has been mentioned above, the strategy for the selection of records from the data base should take into account the problems associated with the selection of a small sub-set from a very large set of records. If one assumes, first of all, that it is necessary to partition the master file on the basis of year of publication and that all materials are covered (i.e. there is a separate *MARC* file for the year 1904, if required), then it will be necessary to process separately accessions corresponding to each year of publication or, where the date of publication is not known, for all years until the item is located.*

To develop the required formula, it is necessary to make appropriate assumptions about the 'intake pattern' of the library. Some outline analyses have been undertaken of 'intake pattern'†; however, it is clear that each institution will have to make its own analysis in terms of 'intake pattern' and proposed matching strategy.

---

* This latter situation is, of course, unlikely to be relevant for cataloguing and is therefore ignored in the following argument.

† Some work is currently being undertaken by, *inter alia*, the university libraries of Newcastle, Bradford, Hull, Birmingham and Aston.

Three points are perhaps worth mentioning. Firstly, if the proposed matching strategy requires a different data file for, say, each year's *MARC* material, then there will be a different proportion of records recovered for each file and it may therefore be necessary separately to cost 'retrieval' of records from each year's file. Secondly, it may be cheaper to create manually any records which would otherwise come from a file with a 'hit' rate in which the overheads involved in scanning the file would be greater than the cost of manual creation of the records. The third point is that the British records available for retrieval only cover materials published since September, 1968 and therefore records corresponding to material published before the date will have to be created manually, unless action is taken with respect to retrospective material. It should, however, be noted that as time proceeds this will become less and less relevant if the proportion of a library's intake decreases with increasing age of material (see figure 3, page 178).

Intake patterns must, of course, be developed in terms of age of material at date of acquisition, coverage by centralized source, and probably by class of material in terms of requirements for precision of cataloguing.

Table 4 gives some provisional figures for the British *MARC* Record Service.* It should be noted that these figures are *BNB's* admitted performance† and cover the period from the 8th January, 1970 (*issue no.* 1046) to the 19th August, 1970 (*issue no.* 1078), except that they do not include records from the first two tapes (1046 and 1047).

Table 4(a) provides a general summary of the contents of each tape (*columns A to D*), the number of these records subsequently replaced (*column E*), the percentage of the total file which are new records (*column F*), correction records (*column G*) and deletion records (*Column H*) and the percentage of new records which, by the end of the period, had been replaced (*Column I*)‡.

Table 4(b) shows the time interval between the issue of a new record and the issue of corrections to those errors which have been detected and actioned by *BNB*.

* These figures are from an (unpublished) analysis of the British *MARC* weekly tapes issued by *BNB*, conducted by D. Millett of the Bodleian Library, Oxford.

† Actual performance is likely to be worse than this as in one—hopefully untypical—sample it was found that there were twice as many errors than those corrected by *BNB*.

‡ It should be noted that these figures assume that new records are only corrected once—in fact, at least one record has been corrected four times.

Table 4(c) shows, for the corrections issued on each tape, the number of corrections referring to each previous tape.

It should be noted that these figures cover a period of intense development of the *BNB* service, and are therefore likely to be rather higher than stabilized production figures. It is understood that *BNB* are, at present, giving attention to the development of procedures both to reduce the rate of occurrence of errors in the *MARC* records, to increase the proportion of errors detected and to reduce the delay in publication of the corrections.

Table 4(d) shows the percentage of records containing errors and the percentage of errors removed, both in relation to the number of weeks since the release of the record. Again it should be stressed that these are actual performance figures during the development phase; on the other hand, they only include errors detected and corrected by *BNB*.

From these figures, it would appear that about 15% of all new records contain errors and, assuming this value, table 4(e) gives the percentage of records still containing errors, x weeks after their issue as new records.

As has been mentioned above, these figures refer only to errors detected and corrected by *BNB* and the actual performance is therefore worse than this. There are however two mitigating criteria, namely that these figures are taken from the experimental period of the British *MARC* Record Service and that they are for all errors in the records. Unfortunately *BNB* have no figures available for the relative proportions of errors in the different data fields and it is therefore impossible to judge what proportion of the errors will be relevant to a given application—for example, 'price' may be crucial to an ordering/accounting system but not relevant to a cataloguing system.

Table 4(e) shows the percentage of records still containing errors eventually detected and corrected by *BNB*, in row 1. If one considers a system, in which r% of errors are detected and removed during local processing at a cost of Cr per record corrected and that R% of all records contain errors not detected by *BNB*. Both r and R have been taken arbitrarily as 10%

Table 4(f) gives the overall percentage of errors for different periods of cumulation, with different delays between the issue of a new *MARC* tape and the publication of the cumulation. For example, with a monthly cumulation in which the new records from the latest two issues of the *MARC* tape are excluded, the percentage of records containing errors is:

$$\frac{(100-r)}{100} (4{\cdot}4 + 0{\cdot}96\ R)\%$$

If 10% of all remaining errors are detected during local processing ($r = 10$) and 5% of all records selected for this activity contain errors not detected by *BNB*, then the percentage of records in the cumulation containing errors will be:

$$\frac{(100-10)}{100} (4{\cdot}4 + 0{\cdot}96 \times 5)\%$$

$$= 8{\cdot}3\%$$

If one assumes that the cost per week of publishing a record which contains an error is C_i (the cost of the inconvenience to the user) and the cost of re-issuing the corrected record is the same as the cost of its original publication, then formulae can be developed for the cost of errors in various forms of record publication. Publication costs are taken arbitrarily from the paper by Cox (1970, b), as are the monthly Schemes 1 and 2 in table 5. Scheme 3, a weekly cumulation system is based on the publication schedule of the published *BNB*. These three schemes show the cumulation of errors as the cumulation sequence proceeds and also give some indication of the cost penalties involved. The costs do not include the 'in-house' procedures to detect and correct the errors—only the printing cost where a record has to be reissued specially to correct a record and the cost of the inconvenience of having erroneous records on the file. The importance of the selection of an appropriate cumulation pattern is evident from these three schemes.

TABLE 4 (a). General summary of weekly tapes

Issue No.	A Total No. of records issued	B No. of new records	C No. of correction records	D No. of deletion records	E No. of records subsequently replaced	F %age of new records	G %age of correction records	H %age of deletion records	I %age of new records replaced
1046	—	—	—	—	50	—	—	—	—
1047	—	—	—	—	198	—	—	—	—
1048	761	458	224	79	45	60·2	29·4	10·4	9·8
1049	585	583	1	1	61	99·7	0·2	0·2	10·4
1050	262	262	0	0	10	100·0	0·0	0·0	3·8
1051	587	587	0	0	25	100·0	0·0	0·0	4·2
1052	526	526	0	0	41	100·0	0·0	0·0	8·8
1053	571	571	0	0	28	100·0	0·0	0·0	4·9
1054	748	633	114	1	78	84·6	15·2	0·1	12·3
1055	694	631	63	0	25	90·9	9·1	0·0	4·0
1056	571	520	50	1	20	91·1	8·8	0·2	3·8
1057	601	535	66	0	39	89·0	11·0	0·0	7·3
1058	529	529	0	0	49	100·0	0·0	0·0	9·3
1059	545	485	60	0	47	89·0	11·0	0·0	9·7
1060	606	570	36	0	62	94·1	5·9	0·0	10·9
1061	708	524	175	9	25	74·0	24·7	1·3	4·8
1062	521	473	46	2	13	90·8	8·8	0·4	2·7
1063	646	646	0	0	44	100·0	0·0	0·0	6·8
1064	539	539	0	0	56	100·0	0·0	0·0	10·4
1065	706	620	86	0	44	87·8	12·2	0·0	7·1
1066	568	533	35	0	36	93·8	6·2	0·0	6·7
1067	583	487	76	20	25	83·5	13·0	3·4	5·1
1068	554	554	0	0	46	100·0	0·0	0·0	8·3
1069	361	361	0	0	72	100·0	0·0	0·0	19·9
1070	667	619	47	1	101	92·8	7·0	0·2	16·3*
1071	563	455	108	0	99*	80·8	19·2	0·0	21·7*
1072	932	785	146	1	269*	84·2	15·7	0·1	34·2*
1073	574	418	155	1	155*	72·8	27·0	0·2	37·0*
1074	922	776	141	5	367*	84·2	15·3	0·5	47·3*
1075	709	536	169	4	210*	75·6	23·8	0·6	39·0*
1076	808	480	322	6	164*	59·4	39·8	0·7	34·2*
1077	769	540	228	1	66*	70·2	29·6	0·1	12·2*
1078	660	553	106	1	99*	83·8	16·1	0·1	17·9*

Issue No.	1	2	3	4	5	6	7	8	9	10	11	12	13	14	15	16	17	18	19	20
1046	0	0	0	0	0	0	0	0	0	0	0	0	0	0	0	0	0	0	0	0
1047	0	0	0	0	0	0	0	0	0	0	0	0	0	0	0	0	0	0	0	0
1048	97	30	16	20	36	4	4	3	2	2	2	2	0	1	1	1	1	0	0	2
1049	1	0	0	0	0	0	0	0	0	0	0	0	0	0	0	0	0	0	0	0
1050	0	0	0	0	0	0	0	0	0	0	0	0	0	0	0	0	0	0	0	0
1051	0	0	0	0	0	0	0	0	0	0	0	0	0	0	0	0	0	0	0	0
1052	0	0	0	0	0	0	0	0	0	0	0	0	0	0	0	0	0	0	0	0
1053	0	2	0	1	0	0	68	7	0	0	0	0	0	0	0	0	0	0	0	0
1054	5	0	35	14	14	17	2	0	0	0	0	0	0	0	0	0	0	0	0	0
1055	2	27	13	0	3	6	9	1	0	0	0	0	0	0	0	0	0	0	0	0
1056	0	9	18	0	0	0	0	0	0	0	0	0	0	0	0	0	0	0	0	0
1057	2	0	0	0	1	0	0	9	9	13	5	0	0	0	0	0	0	0	0	0
1058	0	0	0	0	0	1	0	0	0	0	0	0	0	0	0	0	0	0	0	0
1059	3	33	9	8	5	0	0	0	0	1	0	0	0	0	0	0	0	0	0	0
1060	15	9	3	5	1	3	0	0	0	0	0	0	0	20	0	0	0	0	0	0
1061	20	8	17	3	4	7	23	9	3	11	6	21	15	0	8	0	0	0	0	0
1062	14	22	8	2	0	0	0	0	0	0	0	0	0	0	0	0	0	0	0	0
1063	0	0	0	0	0	0	0	0	0	0	0	0	0	0	0	0	0	0	0	0
1064	0	0	0	0	0	0	0	0	0	0	0	0	0	0	0	0	0	0	0	0
1065	38	31	3	4	5	2	3	0	0	0	0	0	0	0	0	0	0	0	0	0
1066	30	5	0	0	0	0	0	0	0	0	0	0	0	0	0	0	0	0	0	0
1067	17	0	7	1	7	5	14	13	12	0	0	0	0	0	0	0	0	0	0	0
1068	0	0	0	0	0	0	0	0	0	0	0	0	0	0	0	0	0	0	0	0
1069	0	0	0	0	0	0	0	0	0	0	0	0	0	0	0	0	0	0	0	0
1070	47	0	0	0	0	0	0	0	0	0	0	0	0	0	0	0	0	0	0	0
1071	72	13	23	15	0	0	0	0	0	0	0	0	0	0	0	0	0	0	0	0
1072	59	11	7	0	21	12	6	3	7	1	1	0	1	0	0	0	0	0	0	0
1073	140	3	9	2	2	0	0	0	0	1	0	0	0	2	0	0	0	0	0	0
1074	77	60	1	0	0	0	0	0	0	0	1	0	0	0	0	1	0	0	0	0
1075	107	43	11	0	0	4	3	1	2	0	1	0	0	0	0	0	0	0	0	0
1076	139	139	6	4	7	15	2	3	3	1	5	3	2	0	1	1	0	0	0	0
1077	78	31	56	13	21	1	0	2	3	1	5	1	0	1	0	0	0	0	0	0
1078	19	45	13	20	3	0	3	1	0	0	0	0	0	0	0	1	0	0	1	0
Totals	982	521	255	112	130	78	137	52	41	31	26	27	18	24	10	4	1	0	1	2
As percentage of all corrections	40.0	21.2	10.4	4.6	5.3	3.2	5.6	2.1	1.7	1.3	1.1	1.1	0.7	1.0	0.4	0.2	0.0	0.0	0.0	0.1

TABLE 4(c). Correction records for each tape showing tape of original issue

Issue No.	1046	1047	1048	1049	1050	1051	1052	1053	1054	1055	1056	1057	1058	1059	1060	1061	1062	1063
1046																		
1047	0																	
1048	30	97																
1049	0	0	1															
1050	0	0	0	0														
1051	0	0	0	0	0													
1052	0	0	0	0	0	0												
1053	0	0	0	0	0	0	0											
1054	7	68	17	14	1	0	2	5										
1055	0	0	2	7	3	14	35	0	2									
1056	0	0	1	9	0	0	0	13	27	0								
1057	5	13	9	9	0	0	1	0	18	9	2							
1058	0	0	0	0	0	0	0	0	0	0	0	0						
1059	0	0	0	1	0	0	0	1	5	8	9	33	3					
1060	0	0	0	0	0	0	0	0	3	1	5	3	9	15				
1061	8	20	15	21	6	11	3	9	23	7	4	3	17	8	20			
1062	0	0	0	0	0	0	0	0	0	0	0	0	2	8	22	14		
1063	0	0	0	0	0	0	0	0	0	0	0	0	0	0	0	0	0	
1064	0	0	0	0	0	0	0	0	0	0	0	0	0	0	0	0	0	0
Totals	50	198	45	61	10	25	41	28	78	25	20	39	31	31	42	14	0	0

Table 4(c)—continued

Issue No.	1058	1059	1060	1061	1062	1063	1064	1065	1066	1067	1068	1069	1070	1071	1072	1073	1074	1075	1076	1077
1065	3	2	5	4	3	31	38													
1066	0	0	0	0	0	0	5	30												
1067	12	13	14	5	7	1	7	0	17	0										
1068	0	0	0	0	0	0	0	0	0	0	0									
1069	0	0	0	0	0	0	0	0	0	0	0	47								
1070	0	0	0	0	0	0	0	0	0	0	0	13	72							
1071	0	1	0	1	1	7	3	0	0	0	23	7	11	59						
1072	2	0	0	0	1	1	3	6	12	21	15	0	9	3	140					
1073	0	0	0	0	0	1	0	0	0	0	2	0	2	1	60	77				
1074	0	0	0	0	0	1	0	2	0	0	0	0	0	0	11	43	107			
1075	1	0	1	1	1	2	3	5	1	3	3	0	4	3	4	6	139	139		
1076	0	0	0	0	0	0	0	0	1	1	3	3	2	7	21	13	56	31	78	
1077	0	0	0	0	1	0	0	1	5	0	0	2	1	15	1	3	20	13	45	19
1078	0	0	0	0	1	0	0	0	0	0	0	0	1	3						
Totals	49	47	62	25	13	44	56	44	36	25	46	72	101	91	237	142	322	183	123	19

TABLE 4(d). Percentage of errors, eventually detected by *BNB*, remaining and removed

Number of weeks since new records were released		0	1	2	3	4	5	6	7	8	9	10
%age of errors still remaining	A	100·0	60·0	38·8	28·4	23·8	18·5	15·3	9·7	7·6	5·9	4·6
%age of errors removed	B	0	40·0	61·2	71·6	76·2	81·5	81·5	90·3	92·4	94·1	95·4

Number of weeks since new records were released		11	12	13	14	15	16	17	18	19	20
%age of errors still remaining	A	3·5	2·4	1·7	0·7	0·3	0·1	0·1	0·1	0·1	0·1
%age of errors removed	B	96·5	97·6	98·3	99·3	99·7	99·9	99·9	99·9	99·9	99·9

TABLE 4(e). Percentage of records still containing errors, x weeks after issue as new records, assuming that 15% of all new records contain errors which will be detected by *BNB*

	Number of weeks since issue as new record (x)									
	0	1	2	3	4	5	6	7	8	9
1 Percentage of records containing errors which will be detected by *BNB* but have not yet been corrected	15	9·0	5·8	4·2	3·6	2·8	2·3	1·5	1·1	0·9
2 Percentage of records (other than those in row 1) which contain errors not detected by *BNB*	0·85×R	0·91×R	0·94×R	0·96×R	0·96×R	0·97×R	0·98×R	0·99×R	0·99×R	0·99×R
3 Percentage of records corrected during local processing (assumes R=10%)	0·24×r	0·18×r	0·15×r	0·14×r	0·13×r	0·12×r	0·12×r	0·11×r	0·11×r	0·11×r
4 Percentage of records containing errors after local processing (assumes r=10%)	21·1	16·3	13·7	12·4	11·9	11·3	10·9	10·3	9·9	9·7

M

TABLE 4(f). Overall percentage of records containing errors, in cumulated *MARC* files.

Delay in publication (weeks)	Cumulation period			
	Weekly	Fortnightly	Monthly	Quarterly
0	$\frac{(100-r)}{100}(15+0\cdot85R)$	$\frac{(100-r)}{100}(12+0\cdot88R)$	$\frac{(100-r)}{100}(9\cdot6+0\cdot90R)$	$\frac{(100-r)}{100}(6\cdot7+6\cdot93R)$
1	$\frac{(100-r)}{100}(9+0\cdot91R)$	$\frac{(100-r)}{100}(7\cdot4+0\cdot93R)$	$\frac{(100-r)}{100}(6\cdot2+0\cdot94R)$	$\frac{(100-r)}{100}(4\cdot7+0\cdot95R)$
2	$\frac{(100-r)}{100}(5\cdot8+0\cdot94R)$	$\frac{(100-r)}{100}(5\cdot0+0\cdot95R)$	$\frac{(100-r)}{100}(4\cdot4+0\cdot96R)$	$\frac{(100-r)}{100}(3\cdot6+0\cdot96R)$
3	$\frac{(100-r)}{100}(4\cdot2+0\cdot96R)$	$\frac{(100-r)}{100}(3\cdot9+0\cdot96R)$	$\frac{(100-r)}{100}(3\cdot5+0\cdot97R)$	$\frac{(100-r)}{100}(2\cdot8+0\cdot97R)$
4	$\frac{(100-r)}{100}(3\cdot6+0\cdot96R)$	$\frac{(100-r)}{100}(3\cdot2+0\cdot97R)$	$\frac{(100-r)}{100}(2\cdot8+0\cdot97R)$	$\frac{(100-r)}{100}(2\cdot2+0\cdot98R)$

TABLE 5. Some 'typical' publication costs.

Scheme I   (150 new entries per month)

		Number of records containing errors*	Number of extra (replacement) records	Total number of records
1	Jan I	25	0	150
2	Feb I+2	42	0	300
3	Mar I+2+3+Index (I–3)	55	0	450
4	Apr 4	25	5	150
5	May 4+5	42	5	300
6	Jun I+2+3+4+5+6+Index (I–6)	91	0	900
7	Jul I	25	9	150
8	Aug 7+8	42	8	300
9	Sep I+2+...+8+9+Index (I–9)	129	0	1350
10	Oct 10	25	13	150
11	Nov 10+11	42	12	300
12	Dec I+2+...+11+12 (I–12)	159	0	1800

Annual printing cost (assuming no errors) = £2750

Average cost per record printed   = £0·4

Average cost per record issued   = £1·5

Number of errors* × number of months for which record is
  'active'†   = 1183
  at cost of £C_i per record per month   = £(C_i × 1183)

Number of records especially reprinted to remove errors   = 50
  at cost of £0·4 per record printed   = £20·8

Assuming that $C_i = \frac{1}{10}$ of cost per record printed, total extra
  cost = £20·8 + £47·3   = £68·1

* Assumes R = 10 & r = 10, and that a further 10% are removed by each 'in-house' processing. Publication delay = 0 weeks.

† Only includes I month's activity for the annual cumulation.

TABLE 5—*continued*

Scheme 2   (150 new entries per month)

	Number of records containing errors*	Number of extra (replacement) records	Total number of records
1 Jan 1	25	0	150
2 Feb 2 + Index (1–2)	25	8	150
3 Mar 3 + Index (1–3)	25	11	150
4 Apr 4 + Index (1–4)	25	12	150
5 May 5 + Index (1–5)	25	14	150
6 Jun 6 + Index (1–6)	25	15	150
7 Jul 7 + Index (1–7)	25	16	150
8 Aug 8 + Index (1–8)	25	17	150
9 Sep 9 + Index (1–9)	25	17	150
10 Oct 10 + Index (1–10)	25	18	150
11 Nov 11 + Index (1–11)	25	19	150
12 Dec 12‡ + 1 + 2 + 3 + ... + 11 + 12 + Index (1–12)	158	0	1950

Annual printing cost (assuming no errors) = £2285

Average cost per record printed   = £0·6

Average cost per record issued   = £1·26

Number of errors* × number of months for which record
  is 'active'†   = 1164
  at cost of £C_1 per record per month   = £(C_1 × 1164)

Number of records especially reprinted to remove errors = 147
  at cost of £0·6 per record printed   = £88·2

Assuming that C_1 = $\frac{1}{10}$ of cost per record printed, total extra
  extra cost = £88·2 + £69·8   = £158

* Assumes R = 10 & r = 10, and that a further 10% are removed by each 'in-house' processing. Publication delay = 0 weeks.

† Only includes 1 month's activity for the annual cumulation.

‡ December issue also printed separately so that they are not lost in the cumulation.

Scheme 3—based on the *BNB* publication schedule, assuming 150 entries per week. This includes a weekly issue cumulated and indexed in the fourth issue:

	*Number of records containing errors**	*Number of extra (replacement) records*	*Total number of records*
Week 1	39	0	150
Week 2	39	15	150
Week 3	39	19	150
Weeks 4 + weeks 1–3 + Index of weeks 1–4	101	0	600
Also includes total cumulation at each quarter:			
1 Jan 1	101	0	600
2 Feb 2	101	32	600
3 Mar 3	101	44	600
Cumulation‡ 1+2+3 + Index (1–3)	179	0	1800
4 Apr 4	101	0	600
5 May 5	101	32	600
6 Jun 6	101	44	600
Cumulation‡ 1+2+3+4+5+6 + Index (1–6)	302	0	3600
7 Jul 7	101	0	600
8 Aug 8	101	32	600
9 Sep 9	101	44	600
Cumulation‡ 1+2+ ... +8+9 + Index (1–9)	417	0	5400
10 Oct 10	101	0	600
11 Nov 11	101	32	600
12 Dec 12	101	44	600
Cumulation‡ 1+2+ ... +11+12 + Index (1–12)	480	0	7200

Annual printing cost (assuming no errors) = £14,000
Average cost per record printed = £0·46
Average cost per record issued = £1·95
Number of errors* × number of months for which record
   is 'active' = 2000
   at cost of £C_1 per record per month = £(C_1 × 2000)
Number of records specially reprinted to remove errors = 624
   at cost of £0·46 per record printed = £287
Assuming that C_1 = $\frac{1}{10}$ of cost per record printed, total extra
   cost = £287 + £92 = £379

  * Assumes R = 10 & r = 10, and that a further 10% are removed by each 'in-house' processing. Publication delay = 0 weeks.
   † Only includes 1 month's activity for the annual cumulation.
   ‡ Assumes cumulation published one month after last monthly part.

OTHER COST CONSIDERATIONS FOR *MARC*-BASED SYSTEMS

1. One of the situations, which should be considered in the assessment of the viability of a *MARC* record service in a library, is the probability of a search being made for a record which has not yet been released by the central agency. It is, therefore, necessary, where a significant proportion of a library's intake is received immediately on publication of the item, to take into account the relationship between the date of publication of an item and the date of release of the corresponding record by the central agency. No figures have, so far, been published by, for example, the British National Bibliography; however, it can be argued that such figures, if published, may provide an unrealistic basis for assessment of the long-term situation, until the system for the handling and creation of such records has settled down. Nevertheless, such information is important in the assessment of the viability of such services and guidance is necessary, even if it is only as an 'upper bound'.

2. One of the most important criteria in the assessment of the viability of centrally produced machine-readable cataloguing services for current publications is the accuracy of the information on the records when they are released. It is therefore necessary, first of all, that the error rates in such records are carefully assessed, not only by class of record (fiction, non-fiction, juvenile, etc.) but also by the type of error and the data fields in the record which are affected. Such figures are of major importance in the assessment of the cost of the application of corrections or notification of errors in any systems or sources dependent upon the centrally produced records. It is also necessary to establish the patterns of time intervals between the release of the records containing the errors in each class and the notification of the correction by the centralized source.

The importance of these figures depends very much on the type of services and systems adopted by the user institution: for example, an *SDI* service may well be able to tolerate a fairly high error rate as errors may have no permanent effect. On the other hand, the use of the centralized service for the updating and publication of catalogues, could well be penalized, by a high error rate, to an extent greater than the savings inherent in an error-free centralized service, due to the high cost of rectification of the errors. If one assumes that, in conventional systems, the cost of replacement of a set of catalogue cards by a corrected set of cards in a conventional card catalogue is unlikely to be less than the cost of cataloguing a new item, then a number of specific (and probably highly unreliable) lower bound costs are available (Hunt, p. 227). Newcastle University Library, with a 'name' catalogue, a subject catalogue and a shelflist, estimate that, for them, this cost cannot be less than £1.*

3. A more fundamental danger of centralized cataloguing services is the 'loss' of materials due to inaccurate information in the centrally produced records. It is thought that more material is mislaid within present systems than has been lost from them, in many cases.†

Inaccurate information in a centrally produced record could cause the corresponding bibliographical item to be 'lost' by every subscriber to the source. More likely, however, is the fragmentation into parts of homogeneous groups of records. This is particularly likely in respect of subject catalogues. It is thought that in many institutions cataloguers give more attention to the cataloguing rules represented by the precedents in the existing collection than to the formulated rules. Two groups of cataloguers, one producing the records for the central service and the other manually cataloguing material not available from the central service, could well cause homogeneous groups of items to be sub-divided into non-adjacent groups and, until this false sub-division is detected in the local institution, users are likely only to utilize the first group which they find. The present proposal of the British National Bibliography to adopt a subject indexing scheme which is totally untested on any large file (and hence in any real situation) is therefore a matter of considerable concern. (British National Bibliography, 1969*b*).

POSSIBLE LONG-TERM EFFECTS OF CENTRALIZED CATALOGUING

From the above, it would seem that one of the long-term effects of centralized cataloguing might be a substantial diminution in the number of titles held by a library in respect of subjects where bibliographical items have a short 'half-life'. Incautious withdrawal may have a deleterious effect and it will, in these circumstances, be

* C. K. Balmforth; private communication.

† 'A book in the hand is worth ten cards in the drawer'—old Russian proverb. M. W. Grose and M. B. Line, *Library Association record*, vol. 70, 1968, p. 111.

desirable to safeguard the situation by strengthening the Inter-Library Loan System.

Increased effectiveness (perhaps with a reduced cost per item) of the *ILL* system, should make a withdrawal policy less sensitive to error; however, it is interesting to note that if the inter-library communication system can be made 'responsive' in terms of computer-based library systems, then alterations to bookstocks could be made in respect of knowledge of holdings of other nearby institutions.

Furthermore, if regional centres could provide and maintain 'master' bibliographical sources, containing both full bibliographical descriptions and statements of holdings, such that the user library's computer system could retrieve any record 'on-line', then the cost of operation of the entire system (regional centre and network of user institutions) could well be substantially reduced.

GENERAL CONCLUSIONS

1. A centrally produced file of retrospective materials may be of more direct benefit to libraries than the provision of current catalogue material in machine-readable form; indeed it is questionable whether current sources, such as the *MARC* projects, can provide the basis for systems in which cost benefits can be justified directly. This situation cannot be clarified until more detailed information is made available about the performance of the record services.

2. If a sufficient number of institutions were anxious to execute a stock withdrawal policy, then this could well justify, on a cost effective basis, the creation of a high-quality centrally produced file of retrospective material; however, a careful analysis of the true position needs to be undertaken to establish detailed costings for such a project.

3. Considerable advances will have to be made in the inter-institutional facilities (such as *ILL*) to support withdrawal policies, if adopted, and can be much enhanced if total library automation becomes widespread. This will, however, require a policy of *inter-action with* user institutions rather than *distribution to* user institutions.

4. There is a considerable danger in uncontrolled development of central sources without critical appraisal by potential users. There is an urgent need for differences in objectives between central agencies and the user institutions to be exposed and reconciled. Indeed, such

central agencies should heed Lewis' conclusion, reported (elsewhere in this volume) by Jeffreys: '. . . so long as the British National Bibliography continues to remain aware of current problems in organizing and administering bibliographical and cataloguing departments in libraries'.

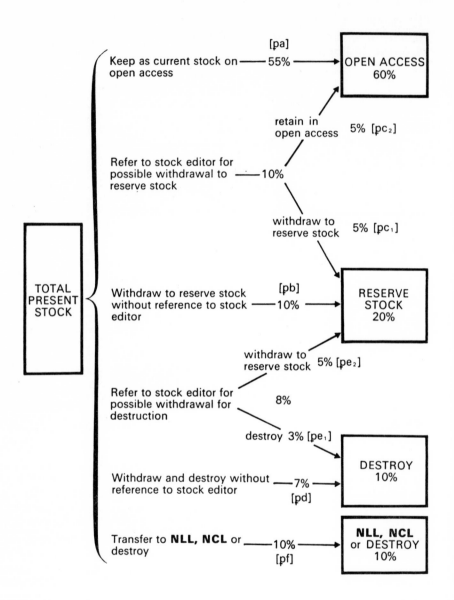

Figure 1. Schematic representation of percentage of items withdrawn or placed in reserve storage in a hypothetical example (see columns F and G of table 2).

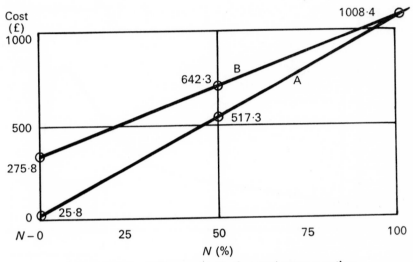

Assumes: c = £1 per minute of central processor time
Rf = £1 per item catalogued manually
Rr = £0·25 per item from centralized source

Figure 2. Cost per 1000 items for creation of full current file (according to the unmodified formula). (See page 158.)

Curve A shows the relationship between the percentage of material not appearing in a centralized source (N) and cost per 1,000 items (with the unmodified formula), assuming that full manual cataloguing costs £1 per item, and that computer time costs £1 per minute of central processor time.

Curve B assumes that the cost of local manual modification of the records from the centralized source is equivalent to the cost of reserve cataloguing (Rr—see page 150), giving the formula

$$£(9+c(0·1+(100-N)/6)+10 \times N \times Rf+(100-N) \times 10 \times Rr).$$

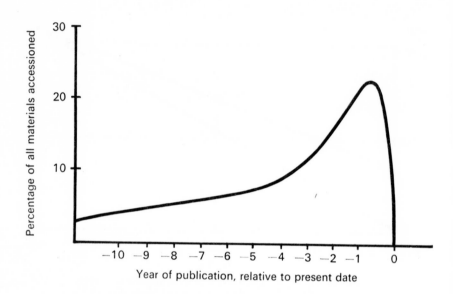

Figure 3. An imaginary intake pattern for a library. (See page 159.)

The proportion of a library's intake published in a given year is assumed to decrease with the increasing age of the material.

The peak of this curve, which is probably in roughly the same place for all libraries, will be most acute in special libraries, where topicality can be assumed to be of particular importance. In public libraries, with a regular demand for recently published English-language material and a selection policy based on *BNB*, it will be little different.

Some factors affecting this curve for university libraries are:

    (a) The need to build a comprehensive collection in many subject fields, in most European languages;

    (b) The creation of new courses of study;

    (c) Inadequate funds, leading to sporadic gap-filling as opportunity arises;

    (d) A relatively large number of gifts and bequests, containing material of all ages;

    (e) A tendency to wait for reviews before purchase;

and (f) An interest in older books for their own sake: special collections material.

   These tend to smooth out the curve; but gifts and bequests can also cause unexpected fluctuations.

SECTION IV

Management Criteria

Management Criteria in the Design of Systems for
Academic Libraries
by N. S. M. Cox

Computer Systems in Academic Libraries—Some
Aspects of Planning and Evaluation
by H. F. Dammers

Some Notes on Costs and Benefits
by N. S. M. Cox and C. K. Balmforth

Management Criteria in the Design of Systems for Academic Libraries

N. S. M. COX

In other papers in this volume, Balmforth, Grose and Jeffreys have reviewed some of the experiences of library automation in the last five years, and both Barraclough, Dews and Smethurst and Cox have outlined current trends and problems in the development of computing techniques for library automation; in addition, Robinson has described a basis for the analysis of the present activities in libraries and Coward, in two papers, has drawn attention to a body of machine-processable data of particular relevance to libraries today.

The aim of this paper is to direct attention to the problems facing management in terms of their responsibility for the design of computing systems, particularly in academic libraries. In doing this, attention is also drawn to other papers, from this volume and elsewhere, supporting the viewpoint that, within the next decade, the management of academic libraries will inevitably be involved in computing systems and showing that it is in the interests of academic libraries *at this time* to concern themselves with the evolution of computing techniques relevant to their discipline.

MAN OR MACHINE?

At the Brasenose Conference on the Automation of Libraries held in Oxford in the Summer of 1966, a paper was given jointly by representatives of The British Museum, The Bodleian Library, Oxford and the University Library, Cambridge (Chaplin, *et al.* 1967). This paper, it was hoped, was a harbinger of the future of the national libraries, and in true scholarly fashion, the authors began their paper with a quotation from Gibbon:

'When men were no longer found, their place was supplied by machines.'

This sentence emphasizes the main underlying problem of librarianship today . . . there is insufficient human resource available to meet all the *present* demands for service in libraries and it is unlikely that there will be sufficient resource to meet the future demands by conventional means. Either library service must deteriorate if demand increases or another means must be found to supplement the existing human resource. More recently than the Brasenose Conference, Dolby, Forsyth and Resnikoff (1968), in their final report on 'An evaluation of the utility and cost of computerized catalogs', summarized their findings as follows:

'A detailed study of several large university and public libraries shows that mature libraries grow at a rate very close to the rate of growth of the Gross National Product. Personnel costs tend to grow at a somewhat faster rate. As the size of the collection increases, the amount of access-per-item must also increase if adequate user access is to be insured. On the other hand the cost of computation is going down rapidly, and the technology to make use of computers in processing bibliographic records is at hand. In this context the primary conclusion of this study is that mechanization of the cataloguing function is not only necessary and desirable, but also inevitable.'
'It is recommended that over the next decade all but the smallest libraries should plan to automate their cataloguing operation. Once the main catalog has been put in machine-readable form, librarians should make use of the information it contains to produce printed book catalogs and special-purpose bibliographies for their users.'
'This same data base should also be used for continuing studies of the contents of the library to insure more efficient management of the collection. Librarians should also give greater thought to the possibility of selling printed copies of their catalogs and special-purpose bibliographies to the general public.'
'Librarians should support the development of text-processing computer languages to reduce programming and operating costs. The library community should establish a standing committee to continually monitor the cost of various library computer operations so that individual libraries will have up-to-date information for their costing activities and the computer industry can be informed as to the effect of new developments in technology on their library customers.'

This report concerns itself solely with the American scene and, although some of the detailed conclusions may be open to question it seems clear that the main conclusions are substantially valid for British libraries as well as those in the United States. It may be of interest to note that, in 1966 at the Brasenose Conference, Laslett pointed out the desirability and urgency of the development of a high-level computer language for use by librarians (Harrison and Laslett, 1967: p. 170). One of the contentions of this paper is that a suitable information processing environment is of primary importance to librarians both because of the facilities which such a language would provide and because of the way in which such an environment would give clarity to the search for standardization of codes of practice in libraries. However, it should be pointed out that, in the context of the report by Dolby, Forsyth and Resnikoff, text processing is only one part of the information processing capability required by libraries.

One of the difficulties in using a computer is getting to know the form or language used to feed in information and instructions. This is at a level of detail unfamiliar to the normal processes of human communication which, in practice, means that some considerable time and effort must be spent in learning a computer programming language. There is a need for a higher-level language which could be used by people without any training in computer science and which could be learnt after a relatively short period of study. Such a language would be more like the accepted words and patterns of normal discourse, simple to use, but flexible enough to deal with various tasks. There is as yet no fully developed higher level language specifically for bibliographical and library purposes, although experimental languages are being developed, for example, *LIBLANG* by Neville Harris at Trinity College Dublin, and *A-CODE* by the Symplegades Research Group at Newcastle. This latter example has been developed as part of the experimental environment of the 'Newcastle File Handling System' which was reported at the 1967 *Newcastle Seminar on the Organization and Handling of Bibliographic Records by Computer* (Cox and Dews, 1967; Dews, 1967; Millar, 1967; Hunt, 1967; Russell, 1967; Grose and Jones, 1967 and Coates and Nicholson, 1967). This work has proceeded (Dews and Smethurst, 1969) but its main importance has been the exploration of the nature of the information processing functions in libraries rather than any of the specific projects. The exploration of the nature of information processing functions in libraries, of course, bears heavily on the nature and function of the libraries; it is not clear in detail as to what university libraries are for . . . nor, for that matter, is it clear what universities are for. The nature of the library may depend quite

N

critically, for example, on whether research or undergraduate teaching is the main aim of the university.

THE NATURE OF THE LIBRARY

Many views have been expressed on the nature of the library from the point of view of information handling (Cox, *et al.*, 1966; Jolliffe, *et al.*, 1967; Overhage and Harman, 1965; Hayes, 1965; and many others). It is suggested here that the library comprizes five basic functions, namely *control, archive, service, co-operation* and *research and development*. This breakdown of activity is not necessarily convenient for looking at other aspects of the library (see, for example, Metcalf, 1965): however, in the context of library systems design, it seems to be closely related to the expenditure of both funds and effort in the library.

1. The *control* function covers, among other things, circulation, stocktaking, maintenance of catalogues and stocks, monitoring of the materials available for purchase, ordering, receipt, accessioning and cataloguing. In academic libraries, this is the dominant function occupying the major part of the human resource and about 50% of the finance; furthermore this function would not be much altered if there were no library users.

2. The *archive* function is mainly concerned with the building up of a representative collection of materials for the present and future generations of users and improving on the shortcomings of collections already built up. In the present financial climate, the majority of the resource allocated to this function may be devoted to the provision of material for the present generation of users in the hope that this will be an adequate basis for future generations. It is salutary to note that if one were to analyse acquisitions over the years, or even the distribution pattern of dates of publication of present collections, one would be able to see the 'good' and 'bad' financial years, rather like detecting the good and bad years by inspection of the rings on a tree-stump.

3. The *service* function, is at present, mainly devoted to personal guidance and assistance for users by members of the library's staff. This aspect of the library is, in particular, underfinanced and the attempts of librarians to provide adequate service in this respect is one of the major contributions to overwork by library staff. The author has never failed to be astonished at the small proportion of the annual library overhead which is devoted to the utilization of the enormous capital investment in library materials. The discussion paper by Dammers offers suggestions as to the way in which this pattern might change in the next decade. However, it is suggested that libraries show a very poor return on capital investment at the present time and that this situation must be rectified.

4. The *co-operative* function stems from the need to support the local service function by interaction with other services and archives, both local and national. At present, for most libraries, this may take the form of co-operative acquisition schemes (e.g. Hunt, 1955*), the provision of inter-library loan facilities by co-operation with the regional library bureaux; the use of the service provided by other libraries (notably perhaps the National Lending Library for Science and Technology) via the regional library bureaux; the use of national cataloguing services such as the British Museum *General Catalogue of Printed Books*, the *BNB* and its associated card services and similar foreign national bibliographies; collaboration in the generation of various union catalogues† such as the *British Union Catalogue of Periodicals;* and subscription to selected information services such as *Beilstein, Chemical Abstracts, Biological Abstracts* and *The Bookseller.*

and 5. The *research and development* function is that part of the activity of the library which contributes to the evolution of techniques of librarianship and may include personal reading by library staff, critical evaluation of new or modified techniques and services such as the new Anglo-American Code, specific research projects such as many of the projects presently being undertaken under the sponsorship of *OSTI* and, in particular, those concerned with the evaluation of the experimental British *MARC* Record Service, and formal discussion and planning concerned with the future of librarianship such as the various British Standards Institution panels.

The Parry Report (1967) devoted six paragraphs to data processing and computers (paragraphs 524–529) in which it was indicated that:

1. 'the increasing availability of data-processing machines is making experiment and use more readily possible on this side of the Atlantic;

2. 'if centralized or shared services should be able to reduce the intellectual efforts, the use of data-processing equipment can reduce the manual;

3. 'it is possible mechanically to keep the information up to date and to present it in different formats;

4. 'the use of data-processing equipment, whilst it enormously increases the output possibilities, demands an analysis of what output is desired before the input procedures are determined;

5. 'while complete library automation cannot be effective until the catalogue data are in machine-readable form, mechanical methods can be applied to separate processes;

6. 'retrieval and storage techniques seem likely to transform the format of publication in some fields;

* See also, for example, 'Parry Report' paragraphs 290-297.

† See also 'Parry Report' paragraphs 530-543.

7. 'in time, the library user may be able to interrogate the computer, at first about the records of documents and eventually about the actual contents of documents;

and 8. 'it is clear that university librarians, whose function is to make it as simple as possible for the scholar to find the literature and the information he wants, should concern themselves actively in research and development.'

In the context of data processing and computers, the report recommended:

1. 'that the [proposed] permanent UGC Sub-Committee on Libraries ... should consider what steps should be taken to secure the maximum degree of collaboration in these [shared cataloguing, etc.] developments;

2. 'that in making decisions about such acquisition and operation of [university computing services], account should be taken of growing library needs;

and 3. 'that, when government policy of supporting research into the broad field of information retrieval is being considered, the significance of its application to university libraries should be borne in mind.'

The most notable recent development in this field is, of course, the report of the National Libraries Committee (Chairman: Dr. F. S. Dainton), published in July 1969. After making detailed recommendations about the management of a future National Libraries Authority, the Committee recommended that 'the feasibility of applying automatic data processing to both the internal management operations and the services of the reference, indexing, bibliographic and administrative divisions of the *NLA* should be studied *in detail and without delay*' [our italics].

At the end of December 1969, the Government set up a project team under the direction of Maurice Line, Librarian of Bath University of Technology, 'to study the feasibility of applying *ADP* to the operations and services of the main material libraries and other organizations providing central services for the country's library system'. This study, costing up to £100,000, will last for about two years.

The speed with which this project was set up shows that central government is aware of the urgent need for an examination of library operations at the national level; the degree to which academic libraries and others will be involved in a national *ADP* library network remains to be seen.

This, then, is the context in which the design of computing systems for academic libraries should be discussed. It would seem, from perusal of the Parry report, that the attitude that the librarian need only be a scholar and that any fool could manage a library must now be dead. Library management is clearly sufficiently complex not to be entrusted to the 'educated' amateurs.

THE SYSTEMS DESIGN TEAM

The design of a computing system for all or part of the university library system will involve both the analysis of the existing activity (see the paper by Robinson), the establishment of the principles on which the system should be based and the costing and functional evaluation of the proposed system as well as the design of the system. To achieve an effective system it is therefore necessary to obtain the services of a group with a capability to conduct all these activities. In addition it is highly desirable that this group should have a special understanding of the nature of libraries and be familiar with current computing techniques for information processing. It is extremely unlikely that a library will be able to build up a group with this level of expertise; however, the library must, in a sense, evolve some sort of design and general computing capability if only to 'vet' the detailed proposals of the main design group, conduct systems evaluation and eventually be responsible for the maintenance of the system. Very few libraries are of a size to warrant a permanent systems design team and it is therefore probable that such a group will have to be obtained from outside the library. There is a fairly close parallel here between the design of a library building and the design of a library information processing system. In the planning of a building the library management committee or planning committee prepares a brief for the architect which is then discussed and a secondary brief prepared during the early stages of design. When the design has been approved, the architect acts as agent to the library during the implementation of this design, organizing and instructing various contractors. An important feature of the design and implementation of a building is the relationship built up between the architect and client both of whom, as the project progresses, obtain a more detailed understanding of each other's problems.

A similar mechanism would seem to be desirable in the planning, design and implementation of a library information processing system; however, a difficulty exists in that there are very few design groups at present capable of undertaking such a project and I would suggest that it is in the interests of library management to encourage the evolution of such services.

This will not be achieved by spreading those computer men and systems analysts, capable of contributing to such a project, around the libraries of this country: they are likely to be much more effective if they are concentrated into a small number of groups. It is probable that the national and copyright libraries are of a sufficient size to maintain their own design groups—for most other libraries the choice would seem to be either the establishment of a design team owned jointly by a number of libraries, or by inviting an outside group to undertake the system design.

It will be preferable to use the design group for a major part of the analysis of the present system, the design of the computer-based system, the control of the implementation of the various phases of this system and some parts of the functional evaluation of this system.

It is of considerable importance that the design group have a real understanding of the nature and function of libraries: too often the library has underrated the information processing problems and too often the computer men have misunderstood the level of complexity of the problems of librarianship.

Unfortunately this does not always come to light (Balmforth, Grose and Jeffreys). Some of the reporting of previous library automation projects seems to have been irresponsible—those concerned should recall the remark of the Polish Nobel prizewinner Henryk Sienkiewicz 'Kobieta nega to dzieto sztuki—kobieta w koszuli to pornografia' (A woman in the nude is art—a woman scantily clad is pornography). I suspect that such academic pornography has cost a considerable amount both in money, effort and time, and has done considerable disservice to librarianship.

SYSTEMS ANALYSIS

If one can assess the parallels between library and similar situations and identify the underlying principles, the design of an information processing system should be approached in two ways, the first being the breakdown of library activity into a number of sub-activities, such as cataloguing, user service, reference, circulation, periodicals handling and so on. Each aspect is to some extent related to the others and it is necessary to establish the details both of the individual activities and of the interrelationships between them. The techniques for conducting this breakdown and the establishment of the detailed functions of each of the aspects has already been discussed in the paper on Systems Analysis by Robinson.

The second approach to the design of systems is concerned with systems capability and relates to the provision of a general environment, the aspect with which the Symplegades Research Group, in Newcastle, was particularly concerned.

Most computing activities, in which the handling of a substantial body of information has been significant, have been designed in an environment where the function, data loading, and the rate of increase of data loading is known. This is true of payroll, banking operations and so on, in fact, many of the applications of data processing which are referred to by Laver (1965). The essential difference between this sort of activity and the activity in libraries, in which a computer is executing a service function, is that in the library these loadings and functions are not nearly so clearly defined.

In some circumstances, for example ordering, accessioning and circulation, there are close parallels between these 'payroll' data processing activities and the requirements for library systems. However, in many other activities—activities on which the effectiveness of the entire library system depends—the function and the loading on the system is at present indeterminate. In five years time, perhaps, when more experience has been gained, this may not be so but at the present time most of the key processing activities are only partially understood.

This distinction may be drawn quite clearly in terms of the concept of a *task* in which the required activity is completely pre-defined and the concept of the computing *environment* which it is hoped will meet tasks which have not yet been defined. In the design of computing systems for libraries, if one takes an overall view, it is therefore of importance to distinguish between *task* and *environment*; this distinction may well depend on the sort of benefits which the management require. If, in fact, library management are looking only for short-term benefits then they are likely to take the view that they can only afford to handle tasks. If, on the other hand, they are looking for longer term benefits, they will probably require to develop an environment in which they propose to meet new tasks when they arise, and here it is likely that the short-term costs will be very much higher.

GENERAL DESIGN CRITERIA

That library management should have the ability to see, in an overall fashion, what a computing system can provide is of major importance. It is therefore relevant to mention here some of the factors influencing the design of the system. I believe that the design of a computing system may have a profound influence on the function of a library; hence, the manager or the management committee must be in a position to appreciate what could be provided and thus make appropriate decisions based on the political and economic climate in which the decisions are required.

A number of elements exist in the design of a computing system; first of all there is the element of the automation of the existing activity, that is the replacement of present function by computerized function; secondly there is the element of re-fashioning the activity to take into account the special capabilities of the computer; and thirdly, and this is the potentially dangerous element, that of altering the system to make it possible to be able to computerize the activity. In this latter situation, there is at present a considerable danger in that the present understanding of the function of libraries by computer personnel and the understanding of computing capability by library personnel is too limited. There seems to be a fairly high tendency to alter the system to make it easier to computerize when this is not an absolute restriction in terms of technical feasibility. Hines and Harris (1966) provide an interesting example of this.

One of the problems in the assessment of the systems design, which has been highlighted in the paper by Robinson, is the difficulty of equating the functions of the proposed system with the properties of the existing system, where these may be heavily bound by contingency, and this may mask some of the unnecessary short-comings.

Various general criteria must be taken into account in the design of systems. These include:

1. the availability of hardware;

2. the design against contingency—the provision, within the designed system, of adequate resource to meet whatever conditions a breakdown of either the hardware or the software system might require;

3. the expectation of life of the system—the length of time before which it is expected that the nature of the tasks to be met has changed sufficiently to require that the system (or parts of it) should be re-designed and re-implemented;

4. the changes in personnel and the availability of personnel to meet the problems associated with the running of the designed system;

5. the resources required to meet the changeover, including:
   5.1 redeployment of staff,
   5.2 selection and recruitment of special staff,
   5.3 training of staff;

6. forecasts of the extent to which the new facilities will change the pattern of demand compared with the availability of resources to meet the demands;

7. anticipation of trends outside the system—change in teaching pattern. information needs within the community, changes in user habits, increase in size of the university, liaison with other establishments, etc.;

8. major changes within the system—is it likely that as the size of the total library system increases, it will become necessary to split the system, for example, into an arts library and a science library, or separate graduate and undergraduate libraries?

and 9. whether the system is to be designed for economy or performance—Marshall* has, on a previous occasion mentioned the problems of design for cash savings and Dammers, in his paper in this volume has stressed the need for increased service.

Management must also be aware of certain features consequent on the introduction of information processing activities into libraries. These include:

1. As the design of the library building influences the activities within it, so the design of the information processing system is likely to influence the activities associated with it.

2. As in a conventional system the requirements are bounded by the constraints and contingencies of the situation in which the system operates, so a computer-based system will also be bounded by similar constraints. Attention should be given to both the requirements of the 'ideal' situation and to the sorts of bounds which might, from time to time, be imposed on the automated system, and the systems design must take the latter into account.

3. The changeover from conventional to computer-based systems should be conducted both so that the activities of the library are not interrupted, and so that adequate 'overlap' is planned when both systems are in operation at the same time—this is likely to place heavy demands on staff and cause some congestion.

* Remark by H. A. J. Marshall in Cox and Grose (1967), p. 181.

4. Users are only interested in improvement in service, and, unless the introduction of computing systems is used for 'sales promotion', any changes in
the user's view of the library, without an improvement in service, will
cause frustration and should be avoided—an aim of the systems design
should be to achieve the changeover without the user realizing that a computing system has been introduced.

5. If wholesale automation is envisaged it is likely that the system will have
to be introduced in phases—to achieve an efficient overall system it will be
desirable to consider the design of the whole system before the first phase is
introduced. The first phase is, therefore, likely to be fairly costly to
introduce.

6. Libraries have to meet a wide range of problems posed by users and may
have to go to some lengths, on occasion, to solve them. A computer-based
system does not as readily permit casual consultation of the library files.
Furthermore, some of these user requests and the actions by the library to
satisfy them are sufficiently rare for it not to be realistic for the systems
analyst to anticipate them. This therefore requires, if standards are to be
maintained in an automated system, that:

6.1 library staff must acclimatize themselves to different accesses to
the working and archive data files—this will require training of
both senior and junior 'counter' staff,

and 6.2 the information processing system should be sufficiently flexible
to permit, perhaps at high cost, the ability to use the system to
answer specific queries.

FUNDAMENTAL DESIGN PRINCIPLES

Melvin S. Day, the Director of the Scientific and Technical
Information Division of the American National Aeronautics and
Space Administration, in a paper (Day, 1965) offered five
keywords—*Service, Timeliness, Decentralization, Compatibility* and
Modernization—as the basic principles for a national information
system and stressed that the system must operate 'not for the sake of
the system or its administrators, but for the sake of the customers'.
It is of importance, in the planning and implementation of this sort
of information system right from the start to lay down, in a similar
fashion, the principles on which the system is to be based. Furthermore, the principles on which you base your system must be agreed
by yourselves, the members of your staffs and your management
committees.

The approach taken in developing the *NASA* programme was to
establish 'a few immutable principles, a sort of fixed geometry into
which all operations must fit', thereafter maintaining as much
flexibility as possible within the boundaries set by these principles.

There are, no doubt, good and bad library management committees: it would seem to me to be the responsibility of the management committee to formulate and explain these principles—probably with considerable advice and assistance from senior library staff—thereafter leaving detailed considerations to the experts—the librarians and the systems designers. I would like particularly to commend those responsible for the management of the library at Trinity College, Dublin, in this respect. There are, no doubt, other institutions in which a clear directive has been given by the management committee; however I suspect that, in general in academic libraries, it will be necessary to educate the management committee in its duties before it is safe to embark on major plans for library automation.

RELATIONSHIP BETWEEN LIBRARY AND DESIGN GROUP

It has been said that librarians get the buildings they deserve (Brown, 1969)—there is a very close parallel here between the design and implementation of a library building and the design and implementation of a library information processing system. Similar to the design of a library building, the better the understanding of the underlying principles of the design of the information processing activity and the more attention given to the detailed briefing of the systems design group, then the better the job. The responsibility of ensuring a good brief, however, should be held jointly by the head of the design group and the librarian and a bad system is generally attributable to both parties. More attention could be given to the safeguards applied by architects to prevent misunderstanding between client and agent.

The architect/client professional relationship is fairly well evolved in libraries but much less experience is available in the professional relationship between systems designer and client. One of the main contributions of the present generation of library management will be to the evolution of this relationship. This will not be achieved without experience and understanding of the problems and expensive mistakes will be made. Two initial steps should be taken:

1. A mechanism should be set up to accumulate experience; this could perhaps take the form of the development of a 'checklist' which should be evaluated in the light of each new project by both library management and

the systems design group. An outline checklist (requiring a great deal of extension) was circulated at the 'Newcastle Seminar'. It could, perhaps, provide part of the basis for a study of this problem.

and 2. Both librarians and computer men should recognize the level of professional competence required in both fields. It seems to be traditional that every library user is an expert librarian, and computer men are (sometimes) library users. We are also only just reaching the point when the nature of information processing functions is becoming understood by computer men. It is of interest to note that the automation project currently in progress in the Library of Congress is costed at about three times their annual budget. In operations of this scale it would seem reasonable to ensure that those responsible for the design are professionally competent and that this is not likely to be realizable 'on the cheap'.

CONCLUSIONS

The view taken in this paper, therefore, is that library automation is an inevitable consequence of the expected demands for service placed on all but the smallest libraries and that management should prepare themselves. They should attempt to assimilate the management problems of all aspects of this automation and, in particular, should concern themselves at this time with their responsibilities in the design and implementation of computer based systems. The key to this is the establishment of the principles of design in their own libraries, and the evolution of a relationship with their design group, rather akin to the architect/client relationship in the design of library buildings. At least as much care should be taken in the selection of a design group as is taken in the selection of the architects for a new library building. It has been stressed that, when automated systems are introduced, they will fundamentally affect the operations of the library, and therefore the basic principles underlying design of the system are of critical importance both to management and to the users of the system.

Finally, it is appropriate to draw a parallel with automation in another field—the father of one of my colleagues, Grose, decided to introduce automation into gardening by purchasing a motor mower. His lawn is now five times as big.

Computer Systems in Academic Libraries—Some Aspects of Planning and Evaluation

H. F. DAMMERS

1. INTRODUCTION

The present paper was intended to discuss 'the functional evaluation of computer systems with particular reference to academic libraries'. Such an attempt, however, would appear to demand:

    1.1. A reasonably representative picture to be available of the type of environment presented by the university library.

    1.2. Consideration of the relationship, the interaction, of specific computer applications with other aspects of library operation. Such interaction may well affect any evaluation profoundly. This has resulted in the view, now gaining ground, that if they are to achieve significant gains in efficiency, libraries should use computers to move towards integrated systems rather than attempt the implementation of separate modules.

    1.3. An assessment of the relationship between computer facilities in the library and those in the university as a whole.

    1.4. Last but not least, some indication of the type and magnitude of future demands on library facilities and of the resources likely to be available to meet such demands.

Considerations such as those indicated above have resulted in a paper that differs in nature from the one originally envisaged; it tends to deal with long term planning and implementation rather than specifically with evaluation.

2. LONG TERM OBJECTIVES

The main objectives one aims at when implementing a computer operated system in the library/information field might perhaps be outlined as follows:

2.1. Greater flexibility of the system to adapt itself to changes in the volume and pattern of demand.

2.2. Improved utilization of existing resources, i.e. greater productivity; the main factor here is labour, which tends to represent the largest cost element, relatively as well as absolutely, in existing systems.

2.3. Better user/system interaction. A variety of reasons (e.g. changes in demand pattern, constraints on supply of adequately trained staff etc.) make it desirable that we should move towards systems that allow the user himself to adjust search strategy and systems performance to meet as closely as possible his specific requirement. Evidence is also accumulating that the use of a human mediator, as far as information retrieval is concerned, may be of doubtful value.

One will note that a straightforward cost benefit or labour saving is not mentioned as an objective in itself. The reason is that such cost assessments tend as a rule to be neither very helpful nor very meaningful in deciding on the merits of a new approach or system. Such aspects are more usefully dealt with in the context of the second objective mentioned, i.e. improved utilization of resources.

3. PRESENT RESOURCES AND THEIR USE

In order to place the resources available in perspective, it may be helpful to try to form an impression of what an average university, if there is such a thing, is like, as far as such an impression can be formed on the basis of a few statistical data. Table 1 gives some overall statistical information relevant to British universities. In connection with currently made comments on the considerable burden which higher education places on the taxpayer, it is of interest to note that ca. $0\cdot6\%$ of the G.N.P. is spent on the ca. $0\cdot4\%$ of the population receiving university education.

In order to arrive at the corresponding data for the 'average' university, we assume that we may divide figures such as those given in Table 1 by about 50; this works out at roughly one university per million inhabitants of this country. We thus arrive at the listing given in Table 2. It may be broadly representative for universities such as those of Bristol, Nottingham and Sheffield. Universities such as Oxford or Cambridge would be about double the average size, whereas newer universities would be only half the average size. The University of London complex stands out as an anomaly being eight to nine times the average size. One will note that ca. 60% of the total

TABLE 1. British universities: Some relevant statistical data

Expenditure per annum	£200 million +
Student population	ca 200,000
Investment since 1945	£500 million +
Staff teaching and research	25,000
other	35,000
total	60,000
Total UK population	ca 55 million
UK gross national product	ca £35,000 million

TABLE 2. The 'average' British university

		Range
Expenditure per annum	ca £4 million	(£500,000–£30,000,000)
Investment since 1945	ca £10 million	
Student population	ca 4000	(500–30,000)
Staff teaching and research	ca 500	
other	ca 700	
total	ca 1200	
Total expenditure on salaries and wages	£2·4 million (60% of total expense)	

TABLE 3. British university libraries: Some tentative statistics on current operations (1969)

Expenditure

Salaries	ca. £4·0 million (ca. 50%)
Books	ca. £2 million (ca. 25%)
Periodicals	ca. £1 million (ca. 13%)
Binding	ca. £½ million (ca. 6%)
Sundries	ca. £½ million (ca. 6%)
	ca. £8 million
	= ca. 4% of total university expenditure
Staff—total	2500–3000
Periodicals (titles)	ca. 150,000
Volumes—total stock	ca. 25 million
increase/annum	ca. 1 million
increase/annum of which books	ca. 750,000

expenditure is concerned with salaries and wages. It is also worth pointing out that the 'average' British university is rather small by current continental and American standards.

Using data given in reports of the University Grants Committee, one can produce a tabulation such as the one given in Table 3, which attempts to reflect the present (1969) situation as regards the university libraries. In this case salaries appear to account for ca. 50% of the library expenditure; the total staff effort involved in library operations in British universities is quite sizeable, i.e. of the order of 2500 for the U.K. as a whole.

Converting these figures to those for the library of the 'average' university, we get a picture as given in Table 4.

A point worth stressing is the total book acquisition. For all universities this might well amount to nearly three-quarter million volumes per annum. (The value of this is nearly £2 million, i.e. ca. $2\frac{1}{2}\%$ of the total value of annual U.K. book purchases). This is probably twice the total number of new books produced annually world-wide (see Table 5). It seems, however, unlikely that the number of different books bought by university libraries will be in excess of say 75,000. This would suggest that a given book may be obtained ca. ten times on average. Only for a very small proportion of the books is a library likely to obtain duplicate or multiple copies. Hence it seems realistic to assume that a given book is bought and catalogued by on average seven different university libraries (range probably 1 to 50).

The above figures were derived mostly from the current University Grants Committee (*UGC*) report 'Returns from Universities and University Colleges'. The data given in the *UGC* Report of the Committee on Libraries, 1967, including estimates provided by *SCONUL* as regards a desirable target for the 'average' university library, give a very similar picture. (Table 6).

The total library budget given in Figure 4 corresponds quite closely with the one indicated by *SCONUL* in 1965 (reprinted as *Appendix 8* of the Parry Report); so does the staff number, but the expenditure on salaries appears to be appreciably higher and, as a result, the acquisition of literature considerably less than suggested by the *SCONUL* standard.

It now seems opportune to have a brief look at the distribution of labour effort in the library. The rather scanty information available on this topic suggests a distribution as indicated in Table 7. It would appear that a very substantial proportion of the labour effort is

TABLE 4. The 'average' British university library

Expenditure	
Salaries	£80,000
Books	£40,000
Periodicals	£20,000
Binding	£10,000
Sundries	£10,000
Total	£160,000
Periodicals (titles)	3000
Volumes total stock	400,000
increase/annum	20,000
increase/annum of which books	15,000
Staff total	ca. 50
Capital value of library stock	say £1 million

For individual libraries these data vary over a range of ratio 1 : 15 or, 1 : 20; for the small libraries, one may have to divide the above figures by 3 to 5; for the larger ones, one may have to multiply them by a factor of 3 to 5.

TABLE 5. Assessment of the number of different books obtained annually by British university libraries

Annual book production (rough approximation)	
A. UK	ca. 25,000 (of which nearly 50% fiction)
B. USSR	ca. 75,000
C. USA	ca. 55,000
D. Others	ca. 100,000–150,000
Total	ca. 250,000–300,000 (of this 35–40% in English)

Rough guesstimate of the proportion obtained in British university libraries

Assumed 60% of books published in UK	15,000	(20%)
Assumed 40% of other books in English	30,000	(40%)
Assumed 20% of other books in foreign languages	30,000	(40%)
	75,000	

o

TABLE 6. Model annual university library budget according to *SCONUL*, 1965

(for university of 3000 undergraduates, 1000 research
students and 500 teaching staff)

Expenditure	£
Salaries	60,000
Books and multiple copies	52,000
Periodicals	21,000
Binding	15,250
Sundries	9,805
	£158,055
Periodicals (titles)	3000
Volumes—total stock	500,000
increase/annum	ca. 20,000
increase/annum of which books	ca. 16,000
Staff—total	50–55

TABLE 7. Staff utilization

	University library	Industrial library
Processing of current accessions (purchasing, cataloguing)	28	4
Reader services (loans—internal, external, circulation, photocopying, counter service, etc.)	12	4
Literature information (bibliography, SDI, etc.)	5	10
Library administration	5	2
	50	20
Research data and company literature processing		12

According to the *SCONUL* report, distribution of staff effort should be as follows: About one-third on reader service, 10% on administration, remainder on processing of current accession. This has been adhered to in the university library tabulation.

The industrial library figures are roughly based on data for the highly computer-oriented Sittingbourne library/information service. In order to make them comparable they have been multiplied by 3.

concerned with adding new information to the library, i.e. acquisition and cataloguing; this rather more so than with the utilization of the information present. One would feel that one of the objectives of computer use might well be to assist in adjusting this situation and shifting the emphasis towards information utilization. In connection with this, it is of interest to give some comparative figures for an industrial/library information service in which the need for information handling rather than document handling features usually quite high. The data in Table 7 bear this out.

A further comparison is given in Table 8. At Shell Research Limited, Sittingbourne, we spend on our centralized library and information services perhaps roughly one-third the amount indicated in Table 4 for the 'average' university library; in this respect, we resemble some of the smaller or newer universities. Also our graduate staff is about one-third of the teaching staff at the 'average' university. Furthermore, our expenditure on books, periodicals and binding is again nearly enough one-third of the corresponding expenditure listed in Table 4. Hence in Tables 7 and 8, the Sittingbourne data have been multiplied by three to make them comparable with those for the 'average' university library.

The Sittingbourne expenditure, however, includes a sizeable item for computer use compensated by a rather lower expenditure on salaries.

TABLE 8. University vs. Industrial library

Expenditure	University library	Industrial library
Literature purchase	£ 55,000	£ 55,000
Total	£160,000	£150,000
Periodicals	3000	2500
Volumes—total stock	400,000	75,000
increase/annum	20,000	7500
increase/annum of which books	15,000	2500
Staff—total	50	20
Users—teaching staff	500	
students	4000	
graduate staff		500
others		1000

The greater emphasis in a science-oriented industrial laboratory on journal literature and its exploitation and the lesser importance attributed to books is clearly suggested in Tables 7 and 8.

Even so, it would appear that the journal usage is of the same order if expressed in relation to the teaching staff in universities and the graduate staff in the industrial laboratories. In both cases, the number of journals taken works out at five to six per staff member.

As regards books, the university library appears to obtain roughly twice as many per user as the industrial research library.

4. EXPECTED USE PATTERN

The universities and hence also their libraries have during recent years experienced a period of rapid growth. Even though we may now be witnessing a phase of restraint, there are several reasons for expecting a further considerable growth in the demands on library/information facilities in universities during the next decade.

TABLE 9. British university libraries: Some factors leading to increased demand during next decade

		Increase	
		Per annum	In 10 years
A.	Proportion general population receiving higher education	10%	250%
B.	Growth of general population	1%	11%
C.	Flow of new literature	6%	80%
D.	More specialization/new subject fields		50–100%

Combined effect of the above factors might increase the demand on library facilities by a factor of 5 in 10 years, i.e. on average by 15-20% per annum.

Some of these have been set out in Table 9. Foremost among the factors likely to cause increased demand is the expected growth in the proportion of the general population receiving higher education. There are now about four students per 1000 of the population. It seems unlikely that we shall reach the present U.S.A. proportion of ca. 20 per 1000 even in ten years time, but it does not seem too far-fetched to assume that we may reach a proportion of ten per 1000 in ten years time. Moreover, the general population is likely to increase over that period by 10–12%. Hence the number of those receiving higher education may well increase nearly three-fold during the next ten years. Perhaps there will not be many new universities; more likely the existing ones will grow from the present average of 4000 students to an average of 10,000 to 12,000; there might then be no universities with less than 4000 to 5000 students, whereas the largest ones may well have to cope with 40,000 to 50,000 students.

As regards the annual flow of new literature, it seems realistic to assume that this will expand by ca. 6% per annum or by about 80% during the next ten years. Specialization, the creation of new subject fields, may well progress at the same pace as the expansion of new literature, i.e. there may be 50 to 100% more subject fields in ten years times than at present. Whatever the pace, this increase in specialization is going to add to the burden of the librarian as it increases the need for revision of classification/indexing procedures, creates more fringe areas and overlap etc.

Somehow it seems unlikely that we shall see the library resources (staff and finance) grow in proportion to the demand, i.e. by a factor of five (or 15–20%) per annum. At most one would expect an increase in proportion to the number of users (students, teaching and research staff). This might raise the annual budget of the 'average' university library to £400,000–£450,000 by 1978/79 (or about 11% per annum). Assuming 3% inflation per annum, it might be as high as £550,000–£600,000. If one is to meet the increased demand indicated earlier, it means that the productivity of the resources available, in particular staff, will have to be increased by 60 to 100% in ten years time or by say 6% per annum. In addition, the university library is likely to be called upon to provide more extensive user services, e.g. *SDI*. This will probably go together with the need for closer user-system interaction.

Hence the case for using computer facilities in university libraries would appear to be a strong one.

It has been suggested that much of the growth in higher education may be absorbed by the polytechnics, thus resulting in a lower cost per student.

A rough analysis shows that this should still leave the universities with a growth potential likely to cause doubling of the library budget in ten years time. Moreover, it may well be considered desirable for cost-efficiency reasons that the existing universities should grow substantially beyond their present average size.

5. SOME POSSIBLE APPROACHES

There have by now been a number of proposals and in several cases steps have been taken to achieve wholesale mechanization/automation of library system. The most ambitious of these proposals is no doubt that involving the automation of the Library of Congress (King *et al.*, 1963). This involves a system about fifty times the size of the average university library, or roughly the size of the combined U.K. university libraries; by any standard it is a formidable undertaking. The holdings total nearly 50 million documents (of which ca. 15 million bound volumes) and the proposal assumes that the automation leading to a network of libraries could be implemented for a sum between $50 and $75 million, i.e. about three times the annual library budget, whereas automation of *LC* alone would cost ca. $30 million or $1\frac{1}{2}$ times annual budget (Table 10). Although the automation was estimated to lead to a ca. 20% lower salary cost by 1972 compared with the projected cost for a manual system, it was felt that the aim of automation should be expansion of services rather than reduction of total operating costs. One point worth noticing is the investment involved in wholesale mechanization. The estimate that this investment will be in the range 1–3 times the annual budget would appear to hold also for smaller systems.

TABLE 10. Library of Congress: Automation

Annual budget—1959	$19·1 million
1961	$22·3 million
1972 (est.)	$38·8 million
Cost of automation—full network	$50–70 million
LC alone	ca. $30 million
Automation cost—hardware	ca. $16·7 million
software	ca. $11·6 million
file conversion	ca. $ 3·3 million
Annual operating cost 1972 automated system	$ 4·5 million
Annual operating cost 1972 manual system	$ 5 million

More than 200 consoles, located throughout the library, were expected to provide instant access to any storage file through the use of console keyboard and display/print facility.

It seems worth mentioning also an example of automation from the European scene. The University Library Bochum (Ruhr-University, Bochum) which now approximates in size to the 'average' British university library, had, as a newly founded library in 1963, the unique opportunity of obtaining a medium-sized computer installation (Siemens 3003) for the sole use of the library. The experience gained during the past five years has recently been reviewed (Pflug and Adams, 1968) and whilst it has apparently not led to a marked cost reduction compared with the conventional library, it has in most cases enabled considerable improvement in the services provided. Implementation has proved slower than envisaged and is now estimated to take ten years rather than the five years originally estimated. The project has shown rather dramatically the severe constraints imposed on automation when the computer system is grafted onto a traditional system approach. Even following the mechanization, the cataloguing costs still consisted for 85% of labour charges. Pflug himself comments on the 'astonishing resistance' of many traditional procedures to efforts to change and improve them. Perhaps it may be some consolation to him to point out that this phenomenon is not unique to the library scene. The resistence to change of well-established procedures, a case perhaps of homoeostasis, has as its positive aspect that it tends to preserve order and stability, its negative correlate however is that it does make innovation often very difficult indeed.

Neither of the cases mentioned is particularly relevant to the problem of implementing computer systems in British university libraries.

Like Bochum, however, they are likely to find that the development towards a large measure of automation will have to be extended over a period of ten years. This seems reasonable; although most of the British university libraries, unlike the Bochum library, are starting now with little or no direct access to computer facilities, the state of expertise and technology will enable much faster progress during the next decade than during the one which started five years ago. Hence one might take as a reasonable time-span for the automation effort the decade 1969–78.

The university librarian will aim to meet the following requirements during the next decade:

1. Meet the considerable increase of library duties resulting from university and literature expansion.

2. Avoid the library budget exceeding the present 4% of the university budget—in fact the libraries can count themselves lucky if they can maintain this share of the university budget—the percentage is more likely to decline as the university grows.

and 3. Expand considerably the literature information services (as distinct from the readers' services). This obviously constitutes an increase in demand which has to be met by improving productivity or by redeployment of existing staff.

The data in Table 7 suggest as areas where one should seek benefit from computer use, the processing of current accessions (purchasing, cataloguing etc.) and readers' services such as circulation, loans (internal and external, photocopying etc.).

With regard to the first item, there appear to be several feasible approaches towards better staff utilization:

1. One can make use of the computer in streamlining and integrating the purchasing/cataloguing procedures as indicated by Pflug and Adams, 1968 (p. 79).

2. One can in this utilize the facilities provided by the British *MARC* Record Service as described by Coward (1970). Here again the method of use will change according to the facilities available. Exchange of records on cards is likely to be replaced by the use of records on magnetic tape and by the use of telecommunication facilities with processing (matching of requests against master file) being done at *BNB*, regionally or on site.

and 3. One can act upon the fact that there is considerable duplication in book purchase (and cataloguing) as indicated earlier and come to mutual arrangements with other university libraries. Perhaps this might result in reducing the number of libraries purchasing the same book from seven to less than half this value. However, in order for this to be feasible, it requires direct communication between the libraries concerned, e.g. via teleprinter services—regular exchange of updated lists of holdings etc. Hence for this to be really feasible and work efficiently, one would again appear to need telecommunication/data processing facilities.

The case for rationalizing the processing of new accessions would appear to be a strong one. According to recent estimates, the cost of cataloguing and associated procedures appears to be of the order of £1 per book. If, as suggested earlier, a given book is bought on average by seven different university libraries, it would seem that ca. £7 is spent on its cataloguing in British universities; this amounts to roughly double its average purchase price. The university libraries buy between them ca. 750,000 books; of the cataloguing effort devoted to these new acquisitions the major part, equivalent to ca. £500,000 or ca. £10,000 per university library, would appear to be concerned with cataloguing books, which are also or have already been catalogued in one or more other university libraries. A situation like this would seem to merit some remedial action by the libraries individually as well as collectively.

With regard to readers' services, various libraries are now using computer-operated loan-control systems. As pointed out by Pflug and Adams (1968: p. 64) computer use enables quicker, and more reliable operation whilst at the same time freeing staff from much repetitive work. Our own experience has indicated that it can reduce the labour effort involved by 50–70%.

External loans seem bound to increase, not only because of mutual arrangements as suggested above, but also because quite apart from this, coverage by a specific library of the total relevant world literature is bound to decrease. This has been indicated in an earlier paper (Dammers, 1968) for an industrial library; it applies no doubt also to the university library. One would hope that in say five years' time a system for on-line use of a lending library, as outlined in the latter paper for journal literature, may begin to come into operation. Such a system would also reduce the need for much photocopying and for binding and associated labour effort. With regard to book loans, one might expect more widespread application of teletype networks for interloan operations. Such a system should interface with the library's own loan-control system; at first via a human operator, at a later stage automatically. Obviously developments of this type would require a large measure of inter-library co-operation.

Computer use should enable the university library to play a much more active part in literature information work, e.g. bibliographies together with indexes can be much more easily and quickly tabulated and indexed via keypunching and use of a *KWIC* indexing program. The library could also act as a useful intermediary between the academic users and data centres such as the *Chemical Abstracts*-based service at Nottingham, *MEDLARS* etc. It could, for instance, send profiles on tape, receive back hits (selected references) on tape and then arrange for printout on site followed by distribution. This would probably provide a more efficient method of operation than the one whereby every university user communicates with the data centre directly.

A variety of possibilities present themselves once the university library has the experience and the amenities to deal with computer-oriented information services.

We will now have to examine what may be involved in the way of systems organization and hardware.

6. SYSTEMS REQUIREMENTS

It is important in developing computer-oriented systems to adhere to a few commonsense guiding principles:

1. One should aim to start modestly, thus not involving an undue amount of capital and labour effort in the initial stages. Even the best planned comprehensive systems have a nasty habit of coming unstuck due to rapidly changing conditions. It is preferable, whenever feasible, to start in a modest but highly adaptive fashion thus building up experience, re-assessing one's goals and adjusting one's course as one goes along.

2. In order to be able to deploy one's resources in the most effective and adaptive manner, one should set one's sights five to ten years ahead. Hence the activities now should be guided by longer-term objectives. In this way, one has at least some reasonable chance of avoiding undue specialisation and obsolescence.

and 3. The investment in capital and labour in each stage of implementation should be justifiable in terms of short-term pay back as well as longer-term gains (growing experience, relevance to long-term objectives). At any stage, one should endeavour to make an effective use of existing technology and know-how.

Taking account of such considerations, we should now see how one might implement mechanization in the 'average' university library.

As indicated earlier, a period of ten years seems to provide a suitable time-scale for the implementation. We will assume that at the end of the period, the library budget will be of the order of £450,000 (ref. para 4). On the basis of present experience, one would expect that expenditure on computer equipment in the fully implemented system might be around 20% of the total budget, hence say £90,000 by the end of the 10 year period. This would cover payment of computer time, rentals, depreciation and maintenance.

This may appear to some to be a rather exorbitant expenditure on computer facilities. However, in order to put this into perspective, it should be stressed that some of the existing systems in libraries are anything but cheap.

In the average university library, the manual card catalogue probably represents an investment of at least one-quarter million pounds and more likely of half-million pounds.

The build up of computer facilities might now be perhaps indicated as given in Table 11. It should be noted that the growth of the library budget is assumed to be in step with the growth of the university, i.e. the library budget is expected to remain at 4% of the university budget. Of the annual increase in funds, ca. 20% is allocated to computer equipment during the first few years; this proportion, however, is likely to increase steadily. Whether this will occur in fact will obviously depend on a multitude of factors influencing the implementation during its course.

TABLE 11. The 'average' university library: Total annual budget and expenditure on computer equipment

Phase	Year	Library budget increasing by 11% pa	Expenditure on computer equipment	In relation to current annual budget (%)
	0	£160,000		
I	1	£178,000	£ 3,500	ca. 2
	2	£197,000	£ 8,000	ca. 4
II	3	£219,000	£13,000	ca. 6
	4	£243,000	£20,000	ca 8
III	5	£270,000	£27,000	ca. 10
	6	£300,000	£36,000	ca. 12
IV	7	£330,000	£46,000	ca. 14
	8	£368,000	£58,000	ca. 16
V	9	£408,000	£72,500	ca. 18
	10	£450,000	£90,000	ca. 20

The library budget is assumed to remain at 4 ca.% of the university budget.

One could visualize implementation in say five phases of two to three years each (Table 12).

Phase I (years 1–3)

Starting with a computer budget of £3500, this phase would see the installation of several keypunches, tape typewriters etc. and use off-line of, for example, the university computer or any other suitable computer system.

During this period one would initiate systems to deal with internal loans, journal holdings and subscriptions, computer production of bibliographies, *KWIC* indexes etc.

Phase II (years 3–5)

The computer budget has now grown to £13,000 and allows the installation of a terminal incorporating card *I/O*, paper *I/O*, fast printer, operating on-line to a suitable computer system, e.g. the university computer.

It means that many of the activities carried out off-line in Phase I can now be carried out much faster on-line. This should also considerably speed up system and program development work.

Phase III (years 5–7)

The computer budget (ca. £27,000) enables the terminal used in Phase II to be replaced by a small-to-medium size library computer system again operating on-line to a central computer system. The library computer would have several magnetic tape units thus enabling the processing of magnetic tape on site. By now the library would be involved in this to a considerable extent, not only for the maintenance of its own library operations (loans, bibliographies, subscriptions etc.) but also for the exchange of data with other data centres in this form (e.g. the *MARC* system, the *CAS* system at Nottingham, the *MEDLARS* system at Newcastle).

Phase IV (years 7–9)

During this phase further development of the library computer system takes place to include several access points (consoles) in the library department, the provision of multi-programming capabilities and disc storage in addition to magnetic tape storage. By this time, the national network may perhaps have developed to such an extent that it will allow on-line access to various data centres, reference libraries etc.

Phase V (years 9–10)

The end of the ten-year development period should see a fully developed system, incorporating graphic displays, on-line query facilities etc., established as part of a larger reasonably integrated information network.

Obviously the above only represents a thumbnail sketch of what a university library might do in the way of implementing a computer-oriented system. However, the course of development outlined appears reasonably well in balance with the possible financial resources, the available technology and overall national developments.

TABLE 12. Computer facilities in university libraries: phased implementation

Phase	Computer budget	Equipment	Applications
I	ca. £3500	Keypunches tape typewriters; off-line computer use	Loans system, journal listing, journal sub-scriptions, bibliographies
II	ca. £13,000	DCT 2000 type terminal +card and papertape read/punch; on-line processing	Building up of files in central computer
III	ca. £27,000	Library computer on-line to large university computer; several magnetic tape units	Processing of magnetic tape files in library. Exchange of tapes
IV	ca. £46,000	Several access points to library computer; tapes and discs, multi-programming capability	Establishing of on-line enquiry systems and display
V	ca. £72,500	Graphic displays; on-line query	Operation as part of large on-line network

The approach outlined would also allow for a gradual building up of experience within the library department as regards computer operation, system development etc.

It might be argued that university development and hence the demand on university libraries is unlikely to progress at the pace suggested earlier (para. 4). The adoption of a more cautious attitude in this respect would, however, not affect the implementation scheme profoundly; it would merely tend to stretch the implementation period from ten years to 12 or 13 years.

7. STAFF REQUIREMENTS

For a development as outlined above to be feasible, a number of conditions have to be fulfilled. One major assumption has already been discussed in some detail, i.e. the expectation that universities will go on growing substantially over the next ten years.

Another major condition is that existing staff can be retrained not only to operate the new facilities effectively but also to play a significant part in system development. This has been shown elsewhere to be feasible (Dammers, 1968); it is also essential if the system is to be well adapted to the library needs.

Moreover, without it the rate of development would be seriously hampered and financial means would prove inadequate.

Table 13 indicates how, during the ten-year period, staff effort might be channelled into computer system operation and implementation. In this tabulation the staff effort on computer activities has been related to computer expenditure by assuming a computer expenditure of ca. £2000 per computer operator/user at the beginning of the ten-year period, rising to £3000 at the end. It has also been assumed that programming and systems development will initially constitute one-third of the computer-oriented staff effort, falling to about one-sixth at the end of the 10-year period, with the total programming and systems development work over the ten-year period amounting to 25 to 30 man-years. It should be noted that the number of programming and systems development staff (four to five by year ten) is considerably less than the overall staff increase during the ten-year period. Hence such specialist staff could, if required, be attracted from outside the library. By and large, however, it is assumed that the staff needed for computer-oriented activities will be found by retraining existing staff.

Such training, particularly in the initial phase, will undoubtedly put a burden on staff resources. Fortunately, experience of the relatively modest systems to be used initially is fairly widespread, hence their introduction may not prove too difficult. Moreover, the library department should be able to obtain support from the university computer centre. Again, however, it should be stressed that if the library wants to be master of its own destiny, it should play a dominant role in its shaping as regards both planning and execution.

A guesstimate of what staff use might look like in the 'average' university library in ten years time is given in Table 14. Various rough assessments on the basis of existing experience suggest that it should be feasible to cope with the greatly increased workload envisaged ten years hence, whilst avoiding a substantial increase in staff numbers. To achieve this will require considerable skill in managing the transition; the proposed development would, without doubt, place a heavy burden on management. It would, therefore, be hardly

TABLE 13. Staff effort devoted to computer implementation during ten year development period

Year	Staff total	Computer Expenditure	Staff effort involved in computer system operation/implementation	
			Total	Programming/ Systems development
0	50			
1	52	£ 3,500	1½	½
2	53	£ 8,000	3½	1
3	54	£13,000	6	1½
4	55	£20,000	8½	2
5	56	£27,000	11	2½
6	57	£36,000	14	3
7	58	£46,000	17	3½
8	59	£58,000	21	4
9	60	£72,500	25½	4½
10	60	£90,000	30	4½
				27

TABLE 14. University libraries: Changes in staff use

	Present	In 10 years time
Processing of current acquisition (purchases and accession)	28	12 (20%)
Readers' service (loans, circulation, copying)	12	12 (20%)
Information service	5	18 (30%)
Computer operations	—	12 (20%)
Library administration	5	6 (10%)
Total number of staff in 'average' university library	50	60

surprising if they view developments of this nature with considerable reservation. However, one is likely to find that in particular the younger staff members concerned in library information work are keenly interested in this type of approach and in general quite capable of acquiring the skills required for its implementation.

8. SOME CONCLUDING REMARKS

The present paper has attempted to give an outline of the possible development of computer-oriented operation in university libraries.

It assumes that during the next decade the demands on the 'average' university library may well increase five-fold, whereas funds are at most likely to increase in proportion to those of the university as a whole, hence at most perhaps by factor of three during the next ten years. Overall productivity should therefore increase by at least 6% per annum.

Only through implementation of suitable computer-aided systems will it be feasible to achieve this improvement in productivity in a flexible and adaptive manner. Implementation along the lines indicated in this paper is likely to produce a change in the deployment of resources as shown in Table 15. It assumes only a minor increase in the number of staff but a considerable increase in their average salary. This will be unavoidable if the required gain in productivity (10–15% in relation to staff resources) is to be achieved.

TABLE 15. University libraries: Changes as reflected in budget

		Present	In 10 years time
A.	Salaries	£ 80,000	£200,000
B.	Books	£ 40,000 ⎫	£100,000
C.	Journals	£ 20,000 ⎭	
D.	Binding	£ 10,000	£ 10,000
E.	Sundries	£ 10,000	£ 50,000
F.	Computer facilities	—	£ 90,000
		£160,000	£450,000

A: Assumes increase in staff numbers by only 2-3% per annum but a rise of 7-8% per annum in average salary.

B and C: Assumes increase at 5-6% per annum.

D: Binding should relatively decline due to use of central data banks for retrieval of journal literature.

E: Increase due to greater need for stationery, tapes, miscellaneous equipment items.

Successful implementation along the lines indicated would at the same time imply economic justification; evaluation in this context amounts to assessing progress against annual targets. Admittedly the approach and targets have only been sketched in a very rudimentary fashion; it is, however, beyond the scope of the present paper to discuss the various aspects in greater detail.

Whether a transition of the type indicated will come about, and in the time scale suggested, will depend in part on interest in university education developing as we expect it should in order to meet the demands of a society undergoing rapid change.

First and foremost, however, it will depend on the determination and skill of those responsible for the management of libraries in bringing such a re-orientation about.

Some Notes on Costs and Benefits

N. S. M. Cox and C. K. Balmforth

When in the past librarians have attempted to justify changes in their system, before some management committee, both the justification and its refutation have been made on 'intellectual' grounds, supported arbitrarily from either side by imprecise costings and differing understandings of the communities being served by the library. In addition, even when the communities are well defined, understandings differ as to the properties and requirements of these groups. This paper attempts to clarify some of the bases for such arguments and suggests that it is high time that attempts be made to develop more effective cost models in terms of the communities served by libraries.

One approach to the problem, that of definition of the objection of a library, has been discussed by Cox (Management criteria in the design of systems for academic libraries). The paper by Balmforth, Grose and Jeffreys quotes both Marshall and Chapin on attitudes towards library budgeting.

The preceding paper (by Dammers) highlights the costs and benefits which are likely to require attempts at justification in the near future.

Another paper by Cox (On the introduction of machine-processable centralized cataloguing services to libraries) illustrates one, fairly straightforward, comparison between a cost (that of initiating a withdrawal policy) and a benefit (that of the space saved in the library as a result), both of which can clearly, though not completely, be expressed in cash terms.

Where both the cost and the saving can be realistically expressed in cash terms, the only problem is that of ensuring that the period between spending the money and obtaining the return is treated realistically. One cannot generally borrow money without paying interest and this should be taken into account in any major cost-benefit study—whether it be a proposed charge in practise or the comparison of two or more alternative schemes.

The justification for expenditure in library systems, however, must be looked at in two ways—the comparison of capital and running costs of two systems in which the end product is identical; and the assessment, in cash terms, of the benefits gained (or lost) in terms of the differences between the end products of the alternative schemes. These 'end products' may, of course, be either saleable commodities or services without direct cash equivalent. This is perhaps most conveniently visualised in terms of a concrete example.

A library decides to study the possibility of the introduction of a partially automated system into its cataloguing department by acquiring a typewriter. This typewriter makes possible the production of several catalogue slips at the same time, using carbon paper rather than manually re-copying the slips. The alternatives open to the library are:

    1.   retain the manual system;
    2a. rent a manual typewriter;
    2b. rent an electric typewriter;
    3a. purchase a manual typewriter;
and 3b. purchase an electric typewriter.

One, only, of these alternatives must be selected and the basis for comparison should include:

    1. Capital cost involved, interest payments on the capital deployed and how this capital is to be recovered;
    2. Running cost of each alternative, including both materials and labour;
and 3. Relative merits and demerits of each alternative other than those of pure cost.

This simple example illustrates some of the difficulties facing library management when attempting to justify changes in their system. Such difficulties, are, of course, magnified greatly when the justification is to be based on the introduction of computing systems to libraries.

If one was to assume, for a moment, that there was an absolute* justification for the introduction of a typewriter, then one is only concerned with the kind of typewriter and whether to purchase it or rent it.

* *Absolute* justification is taken here to imply that no satisfactory alternative exists and that it is not reasonable to cease the operation of the system.

H. A. J. Marshall presented a paper to the 'Newcastle Seminar' (On the justification of automatic data processing) which was circulated as a pre-print but is not published here as changes are being made to the particular costing method it described. The paper attempted to illustrate the method of costing *ADP* projects used in Government Departments, and Marshall stressed that, to undertake comparative costing of alternatives, it was necessary to have estimates of the cost of equipment, computer usage, systems design and so on. In addition, such methods of comparison do not take into account the indirect benefits—the relative merits and demerits—of the alternatives, for these are only relevant to the question of relative economic feasibility.

The basic method is to forecast the costs, over a number of years, of the alternatives including where appropriate a continuation of the present system in its most improved form. A discount factor is applied to the yearly differences between the costs to obtain a present value for the proposed investment. This method is illustrated below.

Marshall points out that such an exercise not only helps to produce a true picture, but has a salutary effect, due to the discipline demanded by detailed costing, in highlighting omissions or inefficient systems design.

From the point of view of library systems, it seems likely that the justification for the system is generally on other than economic grounds. The production of a library, from the point of view of the community which it serves, is measured in large terms associated with the materials available to the users and the speed and convenience, to them, of the method by which the information is provided. It is therefore highly desirable that, if changes in library systems are to be viewed realistically, there should be developed a model of the relationships which exist between the library and the communities which it serves to permit an effective evaluation in cash terms of the services which the library provides to its users. It is not claimed that this is an easy task; however it is a task which should be undertaken for, until such a model is developed and applied, its inadequacies will not be discovered and no progress is likely towards an agreed basis for cost-benefit analysis in libraries, and this 'justification' will continue to be argued on doubtful 'intellectual' grounds.

One can, however, limit the area of doubt in considering the replacement of existing library systems. Let us assume a proposal to replace an existing system by a new system. Many of the features of the old system will be exactly mirrored in the new. Some of the desirable features of the old system may be lost and a number of both desirable and undesirable features will occur in the new system. One can, therefore, compare the efficacy of the two systems in a fairly arbitrary fashion.

If one disregards the features common to both systems, one can develop a table of advantages and disadvantages gained and lost. Some of these may cancel out as being of the same order of magnitude leaving a residual difference in performance between the two systems. One is then left with a comparison between this difference in performance and the difference in costs.

This may be illustrated in terms of the proposed acquisition of a typewriter.

Alternative 1
> *Maintain the existing manuscript system, but improve it by using carbon paper to give multiple copies.*
> Capital outlay: Nil.
> Operating cost: 150 sets of cards per man-week;
> carbon paper £0·40 per man-week.

Alternative 2a
> *Rent a manual typewriter*
> Capital outlay: Nil.
> Operating cost: 200 sets of cards per man-week;
> typewriter rental (including maintenance) £1·25 per week;
> carbon paper £0·66 per man-week.

Alternative 2b
> *Rent an electric typewriter*
> Capital outlay: Nil.
> Operating cost: 220 sets of cards per man-week;
> typewriter rental (including maintenance) £2·40 per week;
> carbon paper £0·73 per man-week.

Alternative 3a
> *Purchase a manual typewriter*
> Capital outlay: £102
> Operating cost: 200 sets of cards per man-week;
> servicing of typewriter £0·09 per week;
> carbon paper, ribbon, etc. £0·66 per man-week.

Alternative 3b

    Purchase an electric typewriter
    Capital outlay: £328
    Operating cost: 220 sets of cards per week;
    servicing of typewriter £0·28 per week;
    carbon paper, ribbon, etc. £0·73 per man-week.

If the operator of the system is paid £1,600 p.a. (including superannuation, etc.), works for 49 weeks per year, is away sick for, on average, one week per year, and the required annual production of catalogue cards is 50,000 sets per year, one can compare the cost of the various alternatives. Depreciation of the typewriters is taken as fixed equal sums over seven years.

Alternative 1

    Capital outlay: Nil
    Number of operators required: 7 giving capacity of 50,400 sets of cards p.a.

Annual operating cost: Personnel	£11,200	
Materials	£ 134	
Total	£11,334	

Alternative 2a

    Capital outlay: Nil
    Number of operators required: 6, giving capacity of 57,600 sets of cards p.a.

Annual operating cost: Personnel	£ 9,600
Equipment rental	£ 360
Materials	£ 190
Total	£10,150

Alternative 2b

    Capital outlay: Nil
    Number of operators required: 5, giving capacity of 52,800 sets of cards p.a.

Annual operating cost: Personnel	£8,000
Equipment rental	£ 573
Materials	£ 175
Total	£8,748

Alternative 3a

    Capital outlay: £612
    Number of operators required: 6, giving a capacity of 57,600 sets of cards p.a.

Annual operating cost: Personnel	£9,600
Equipment maintenance	£ 27
Materials	£ 190
Capital depreciation	£ 87
Total	£9,904

Alternative 3b

    Capital outlay £1,640
    Number of operators required: 5, giving a capacity of 52,800 sets of cards p.a.

Annual operating cost: Personnel	£8,000	
Equipment maintenance	£ 70	
Materials	£ 175	
Capital depreciation	£ 234	
Total	£8,479	

Note the disparity in material cost in both the *a* and *b* alternatives. This cannot be justified, as both machines have identical materials requirements. The disparity arises from costing the materials on the basis of the capacity of the operators rather than their throughput. Materials cost for the typewriter systems ought to be £170 in all cases. On the other hand, complete units are required (i.e. whole typewriters and whole people) even though this gives space capacity.

This exercise illustrates the way in which a check can be made on costing and on assumptions about the operation of the system.

More complex situations, such as the introduction of computing systems, will require proper discounted cash flows to be determined, particularly where high capital investment (and associated interest charges and depreciation) provides a major contribution to the running costs.

A table of the type shown below is of use in determining the acceptability of a new system:

	Old System			New System
A	Undesirable features to be lost in new system		D	Undesirable features gained with new system
B	features common to both systems	(B=E)	E	features common to both systems
C	desirable features lost in new system		F	desirable features gained in new system

The test of acceptability is therefore whether the increase in cost (which may be in fact negative) is less or greater than the total net gain of desirable features $(A - D + F - C)$.

To illustrate some of the problems of determining cash values, even on a 'difference' basis, some of the features which might be compared in a 'typical' order system are given below:

A.   *Undesirable features lost in the new system*
1. Large manually-maintained files, with problems of filing and storage.
2. A separate accounts system, necessitating transfer and re-creation of records.
3. Manually extracted lists of overdue books and books received.

and 4. Other manual duplication of a single central file or parts of it.

C.   *Desirable features lost in the new system*
1. Immediate access and up-dating.

and 2. Library control over all parts of the operation.

D.   *Undesirable features gained in the new system*
1. Dependence on a machine, probably not owned by Library.
2. Possibly similar dependence on non-Library staff for system development, etc.
3. Up-dating at intervals only.
4. Form of record dictated by machine requirements.
5. Regular and perhaps expensive changes in system due to developments in hardware.

and 6. Cost of systems analysis and development, extra to the actual running costs.

F.   *Desirable features gained in new system*
1. Ability to print out listings and selection at will, without further manual intervention.
2. Protection against wage-inflation, by reduced dependence on staff.
3. Increased financial control.
4. Possibility of system checking for duplicating (by *ISBN* for example), thus reducing inadvertent duplication.
5. Reduced space needed to house the system.
6. Greater convenience and legibility of book form printout, compared with cared-file.
7. Records available to accessioning and cataloguing sections in machine-readable form.

and 8. Centrally-produced machine-readable records available.

The basic staff being either junior or acquisitions clerks or key-punchers, are probably comparable in cost; but the new system provides benefit not otherwise attainable without extra staff.

Such an analysis also has the advantage that it is of great assistance to a systems analyst as well as for cost justification, and indeed one further justification of any analysis might well be that for librarians to look critically at their processes at this level of detail can be nothing but salutary.

In employing criteria of this kind when attempting to justify a new system to a lay committee it is of course crucial to establish a common basis of agreement before embarking on a detailed exposition of cost and benefit. If no common undertaking exists about the objectives of the library and the needs of the community none but the most general enquiries ('may books be borrowed?') can be answered—and not always those.

TAILPIECE

Automation and Librarians: discussions at the Newcastle Seminar on the Management of Computing Activity in Academic Libraries
by C. J. Hunt

References

Glossary

Index

Automation and Librarians: discussions at the Newcastle Seminar on the Management of Computing Activity in Academic Libraries

C. J. HUNT

The papers presented at the Newcastle Seminar on the Management of Computing Activity in Academic Libraries were preprinted. Each session consisted of a brief presentation of a paper, followed by extensive discussion which ranged over three broad areas—cost justification of library systems, both automated and manual: the initiation and staffing of computing activity in academic libraries; and the relationship between individual libraries and a national library system. The intention of this paper is to record some of the salient points made in the discussions.

Mr. H. A. J. Marshall, of H.M. Treasury, during the introduction to his paper mentioned that he had originally been asked to give a paper on cost justification in academic libraries. However, he had no doubt that 'this particular nasty job' was entirely for the librarian, and he could advise only on methodology. There was a general feeling expressed at almost every session of the Seminar that proper costing is fundamental to the development of automated library systems, but considerable divergencies in result emerged from the various libraries that had attempted it on specific manual systems. Stated costs for cataloguing varied from 'about ten shillings' to 'over a pound' per item; one library's figure was 16/7½d., which Mr. Marshall found 'too misleading for words, because it is just too accurate'.

Differences in methodology of costing apart, a fundamental difficulty in comparing a particular system in one library with the same in another, or with a mechanized system, is that library procedures frequently tend to be old, overstrained and run-down, producing far from ideal results. To obtain meaningful figures it is often necessary to cost not what *is being done* but what *should be done* for the system to achieve its full purpose. By this extended yardstick mechanized systems become more feasible.

The relatively few people employed in British academic libraries, combined with the fact that staff costs are much lower than in the United States although computer costs are much the same, make it difficult to draw up a case for computerizing a system by proving the overwhelming argument that money would be saved by using a computer; the indirect benefits offered—those 'extras' which a manual system cannot give—have to be measured and their value proved.

There was considerable argument about the costing of computer time. In most universities, the library is given this time without charge by the computer department. Professor E. S. Page of the University of Newcastle upon Tyne Computing Laboratory felt that it was nonsense to consider charging for a service which almost literally cost the computer installation nothing, as the machine would otherwise be standing idle in the intervals between its proper task of carrying out research. Mr. Marshall argued that, even if no charge were made, the system should be costed as though it were, for otherwise the costing would have no validity. While most librarians tended to agree with the principle they doubted the practical utility of assuming that the library existed in a market situation within the university. It was possible, however, that in the future libraries might be in just this position if there were changes in the policy of the Computer Board.

In H.M. Treasury apparently the term 'computeritis' is used to describe the state of mind of those 'who have spent three or four months working like the devil on a scheme, and when they come off at the end it isn't worth doing; it's very hard indeed to drop it, and they are going to bend over backwards to find some justification.' This state of mind is not unknown among librarians, and there was much talk at the Seminar about how libraries should enter the brave new world, and a little detail about how in fact some of them had done so. The metaphor of the architect's relationship with his librarian client was much invoked, although it was forcibly pointed out that, judging by past experience, this was not altogether a hopeful comparison.

A professional systems design team available for consultation and for hire to carry out specific tasks would allow the rare and expensive expertise in this field to be shared by many libraries. Some libraries have created the post of systems analyst within their own staff hierarchies, but this could lead to potential clashes of authority within the staff structure; a professional team called in from outside avoids the danger of such conflict.

Most British academic libraries which began computing activity early did so in rather less than a formal spirit of scientific management. Accident, the fortuitous interplay of personalities, and even the atmosphere of the Senior Common Room bar were apparently the most important factors. Library computing activity began because computer time was available, and costing was very much a secondary activity. Those pioneering days, however, are now most definitely over, to be succeeded by a hard-headed consciousness that such adventures cannot be entered into lightly.

One significant point, mentioned by a number of librarians at the Seminar, was that little difficulty had been found in getting library staff to adapt themselves to mechanized systems. A week's hard work at a programming course was enough for basic concepts and—as important—the jargon, to be picked up. The revolutionary implications of computerized techniques are sufficient to inspire younger staff to work at them with unbounded enthusiasm.

Inevitably much of the discussion was about 'standardization' and 'centralization'. The overwhelming pressure forcing individual libraries to become 'part of the maine' is undoubtedly the ever-increasing volume of literature being produced and the consequent relative decrease of any one library's coverage of this literature. Running a close second to this is the desire to lessen the duplication of work in British academic libraries, to take the most skilled staff away from processing and put them into reader services. Mr. R. E. Coward of the British National Bibliography Ltd. remarked that 'American university libraries will go to almost any length to avoid cataloguing themselves'. Until recently this has not been a feature of their British equivalents; now, however, enthusiasm for centralized cataloguing is matched only by the frustration of trying to adopt it. The computer does not offer an easy way out of traditional dilemmas; it intensifies them.

Project *MARC*, as a means of providing machine-readable records for local catalogue use, was the subject of much discussion, and a number of fundamental difficulties were raised and examined, if not solved. These included the problems of matching books and records, which will become more and more expensive as the file of records grows, particularly if the file is 'linear', and of continuing to catalogue books locally because no machine-readable records have been centrally produced—the number of these will become smaller and smaller as international coverage increases and work is done on converting retrospective files. The most acute problem, however, and one central to all the discussions at the Seminar, was the future nature of local catalogues. What should be their physical form? On-line interrogation would appear to be too expensive, even if desirable, which in many cases is doubtful. Using centrally-supplied magnetic tapes to print out catalogue cards locally does not appear to be a very useful operation. The attractive alternative of a regularly cumulated book catalogue is the obvious choice—but the length of each record becomes a dominating economic factor, which it never has been in a card catalogue. What information should be in a catalogue, and how should it be arranged? In the past librarians have manually altered, added or deleted information, particularly the form of the descriptors governing the arrangement, to fit the local catalogue file. The costs of doing this are not trivial, and form the basic reason why many librarians have never used purchased catalogue cards. The computer costs of such alterations are not only more substantial but more obvious. Local deviations from national standards require far more rigorous examination and justification than in the past.

Up to now, the use of computers has been dominated by local circumstances. No British library has a computer of its own; each uses the machine of its parent body. The national libraries, without parent bodies owning computers, have therefore been rather at a disadvantage in experimentation—their schemes have been subject to Treasury cost analysis from the start. The future pattern of use of computers is uncertain; it may well be that the best development would be a national computer grid explicitly for library use. In any case standards must be set to allow systems to become compatible and economic. At the moment libraries are autonomous institutions —at least from each other. If they are to retain their independence, agreed solutions to these problems must be found, or the solutions will be imposed from above.

The overall impression gained at the Seminar was that academic librarians are now very much aware of the potential advantages of computerization and are prepared to recognize the changes in procedure and emphasis consequent upon the introduction of mechanized systems. Perhaps the fundamental danger now facing these librarians is that they may accept a greater simplification of the library function than is really essential and this could lead to unnecessary long-term damage.

References

Adams, B. *See* Pflug and Adams (1968).

Adkinson, B. W. and Stearns, C. M. (1967). Libraries and machines—a review. *American documentation*, Vol. 18, July 1967.

Allen, J. A. (1969). A computerized issue system in Brighton Public Libraries. *Program*, Vol. 3, No. 3/4, 115–119.

Annual review of information science and technology, Vol. 1, 1966 (in continuation). New York, Interscience for American Documentation Institute.

Ash, L. (1963). Yale's selective book retirement program. Hamden, Conn., Archon Books.

Association of Research Libraries (1970). Minutes of the 75th meeting, January 1970, p. 115. Washington, D.C.

Austin, D. *see* British National Bibliography (1969b).

Average book prices (1968). *Library Association record*, Vol. 70, No. 9, September 1968, p. 233.

Average book prices (1969). *Library Association record*, Vol. 71, No. 8, August 1969, p. 246.

Avram, H. D. (1968). *The MARC pilot project: final report on a project sponsored by the Council on Library Resources, Inc.* Washington, D.C. Library of Congress, 183 p.

Batty, G. D. (ed). *See* Davie (1966); Howard (1967).

Bearman, H. K. G. (1968). Library computerization in West Sussex. *Program*, Vol. 2, No. 2, July 1968, p. 53–56.

Becker, J. (1965). Using computers in a new university library. *ALA bulletin*, Vol. 59, October 1965, p. 823. (Includes a short bibliography of articles about the library of Florida Atlantic.)

Bennett, F. (1968). Mergers and catalogues. *Library Association record*, Vol. 70, No. 4, April 1968, pp. 100–102.

Birmingham libraries joint research on British *MARC* (1969). *Catalogue and index*, No. 13, January 1969, p, 12.

Blackwell, J. (1970). The impact of mechanization on the book world. *Aslib proceedings*, Vol. 22, No. 3, pp. 102–108.

Bochum. University Library. *See* Pflug (1968).

Bregzis, R. (1965). The Ontario new universities library project—an automated bibliographic data control system. *College and research libraries*, Vol. 26, November 1965, p. 495.

Bregzis, R. (1967). *The University of Toronto/MARC pilot project*, in Cox and Grose (1967).

British National Bibliography (1968). *BNB MARC* documentation service publications. No. 1: *MARC* record service proposals, presented by R. E. Coward. London, British National Bibliography, Ltd.

British National Bibliography (1969a). *BNB MARC* documentation service publications. No. 2: *MARC II* specifications (March 1969). London, British National Bibliography, Ltd.

British National Bibliography (1969b). *BNB MARC* documentation service publications. No. 3: PRECIS; a rotated subject index system, by Derek Austin and Peter Butcher. London, British National Bibliography, Ltd.

Brown, H. F. (1969). *Academic library planning:* paper presented to the University College and Research Group of the Library Association, January Meeting, 1969.

Bryan, H. (1966). American automation in action. *Australian library journal*, Vol. 15, August 1966, p. 127. (Reprinted in *Library journal*, Vol. 92, No. 2, January 15, 1967, p. 189).

Butcher, P. *see* British National Bibliography. (1969b).

Camden. *Borough. Libraries and arts department* (1970). Notes on computer charging. *Staff information sheet* No. 9, 1–4.

Cammack, F. M. (1965). Remote-control circulation [at the University of Hawaii]. *College and research libraries*, Vol. 26, May 1965, p. 213.

Carroll, D. E. (ed). *See* Chapin (1967), Payne (1967).

Carter, K. (1968). Dorset county library: computers and cataloguing. *Program*, Vol. 2, No. 2 (1968) pp. 59–67.

Cataloguing by computer (1966). *ICT data processing journal, 28*. (Reprinted in *An Leabharlan*, Vol. 25, No. 1 (1967) pp. 26–29.)

Cayless, C. F. and Kimber, R. T. (1969). The Birmingham libraries cooperative mechanization project. *Program*, Vol. 3, No. 2, pp. 75–79.

Chapin, R. E. (1967). Administrative and economic considerations for library automation, *in* University of Illinois Graduate School of Library Science: *Proceedings of the 1967 Clinic on library applications of data processing.* Edited by D. E. Carroll. pp. 55–69. Champaign, Illinois, Illini Union Bookstore.

Chaplin, A. H., Shackleton, R. and Oates, J. C. T. (1967). *Needs and aims: the situation at the British Museum, the Bodleian Library, Oxford and the Cambridge University Library*, in Harrison and Laslett (1967).

Childers, T., *et al* (1967). *Book catalog and card catalog; a cost and service study.* Towson, Maryland, Baltimore County Public Library. Includes reprints of the articles by Robinson (1965) and Kieffer (1966).

Clapp, V. W. (1967). Retrospect and prospect [on co-operative and centralized cataloguing]. *Library trends*, Vol. 16, No. 1, July 1967, pp. 165–175.

Coates, E. J. and Nicholson, I. (1967). *British Technology Index—a study of the application of computer processing to index production*, in Cox and Grose (1967).

Coblans, H. (1966). *Use of mechanized methods in documentation work.* London, Aslib.

Coward, R. E. (1967). *United Kingdom MARC record service*, in Cox and Grose (1967).

Coward, R. E. (1968). *MARC* project. *Assistant librarian*, Vol. 61, pp. 174–175.

Cowburn, L. M. and Enright, B. J. (1968). Computerized U.D.C. subject index in The City University Library. *Program*, No. 8, January 1968, p. 1.
(In the same issue of *Program* D. G. Hanson gives the computer program for this subject index.)

Cox, N. S. M. (1970*a*). The Newcastle File Handling System—phase 1: an experimental information processing environment. *Bull. I.M.A.*, Vol. 6, No. 1, April 1970, pp. 47–41.

Cox, N. S. M. (1970*b*). *Present-day performance standards.* Paper presented to the Oriel Computer Services Limited/Kynoch Press Seminar on *The Integration of computer-based information into printing techniques*, 17th April, 1970.

Cox, N. S. M. and Davies, R. S. (1970*a*). On the communication of machine-processable bibliographical records. Part I: an analysis of the draft British Standard. *Program*, Vol. 4, No. 3, pp. 89–98.

Cox, N. S. M. and Davies, R. S. (1970*b*). On the communication of machine-processable bibliographical records. Part II: the 'Newcastle' communications format. *Program*, Vol. 4, No. 3, pp. 99–115.

Cox, N. S. M. and Davies, R. S. (1970*c*). On the communication of machine-processable bibliographical records. Part III: the communication format access-language. *Program*, Vol. 4, No. 3, pp. 116–129.

Cox, N. S. M. and Davies, R. S. (1970*d*). The indexing of records in the Public Record Office. University of Newcastle upon Tyne, Computing Laboratory.

Cox, N. S. M. and Dews, J. D. *The Newcastle File Handling System, in* Cox and Grose (1967).

Cox, N. S. M., Dews, J. D. and Dolby, J. L. (1966). *The computer and the library; the role of the computer in the organization and handling of information in libraries.* Newcastle upon Tyne, University Library.

Cox, N. S. M. and Grose, M. W. (eds.) (1967). *Organization and handling of biblio-graphic records by computer.* Newcastle upon Tyne, Oriel Press.

Crisis in L.C. card service (1970). *Catalogue and Index*, No. 18, April 1970, p. 13.

Dainton, F. S. [report]. *See* National Libraries Committee (1969).

Dammers, H. F. (1968). Integrated information processing and the case for a national network. *Information storage and retrieval*, Vol. 4, pp. 113–131.

Dawson, J. M. (1967). The Library of Congress: its role in co-operative and centralized cataloging. *Library Trends*, Vol. 16, No. 1, July 1967, pp. 85–96.

Davie, C. K. (1966). Administration and the computer: the context for libraries. *In The library and the machine*, ed. C. D. Batty, pp. 4–20. Scunthorpe, North Midland Branch of the Library Association.

Davies, J. (1965). *Automatic data processing and the public library.* In Library Association. Proceedings, papers, summaries of discussions at the Public Libraries Conference held at Eastbourne 1965, pp. 17–26.

Davies, J. R. (1960). Punched cards in the library and information fields. *Aslib proceedings*, Vol. 12, No. 3, pp. 101–108.

Davies, R. S. *see* Cox and Davies (1970).

Day, M. S. (1965). *Applications of basic principles in the design and operation of a large information system, in* Rubinoff, M. (ed.), *Towards a national information system*, London, Macmillan, 1965.

De Gennaro, R. (1968). Automation in the Harvard College Library. *Harvard Library bulletin*, Vol. 16, No. 3, July 1968, p. 217.

Dewey, M. (1877). Co-operative cataloging. *Library journal*, Vol. 1, January 1877, p. 170.

Dews, J. D. (1967). *The Union List of Periodicals in Institute of Education Libraries*, in Cox and Grose (1967).

Dews, J. D. and Smethurst, J. M. (1969). *The Union List of Periodicals in Institutes of Education processing system*, [Symplegades, No. 1], Newcastle upon Tyne, Oriel Press Ltd.

Dix, William S. (1967). Centralized cataloging and university libraries—Title II, Part C, of the Higher Education Act of 1965. *Library Trends*, Vol. 16, No. 1, July 1967, pp. 97–111.

Dolby, J. L., Forsyth, V. and Resnikoff, H. L. (1968). *An evaluation of the utility and cost of computerized library catalogs*, U.S. Department of Health, Education and Welfare, Final Report, Project No. 7-1182.

Dougherty *see* Leonard (1969).

Driver, E. H. C., Duchesne, R. M., Hall, A. R. and Wilkins, D. J. (1970). The Birmingham Libraries' cooperative mechanisation project: a further report. *Program*, Vol. 4, no. 4, October 1970, pp. 150–155.

Duchac, K. (1967). Evaluation of the processing centers. *Library Trends*, Vol. 16, No. 1, July 1967, pp. 14–22.

Duchesne, R. M. (1969). Birmingham libraries co-operative mechanization project. *Program*, Vol. 3, nos. 3/4, pp. 106–110.

Duchesne, R. M. *see also* Driver, *et al.* (1970).

Edmunds, H. P. *See* King, *et al.* (1963).

Enright, B. J. *See* Cowburn and Enright (1968).

Flood, M. M. *See* King, *et al.* (1963).

Florida Atlantic University. *See* Becker, (1955); Perreault (1964).

Foster, F. G. (1967). *Standard numbering in the book trade: an inquiry carried out by the Publishers Association*. London, Publishers Association.

Forsyth, V. *See* Dolby, Forsyth and Resnikoff (1968).

Fussler, H. H. and Simon, J. L. (1969). Patterns in the use of books in large research libraries. Chicago, Chicago University Press.

Goldhor, H. (ed.). *See* Hayes (1965).

Grose, M. W. and Jones, B. (1967). *The Newcastle University Library order system*, in Cox and Grose (1967).

Grose, M. W. *see also* Cox and Grose (1967).

Hall, A. R. (1969). On the *MARC:* the Birmingham Public Libraries' co-operative mechanization project. *BPL bulletin*, No. 31, 1–2.

Hall, A. R. *see also* Driver, *et al.*, (1970).

Hall, A. T. (1969). Some questions about the *MARC* project. *Library Association record*, Vol. 71, pp. 275–276.

Hanson, D. G. *See* Cowburn and Enright (1968).

Harris, J. L. *See* Hines and Harris (1966).

Harrison, J. and Laslett, P. (eds.). (1967) *The Brasenose conference on the automation of libraries:* proceedings of the Anglo-American conference on the mechanization of library services, 30 June–3 July, 1966., London, Mansell.

Harman, R. J. (ed.). *See* Overhage and Harman (1965).

Hawgood, J. and Morley, R. (1969). Project for evaluating the benefits from university libraries. Final report. University of Durham.

Haynes, R. M. (1965). Implications for librarianship of computer technology, *in* Goldhor, H. (ed.), *Proceedings of the 1964 clinic on library applications of data processing*, Champaign, Illinois, University of Illinois Graduate School of Library Science.

Hines, T. C. and Harris, J. L. (1966). *Computer filing of index, bibliographic and catalog entries*. Newark, N. J., Bro-Dart Foundation.

Howard, R. (1967). Greenwich libraries computer catalogue, *in Libraries and machines today*, edited by C. D. Batty, pp. 3–12. Scunthorpe, North Midland Branch of the Library Association.

Hunt, C. J. (1967). *The computer production of catalogues of old books*, *in* Cox and Grose (1967).

Hunt, K. G. (1955). *Subject specialization and co-operative book purchase in the libraries of Great Britain*. London, Library Association (Pamphlet no. 12).

Jain, A. K. (1966). Sampling and short-period usage in the Purdue Library. *College and Research libraries*, Vol. 27, No. 3, May 1966, pp. 211–218.

Jeffreys, A. E. and Wilson, T. D. (eds.) (1970). U.K. *MARC* Project: proceedings of the seminar organized by the Cataloguing and Indexing Group of the Library Association at the University of Southampton, 28–30 March 1969. Newcastle upon Tyne, Oriel Press.

Johnson, G. (1966). What the public wants from computers. *Aslib proceedings*, Vol. 18, No. 9, pp. 239–245.

Jolliffe, J. W. (1968). The tactics of converting a catalogue to machine-readable form. *Journal of Documentation*. Vol. 24, No. 3, pp. 149–158.

Jolliffe, J. W., Line, M. B. and Robinson, F. (1967). *Why libraries differ—and need they?*, *in* Cox and Grose (1967).

Jones, B. *See* Grose and Jones (1967).

Journal of library automation. Vol. 1, March 1968 (in continuation). Chicago, Ill., Information Science and Automation Division of the American Library Association.

Kennedy, R. A. (1968). Bell telephone laboratories' library real time loan system (BELLREL). *Journal of library automation*, Vol. 1, pp. 128–146.

Kieffer, P. (1966). The Baltimore County Public Library book catalog. *Library resources and technical services*, Vol. 10, No. 2, Spring, 1966, p. 133-42.

Kimber, R. T. (1967). Computer applications in the fields of library housekeeping and information processing. *Program*, No. 6, p. 5.

Kimber, R. T. (1968). An operational computerized circulation system with on-line interrogation capability. *Program*, Vol. 2, No. 3, pp. 75–80.

Kimber, R. T. *see also* Cayless and Kimber (1969).

King, G. W., Edmundson, H. P., Flood, M. M., Kochen, M., Libby, R. L., Swanson, D. R. and Wylly, A. (1963). *Automation and The Library of Congress*: A survey sponsored by the Council on Library Resources, Inc., Library of Congress, Washington, D.C., USA.

Kochen, M. and Segur, A. B. (1970). 'Effects of cataloging volume at the Library of Congress on the total cataloging costs of American research libraries'. *Journal of the American Society for Information Science*, Vol. 21, No. 2, March/April 1970, pp. 133–139.

Kochen, M. *See also* King, *et al.* (1963).

Laslett, P. (ed.). *See* Harrison and Laslett (1967).

Laver, F. J. M. (1965). *Introducing computers*, London, H.M.S.O.

Leonard, L. E. (1968). Co-operative and centralized cataloging and processing: a bibliography, 1850–1967. Illinois University, Graduate School of Library Science (Occasional papers, no. 93).

Leonard, L. E., Maier, J. L. and Dougherty, R. M. (1969). Centralized book processing: a feasibility study based on Colorado academic libraries. New Jersey, Scarecrow Press.

Lewis, P. R. (1967). *BNB* printed cards: distribution and use in British libraries. *Catalogue and index*, No. 8, October 1967, pp. 8–10.

Libby, R. L. *See* King, *et al.* (1933).

Library of Congress. Processing Department (1960). The cataloging-in-source experiment. 1960.

Line, M. B. (1966). Automation of acquisition records and routine in the University Library, Newcastle upon Tyne. *Program*, No. 2, p. 1.

Line, M. B. (1968). *The functions of the university library*, in W. L. Saunders, ed.: University and research library studies, Oxford, Pergamon Press.

Line, M. B. *See also* Jolliffe, Line and Robinson (1967).

Lingenberg, W. (1968). *Computer applications in libraries of the Federal Republic of Germany: commentary on a questionnaire by G. Pflug on the state of automation in German libraries in April 1968* (Typescript).

Lynch, M. F. (1966). Computers in the library, *Nature*, Vol. 212, December 24, 1966, p. 1402.

McCune, L. C. and Salmon, S. R. (1967). Bibliography of library automation. *ALA bulletin*, June, 1967 p. 674. [377 items. General and miscellaneous; General (Library of Congress); Acquisitions; Cataloging; Cataloging (automatic typewriters); Cataloging (book catalogs); Cataloging (filing); Cataloging (Library of Congress); Circulation; Serials; Systems Analysis; Total systems.]

Maier, J. M. *See* Leonard (1969).

Maidment, W. R. (1965). The computer catalogue in Camden. *Library world*, Vol. 68, No. 781, p. 40.

Maidment, W. R. (1966). Book issue control by computer within a locally integrated system. *Aslib proceedings*, Vol. 18, No. 9, pp. 246–253.

Maidment, W. R. (1968). Computer methods in public libraries. *Program*, Vol. 2, No. 1, p. 1.

Markuson, B. E. (1964). *Libraries and automation;* proceedings of the Conference on libraries and automation held at Airlie Foundation, 1963. Washington, Library of Congress.

Markuson, B. E. (1965). The United States Library of Congress automation survey, *Unesco bulletin for libraries*, Vol. 19, No. 1, January/February 1965, p. 24.

May, W. J. (1954). The boys' book of crystal sets and simple circuits. London, Bernards. [This is the only book left on crystal sets!]

Meakin, A. O. (1965). Production of a printed union catalogue by computer. *Library Association record*, Vol. 65, No. 9, September 1965, p. 311.

Metcalf, K. D. (1965). *Planning academic and research library buildings*, New York, McGraw Hill.

Millar, D. G. (1967). *An analysis of survey data*, in Cox and Grose (1967).

Morley, R. *See* Hawgood and Morley (1969).

National Libraries Committee, (1969). *Report*, London, H.M.S.O.

Oates, J. C. T. *See* Chaplin, Shackleton and Oates (1967).

Overhage, C. F. J. and Harman, R. J. (eds.) (1965). *Intrex—report of a planning conference on information transfer experiments*, Cambridge, Mass., M.I.T. Press.

Pace, S. A. (1970). *Production and display standards*. Paper presented to the Oriel Computer Services Limited/Kynoch Press seminar on *The integration of computer-based information with printing techniques*, 17 April, 1970.

Parry, T. (1968). University libraries and the future. *Library Association Record*, Vol. 70, No. 7, September 1968.

Parry, T. [report]. *See* University Grants Committee (1967).

Payne, C. T. (1967). An integrated computer-based bibliographic data system for a large university library: problems and progress at the University of Chicago, *in* University of Illinois Graduate School of Library Science: *Proceedings of the 1967 Clinic on library applications of data processing*, edited by D. E. Carroll, pp. 29–40 Champaign, Illinois, Illini Union Bookstore.

PEBUL. Final report. *See* Hawgood and Morley (1969).

Perreault, J. M. (1964). The computerized book catalog at Florida Atlantic University. *College and research libraries*, Vol. 25, No. 3, May 1964.

Pflug, G. (1968). Experiences and problems of electronic data processing encountered by the University of Bochum Library, *Aslib proceedings*, Vol. 20, No. 11, November 1968, p. 492.

Pflug, G. *See also* Lingenberg (1968).

Pflug, G. and Adams, B. (1968). *Elektronische Datenverarbeitung in der Universitäts-bibliothek Bochum*. Ergebnisse-Erfahrungen-Pläne, Pressestelle der Ruhr-Universität Bochum, pp. 147.

Program: news of computers in British (university) libraries. No. 1, March 1966 (in continuation). The Queen's University of Belfast, School of Library Studies. The word 'university' was dropped from the sub-title with the appearance of Vol. 2, No. 1 in April 1968, when *Program* extended its coverage to include public and special libraries. It will in future be closely linked with the Mechanization Group of Aslib.

Project for evaluating the benefits from university libraries. *See PEBUL*.

Purdue. University Library. *See* Jain (1966).

Reimers, P. R. (1967). The effective use of bibliographic information and the role of automation in this process. *Libri*, Vol. 17, No. 4, p. 305. [A short description of the *MARC 1* project of the Library of Congress. The Summer 1968 issue of *Library resources and technical services*, Vol. 12, No. 3, was largely devoted to Project *MARC*.]

Resnikoff, H. L. *See* Dolby, Forsyth and Resnikoff (1968).

Richmond, P. A. (1966). Note on updating and searching computerized catalogs. *Library resources and technical services*, Vol. 10, No. 2, Spring 1966, pp. 155–160.

Robinson, C. W. (1965). The book catalog: diving in. *Wilson library bulletin*, Vol. 40, November 1965, p. 262.

Robinson, F. *See* Jolliffe, Line and Robinson (1967).

Rubinoff, M. (ed.). *See* Day (1965).

Russell, J. H. (1967). *A computer-produced bibliography, in* Cox and Grose (1967).

Salmon, S. R. *See* McCune and Salmon (1967).

Saunders, W. L. (ed.). *See* Line (1968).

Shackleton, R. *See* Chaplin, Shackleton and Oates (1967).

Shackleton, R. *See also* University of Oxford (1966).

Shaw, R. R. (1965). Machine application at the University of Hawaii. *College and research libraries*, Vol. 26, September 1965, p. 381.

Simon, J. L. (1967). How many books should be stored where?—An economic, analysis. *College and research libraries*, Vol. 28, No. 2, March 1967, pp. 92–103.

Simon, J. L. *See also* Fussler (1969).

Standard book numbering agency (1967 and 1968). *Standard book numbering* [1st and 2nd ed.]. London, Standard Book Numbering Agency.

Stearns, C. M. *See* Adkinson and Stearns (1967).

Stein, T. (1964). Automation and library systems. *Library journal*, Vol. 89, July 1964, p. 2723–34.

Stuart-Stubbs, B. (1966). *Conference on computers in Canadian libraries, Université Laval, Quebec, March 21–22, 1966,. A report prepared for the Canadian Association of College and University Libraries.* University of British Columbia Library. (Quoted in *Program*, No. 6, July 1967, p. 9).

Swanson, D. R. *See* King, *et al.* (1963).

Trueswell, R. W. (1965). A quantitative measure of user circulation requirements and its possible effects on stack thinning and multiple copy determination. *American documentation*, Vol. 16, No. 11, January 1965, pp. 20–25.

Trueswell, R. W. (1969). Some behavioral patterns of library users, the 80/20 rule. *Wilson library bulletin*, January 1969, pp. 458–461.

University Grants Committee (1967). *Report of the Committee on Libraries* [Parry Report], H.M.S.O., London.

University Grants Committee (1968). *Returns from Universities and University Colleges, Academic Year 1965–66.* H.M.S.O., London.

University of Hawaii. *See* Cammack (1965).

University of Illinois. Graduate School of Library Science. *Clinic on library applications of data processing.* Urbana, Illinois, Illini Union Bookstore. (This 'clinic' has been held annually since 1963. The proceedings of each meeting are published.)

University of Newcastle upon Tyne (1968 and 1969). Catalogue Computerization Project, *First and second interim reports.* [Deposited at NLL].

University of Oxford (1966). *Report of the Committee on university libraries. (Chairman R. Shackleton)* Oxford, Oxford University Press.

Unlocking the Computer's Profit Potential (1968). McKinsey and Company, Inc., New York.

Use of *BNB MARC* tapes in a group of Birmingham Libraries (1968). *OSTI news-letter*, (December 1968), 2.

Vann, S., *et al.* (1966). Processing centers for public libraries: a tentative list. *Library resources and technical services*, Vol. 10, Fall 1966, pp. 489–492.

Veasey, W. I. (1968). Comparative index to periodical prices (*Library Association record*, Vol. 70, No. 8, August 1968, p. 202.

Veasey, W. I. (1969). Comparative index to periodical prices (*Library Association record*), Vol. 71, No. 8, August 1969, p. 244.

Wells, A. J. (1968). Shared cataloguing: a new look at an old problem. *Aslib proceedings*, Vol. 20, No. 12, December 1968, pp. 534–541.

Wilkins, D. J. *see* Driver, *et al.* (1970).

Wilson, C. W. J. (1969). Comparison of U.K. computer-based loans systems. *Program*, Vol. 3, Nos. 3/4, pp. 127–146.

Wilson, T. D. *See* Jeffreys (1970).

Woods, R. G. (1966*a*). Use of an *ICT* 1907 computer in Southampton University Library. *Program*, No. 1, March 1966, pp. 1–3.

Woods, R. G. (1966*b*). Use of an *ICT* 1907 computer in Southampton University Library. Report No. 2. *Program*, No. 3, October 1966, pp. 1–3.

Woods, R. G. (1968). Use of an *ICT* 1907 computer in Southampton University Library. Report no. 3. *Program*, Vol. 2, no. 1, April 1968, pp. 30–33.

Woods, R. G. (1969). Use of an *ICT* 1907 computer in Southampton University Library. Report no. 4. *Program*, Vol. 3, nos. 3/4. November 1969, pp. 111–114.

Wylly, A. *See* King *et al.* (1963).

Glossary

This glossary is intended to throw some light on library jargon for computer-people; and on computer jargon for librarians. It is neither exhaustive nor particularly precise, and readers who wish for further enlightenment are advised to seek it on the one hand in the Glossary to the *Anglo-American Cataloguing Rules (British Text)* 1967, pp. 266–269; and on the other in the *Penguin Dictionary of Computers*, by Anthony Chandor and others, 1970.

Italics indicate a further reference under the word italicised.

Added Entry In a library catalogue, a card or other descriptive unit, containing the same information as the *Main Entry*, but having as its filing heading some other keyword than that selected for the Main Entry: e.g. title, series, editor, illustrator, translator. Its purpose is to give access to the catalogue at various points, based on a prediction of what information the reader may bring with him.

Automatic data processing (ADP) Processing of records by automatic equipment, often computers; however, sometimes used, in contrast to *EDP*, to indicate the use of electro-mechanical (non-computer) equipment.

Algorithm Often loosely used to mean a series of instructions given to the computer to enable it to deal with a specific problem. The term has a more formal description, which is not readily comprehensible to the amateur!

Assembly language A symbolic programming language, based directly on the *hardware* functions of a specific computer, which is translated into *machine code* for operation on the computer.

Automation The operation of any system or process by the use of automatic devices, without intervention by human (manual) techniques. May refer to mechanical as well as computer devices.

Batch Processing (Off-line) In contrast with *on-line working* batch-processing implies the collection of data for processing in large quantities (e.g. overnight). This method is cheaper than on-line, but is not suitable if an immediate response is essential.

Bit A *binary* digi*t*, i.e. a digit in binary notation: either 0 or 1.

Byte A set of eight binary digits (see '*bit*') regarded as a unit; often a sub-division of a word, the basic unit of computer memory, used for the storage of representations of characters.

Central processor (Central processing unit; CPU) The main section of a digital computer, containing memory unit, arithmetic unit and control section. It is on the size of the CPU that the computer's ability to perform tasks depends.

Character set That collection of characters (e.g. numerals, letters, punctuation marks, typographic signs, etc.) recognised by a particular computer system as acceptable and valid. There are several standard sets, including EBCDIC (Extended Binary-Coded-Decimal Interchange Code) and ISO

241

(International Standards Organisation).

Compiler A program which converts a program, written in either a *high-level language* or in *assembly language*, into the sequence of *machine code* instructions which are actually obeyed by the computer.

Computer-generated microfilm See *Computer output on microfilm (COM).*

Computer output on microfilm (COM) Technique whereby, instead of comparatively slow output on peripheral devices such as the line-printer, the computer prints direct on to microfilm at approximately the same rate as it can transfer information internally (up to 120,000 characters per second).

Computer typesetting The use of automated techniques for setting type. This permits not only automatic justification but also control of layout and pagination, and the generation of indexes. This term often embraces both the computers and computer methods involved, as well as any special *peripheral devices.*

Corporate author In a catalogue entry, the body responsible for the production of the book concerned, when not a personal author but a corporate body, such as a Company or Institution.

Current awareness The provision of information, shortly after publication, about current work being done in a particular field of interest. Frequently takes the form of analysed contents pages of periodicals, but can also be produced, for example, as a by-product of machine-based acquisitions/cataloguing operations.

Data bank A collection of records maintained for some specific purpose and accessible to a variety of users who will extract information and/or records from it for local use, often by direct access on-line. The collection of records is generally in machine-readable form (i.e. on magnetic tape, punched cards, etc.).

Data base A body of machine-readable records, regarded as a homogeneous collection for some purpose, but not created solely for a specific application (c.f. *data bank*). This term is also used to mean the format in which machine-readable records can be stored.

Data field See *Field.*

Data link A connection by which machine-readable data can be transmitted between locations remote from each other.

Diary One method used in surveying library use or library systems. Readers or library staff fill in pre-printed forms indicating their movements/objectives/occupations during a particular time, for analysis by a systems analyst or other survey staff.

Disc (i.e. magnetic disc) A computer storage device giving *random access* to data recorded on it. Generally much faster and more economical than *linear access*. Functions rather like a gramophone disc, with pick-up via one or more read/write heads, except tracks are concentric (unlike the gramophone spiral track) and that generally it is possible both to read and write information to the disc on both surfaces simultaneously. It is often possible to remove one disc and replace it with another on the *peripheral device*, thus providing different information to the system.

Drum (i.e. magnetic drum) A computer storage device in the form of a drum. Usable for direct-access applications. Similar to a phonograph cylinder, except that tracks are separate rather than spiral. Normally drums are permanently attached to the system.

Electronic data processing (EDP) Processing of records by electronic equipment (i.e. computers). Used sometimes in contrast to *ADP*, which may also indicate the use of automatic non-computer methods.

Field A particular area of a computer record, e.g. in library records the author or date of publication of a book. Fields may be of fixed or variable length, depending on the operation of the computer being used and on the needs of the user.

File A collection of *computer records*, organized in some way; not necessarily sorted in any order, but having some relationship with each other such as a common source or format.

File-handling system A facility for the manipulation by computer of collections of records containing data. The development of such systems was made necessary by the fact that the computer is suited primarily to the high-speed manipulation of numeric records, and has to be managed in a totally different way when handling other types of data such a library records.

Fingerprint (in Project LOC) A method of identifying books, based on the recording of letters from fixed locations within the volume to provide points for comparison. See p. 50.

Flow-charting The graphic representation of a process, either a system or a computer program, to facilitate the checking of its logical construction, and to record it for future development. A flowchart consists of a number of labelled symbolic areas connected by lines showing by arrows the direction in which control is transferred from initial input to eventual output.

Hardware Computer machinery, as opposed to the programs which operate it—the *software*.

High-level language A computer programming language intended to allow the greatest ease of writing for the user. Unlike the *machine-language* which consists of instructions in a form immediately acceptable to the machine, a high-level language (FORTRAN, COBOL, ALGOL) is recognisable as statements in pseudo-English, or in mathematical notation; and each high-level instruction will correspond to several instructions in machine-code, into which it must be converted by a *compiler* before processing can begin.

Housekeeping Library routines, operating daily, carrying out the basic work of the library: ordering, cataloguing, controlling circulation of books. For computer applications, housekeeping is contrasted with *information retrieval*. Also used of programs written to control input and output operation on the computer.

Information Retrieval The handling by computer of collections of data, such as bibliographic records, to extract information needed for specific purposes by individual users.

Integrated system In a library, an automated system of which all parts have been planned as parts of a whole, so that each is compatible with the others and all make the most economical and efficient use of available resources (for example, details relating to a book, generated at the order stage, are used in cataloguing, issue records, binding records, stocktaking, and, if necessary, withdrawal, without at any stage needing to be re-created).

Interface Generally, the connexion between two units of a computer. More specifically, the complex connexions between a central processing unit and its peripheral units.

International standard book number (ISBN) A unique identifier, originally for British books (Standard Book Number), now being adopted in other countries. It now consists of nine digits of which the first is a country code; the next group represents the publisher and the last the individual title. A tenth digit is a check digit, by which the accuracy of transcription of the number may be verified. The ISBN is increasingly used as a record identification key for machine handling, for example in MARC. The original British SBN lacks the country code at the beginning.

Joint author One of two or more

authors of a book or other publication, where all the authors are of equal standing and have equal responsibility for the final publication. Usually *added entries* will be created for all joint authors.

Key One of the marked levers or buttons on a keyboard (as on a typewriter (see next entry)). More importantly, a group of symbols used as an identifier for a record (e.g. sort-key). The ISBN is a key of this type.

Key-punching (Keyboarding) The use of a keyboard-operated machine (e.g. card punch, paper-tape punch) to punch data manually into an input record.

Line-printer Computer peripheral device for printing out information a line at a time. The speed, which can be from 300 to 2,000 lines per minute, is much higher than that of devices printing one character at a time, but the graphic quality can be very low, and lower case letters are often not available.

Linear access The only kind of access to records on *magnetic tape*, when a reel of tape must be scanned along its length in a search for particular records. Slow and costly compared with *random access on discs*.

Linear programming An aspect of mathematical programming, dealing with the maximization or minimization of a linear function of a set of variables. Of great use in costing operations and finding the most effective ways of allocating resources.

Machine code The programming 'language' used internally in a computer. Instructions may be written in machine code by programmers, but are more often written in a *high-level language* which is then converted to machine code for processing.

Machine format The structure of a record which can be handled by machine, needing, for example, a method of identifying *fields* either by attached indicator tags or by some

form of directory at the beginning of the record, giving the starting point of each field.

Machine-readable Capable of being manipulated (sorted, merged, corrected) on a computer, and output onto peripheral devices.

Magnetic tape A common form of storage medium used in the computer. Can hold much more information than paper tape (say 550 characters per inch) and may be used as an input medium for faster transfer (about 40,000 characters per second) than can be achieved with *paper tape*.

Main entry In a library catalogue, the master record describing one particular book or other bibliographic unit. The heading used for filing will most often be the name of the person or body responsible for the production of the book; and the information will usually be repeated under different headings (see *Added entry*).

MARC (Machine-readable cataloguing Project) This Project, providing machine-readable records for cataloguing and other purposes, originated with the Library of Congress and has been developed jointly with the British National Bibliography. See pp. 126 ff.

On-line On-line working means direct access to the computer processor from a terminal, and a short response-time when a message or instruction is keyed in. Contrasts with *batch-processing*. On-line access is expensive, but may be necessary, e.g. for circulation records, or for file-editing, or, especially, for the retrieval of information on demand.

Paper Tape Common input medium for the computer, in which characters are indicated by holes punched across the tape according to whatever code is used. The number of holes across the tape (tracks) may vary between 5 and 8 depending on the machine and the code system used. Much less bulky than *punched cards* and can be read at above 1000 characters per second, although punched cards are probably easier to correct.

Parameter An item of information used in a computer process and which can take different values as the process is repeated. Defines the area of an operation by setting numerical limits.

Peripherals Devices connected to the *Central Processor Unit* of a computer for input, output or storage, e.g. card punch, magnetic disc, tape reader.

Mechanization The control of processes by the use of machines, usually, but not necessarily, computers. See *Automatic data processing* and *Electronic data processing*.

Multi-processing Operation of a computer system having more than one processing unit, able to function simultaneously.

Multi-programming A technique developed in order to use a computer's processor more efficiently, by having more than one program present in memory at the same time. Since different programs call for different uses of the control processor in relation to peripheral devices, multi-programming can be used to permit the most economic combinations of work to be performed, provided that no program is able to interfere with the operation of another.

Optical character recognition (*OCR*) A means of inputting data to a computer, whereby printed characters are read by light-sensitive devices. Special forms of type have been designed for the purpose.

Print-out The printed output, in legible form, from a computer device, such as a tape-typewriter or a line-printer.

Profile The particular subject interests of an individual library user or research worker expressed as classification keys (e.g. Dewey class numbers) and used to retrieve from a data file those items of current interest (cf. *current awareness*).

Punched Card Common form of computer input (cf. *paper tape, magnetic tape*) in which holes are punched in a card (the most usual being one divided into 80 columns), by an operator using a card-punch. Punched cards are also used in other types of data-processing machinery.

Random access The obtaining of information from a computer via devices such as disc store and magnetic drum, with which it is not necessary to search serially (see *magnetic tape, linear access, disc, drum*).

Real time A real-time computer system is one in which data put in is processed as it is produced, giving an immediate response. Necessary, for example, in process control and some information retrieval systems, where it is essential to maintain a completely up to date central file and draw on it. Often used loosely together with *on-line*. Real-time operations must be on-line, but on-line devices may have a fairly slow response time, not strictly operating in real time.

Record A set of data elements, forming a unit. Records are combined to make *files*.

Routine A program or part of a program (input routine, error routine).

Serial access. See *Linear access.*

Shelf-list A record, in the order in which they stand on the shelves, of the books in a library's stock. Used for checking stock at stocktaking, stock control, subject access (when no subject catalogue is available).

Software The programs written for a computer, as opposed to the actual machinery (*hardware*). Usually used to describe those programs supplied by a manufacturer to facilitate the use of the machine, rather than the specific programs written by users themselves.

Standard Book Number (*SBN*). See *International Standard Book Number* (*ISBN*).

Stock editor A member of the library's staff responsible for the control of the stock, especially the weeding out of obsolescent material and the replacement of missing items.

Sub-field A division of a *field*, e.g. in the *MARC* record the various sections of the heading: dates, epithets, etc.

System Interrelated objects forming a unit, usually interacting to produce some specified result, e.g. in date-processing, humans (creating the *software* interact with machines (*hardware*)) to manipulate information, say to produce a library catalogue.

Systems analyst A person who works on the definition and creation of systems, by investigating existing systems, describing them, evaluating them and where necessary designing replacements. A major part of the analyst's work is documentation: recording in detail the systems described and created, as a basis for agreement and future development.

Teleprinter, teletypewriter Types of *terminal* device, using a typewriter-style keyboard.

Terminal A device for input/output, connected to a computer system. Types of terminal include *visual display units, teleprinters, teletypewriters*.

Time-sharing A high-speed system for carrying out different operations almost simultaneously, switching from one to another according to a set of predetermined priorities and sequences.

Union catalogue A library catalogue containing, in one sequence, records of the holdings of more than one library or collection.

Visual display unit (VDU) A computer *terminal* resembling a television screen, upon which information is displayed from the computer memory. VDUs also have facilities for input by keyboard. Usually taken to mean a screen capable of displaying a given restricted set of characters, but can mean a screen capable of displaying line drawings.

Index

This index is constructed on principles tending to produce brief indexing terms and to avoid introducing sub-headings wherever possible. No references are made from general to specific terms or vice versa. For subjects which are referred to frequently in passing, only major references are indexed. Personal names do not appear in the index.